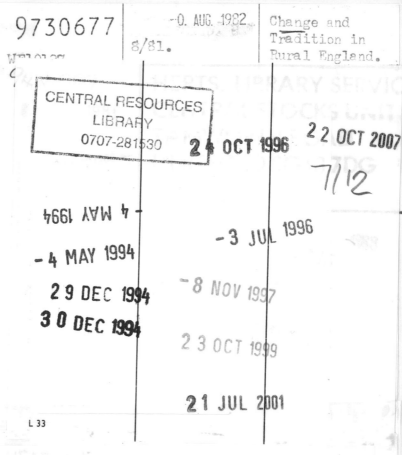
	From Area codes 01923 or 0208:	From the rest of Herts:
Renewals:	01923 471373	01438 737373
Enquiries:	01923 471333	01438 737333
Minicom:	01923 471599	01438 737599

L32b

D1486196

Change and Tradition in
Rural England

By the same author

The Uses of Poetry, 1978
Readings, 1974
CAMBRIDGE UNIVERSITY PRESS

Distant Voices, 1978
HEINEMANN EDUCATIONAL BOOKS

CHANGE AND TRADITION IN RURAL ENGLAND

An anthology of writings on country life

CHOSEN AND EDITED BY
DENYS THOMPSON

CAMBRIDGE UNIVERSITY PRESS

CAMBRIDGE

LONDON · NEW YORK · NEW ROCHELLE
MELBOURNE · SYDNEY

Published by the Press Syndicate of the University of Cambridge
The Pitt Building, Trumpington Street, Cambridge CB2 IRP
32 East 57th Street, New York, NY 10022, USA
296 Beaconsfield Parade, Middle Park, Melbourne 3206, Australia

First published 1980

Printed in Great Britain by The Anchor Press Ltd
and bound by Wm Brendon & Son Ltd
both of Tiptree, Essex

British Library cataloguing in publication data
Change and tradition in rural England.
1. England – Social life and customs – Sources
2. Country life – England
I. Thompson, Denys
942'.00973'4   DAII0   79–41613
ISBN 0 521 22546 9

CONTENTS

4   THE FUTURE

ILLUSTRATIONS

ACKNOWLEDGEMENTS

The editor wishes to thank Michael Black for his help, and the following authors, or their representatives, and publishers for permission to reprint copyright passages: Adrian Bell for his *Scrutiny* article and passages from *A Countryman's Notebook* and his anthology *The Open Air*; the Cambridge University Press: M. K. Ashby, *Joseph Ashby of Tysoe*; Thomas Hennell, *Change in the Farm*; Walter Rose, *Good Neighbours* and *The Village Carpenter*; and *The Journals of George Sturt*; the Hogarth Press: *Life As We Have Known It*, edited by M. L. Davies; the Oxford University Press: Flora Thompson, *Lark Rise to Candleford*; Raymond O'Malley, *One-Horse Farm*; and George Allen and Unwin, Ltd: Mary Palmer, *Writing and Action*.

GENERAL INTRODUCTION

This book illustrates the mainstream of English writing on the country from the time of Cobbett to about the middle of the present century. The authors represented (apart from Jefferies) are mostly concerned with the people working in it rather than with the beauty of the landscape; and what they say has implications for us and our problems in the 1980s. It is in no way an exercise in nostalgia. However often he looked back, Cobbett aimed at improving the lot of the labourer; Hardy knew that there was no return, since he wrote to preserve for his own satisfaction 'a fairly true record of a vanishing life' (General Preface to *Novels and Poems* (1912)); and Jefferies declared in *Round About a Great Estate* (1880) 'My sympathies and hopes are with the light of the future, only I should like it to come from nature. The clock should be read by the sunshine, not the sun timed by the clock.' And Sturt, the greatest of writers, other than novelists, on the country, was explicit: 'The more I examine it, the more I grow sceptical of the well-being of the people, in these "good old times" ' (*Journals*, p. 622). His main concern was for the future, to enable people to become something better than peasants.

It did not take long for England to become an industrial rather than an agricultural country; and only in living memory has agriculture itself become a branch of industry. Adrian Bell writes in a letter: 'I find it almost impossible to believe that the yet living *Me* went to farm in Suffolk in a parish which *had not in it a single power-driven machine* but one old steam engine. And a windmill turned busily in real business in the ever-blowing winds of high Suffolk.' The change to a fully industrial society has affected the lives, aspirations and expectations of us all; it shapes our terms of reference. The farm worker has psychologically long been a town bird, as Lawrence observed years ago, and the land itself is too often an extension of the processing factory. Plants are raw material for packaging or freezing, animals are machines to be minded before they are fed on to the conveyor belt.

Ever since Plato proposed that the ideal community would be a city of specialists, writers have contrasted town with country life. The Greeks had no real cities, but the Romans had, and when their cities became noisy and dirty and centres of crime they satirised them and extolled the rural way of living. The Roman complaints were echoed by English authors. Smollett in *Humphry Clinker* (1770) wrote about London as an overgrown dropsical monster; Johnson established himself by a version of Juvenal on the horrors of metropolitan life. The line has continued with the records by Mayhew, Dickens, Jack London and others of what they found in the capital; and Jefferies in his compelling *After London* (1885) forecast its utter ruin and the un-idyllic restarting of civilisation in the wild. However the town–country antinomy does not open up a helpful approach or enable us to decide which of the many volumes on rural life have something to say to us in the 1980s.

For the purposes of this book – to see if our rural past can assist with our problems – the writers who matter are those who have noted the impact on people of enclosures and the industrial revolution. The final wave of enclosures early last century co-incided with the growth of industry, without causal connection; but both factory owner and enclosing squire were profiteers who ill-treated those whose work produced the profits. The townsman Blake in 'London' exposed the cruelty that came with the strengthening of the cash nexus, and he took for granted the primacy of agriculture:

The sword sung on the barren heath,
The sickle in the fruitful field:
The sword he sung a song of death,
But could not make the sickle yield.

Later, in the prophetic *Vala* (Night the Seventh) he execrates the destruction of the old order and the replacement of the 'arts of life' by the rhythm of the machine; and seems to foretell that war is inherent in technological progress:

Then left the sons of Urizen the plow and harrow, the loom,
The hammer and the chisel and the rule and compasses.
They forg'd the sword, the chariot of war, the battle ax,
The trumpet fitted to the battle and the flute of summer,
And all the arts of life they chang'd into the arts of death.
The hour glass contemn'd because its simple workmanship
Was the workmanship of the plowman, and the water wheel
That raises water into cisterns, broken and burn'd in fire
Because its workmanship was like the workmanship of the
  shepherd,
And in their stead intricate wheels invented, wheel without wheel,
To perplex youth in their outgoings and to bind to labours
Of day and night the myriads of Etermity, that they might file
And polish brass and iron hour after hour, laborious workmanship,
Kept ignorant of the use that they might spend the days of wisdom
In sorrowful drudgery to obtain a scanty pittance of bread,
In ignorance to view a small portion and think that All. . . .

While Blake was writing others were noting the results of enclosures. In the 1780s John Byng, later Lord Torrington, wrote in his diary: 'As a sportsman I hate enclosures, and as a citizen I look on them as the greedy tyrannies of the wealthy few, to oppress the indigent many, and an iniquitous purchase of invaluable rights.' In 1800 Arthur Young,[1] an ardent believer in improving agriculture, admitted that the enclosure of 'waste' land, however

productive it might be, deprived the poor of their stake in the
land and turned peasants into paupers: 'The poor look to facts,
not meanings; and the fact is, that by nineteen enclosure bills in
twenty they are injured, in some cases grossly injured.' In a letter
of 1802, seeking the interest of Charles James Fox in his poems,
Wordsworth deplored the decline of the 'estatesmen', the small
hereditary landowners of the Lake District, and noted that 'by the
spread of manufactures through every part of the country . . . the
bonds of domestic feeling among the poor have been weakened,
and in innumerable cases entirely destroyed'. Further, in Book
VIII of *The Excursion* he described the 'outrage done to nature' –
the destruction of the organic relation of man to man, the imposition of the inhuman rhythm of the factory system, the miserable
slums for near-serfs and the plight of the victims. He showed too
how families were broken up by the labour of children and
women, and by the treatment of men as machines.

For all their differences, Young, Wordsworth and Cobbett
agreed that every labourer should have a stake in the land.
Cobbett in particular spelled this out; what he wanted was a
nation of small farmers or cottagers, with allotments and common
rights, and to help them he wrote various handbooks of practical
advice. He detested a wide range of human types and institutions;
he could be inconsistent, sometimes with a bullying manner – but
his instincts were sound. He recorded the worsening lot of ordinary men and women in a lively prose, never far removed from
vigorous speech. He had an eye for a beautiful landscape when the
beauty was an effect of good agriculture. However much we may
dislike some of his prejudices, we have to recognise that a page or
two of his is worth more than all the works of the political
economists of his day.

Progress – the advance of industry and the decline of agriculture
as a way of life – continued without check; and on Cobbett's
death in 1835 there was none to continue his fight. Richard
Jefferies (1848–87) was an exquisite observer of nature, but he did

not quickly overcome the limitations of his background and his start as a Tory journalist. In Edward Thomas's words, 'He does not dwell on the possibility that there is something deeply wrong . . . when the land is left idle and only the men who could till it suffer' (*Life of Richard Jefferies*, p. 15). He attacked labourers for their 'communism', and he was completely uncritical of such activities as coursing and the poisoning of magpies, revealing his 'callousness and his careless acceptance of things as they are'. Not till he himself was racked by pain and poverty did he write with full sympathy for the people who dwelt in the country he described so beautifully. Though peerless as a recorder of the English scene at its most lovely, he did not see what was happening.

George Sturt (1863–1927) continued the purposeful observing of Cobbett. Much more of a thinker than his predecessor, he came in the end to respect him, after an initial dislike. Sturt had literary ambitions and corresponded a good deal with Arnold Bennett, but in 1884 he had to take over the family wheelwright's shop. Though it gave him wonderful material, the business was uncongenial, and eventually he was able to give it up and pursue his main interest in writing. He completed novels and a book on aesthetics, but it is his half-dozen books on rural life and industry, given unity and direction by his *Journals*, that establish him as a writer to be taken very seriously. His distinction lay in his ability to see a main current in a number of small changes.

In *The Bettesworth Book* (1901) Sturt described the working of the folk mind in, and the variety of skills exercised by, the man he employed, a variety that suggested that there was no such thing as an unskilled agricultural labourer. (This and other books up to and including *Change in the Village* were published under the pen-name of George Bourne.) In *Memoirs of a Surrey Labourer* (1907) he presented a full picture of the same man. Dragged up as an orphan, he had started life without advantages, and by modern standards he always appeared dirty: yet he displayed great good sense, a receptive mind, dignity and cheerfulness, together with a never-failing gift of expression. Tradition and religion had offered him little, yet Sturt was able to describe him thus, in his old age:

Alone, of his own inborn instinct for being a decent man, he strove through all his life, not to be rich, but to live upright and unashamed. Fumbling, tiresome, garrulous, unprofitable, lean and grim and dirty in outward appearance, the grey old life was full of fight for its idea of being a man; full of fight and patience and stubborn resolve not to give in to anything which it had learnt to regard as weakness . . . think of the patient, resolute spirit, which had almost never indulged its weaknesses, but had its self-respect, its half-savage instincts towards righteousness, its smothered tastes, its untold affections and its tenderness.

Bettesworth was not a peasant, but his recollections were evidence of a vanished peasant economy. This is the subject of *Change in the Village*, Sturt's next and, after the *Journals*, his most important book.

Sturt was always realistic about the peasant way of life. The village he wrote about, originally settled by squatters, was turning into a suburb. It had its seamy side, with squalid and brutal features; it did not lack vice and tragedy. But enough of an older order was left to show that there had once been a civilisation that gave coherence to life, and that despite harshness and poverty the daily round had been varied and interesting, providing scope for men to be men and to live while earning a living. By pointing the contrast with the industrial system, Sturt identified problems that have been rediscovered by writers on the failure of the work-for-leisure formula to afford satisfaction – the extent for example to which the fragmentation of work disorganises the rest of life and makes talk of 'job enrichment' sound futile. In *The Wheelwright's Shop* (1923) he wrote sensitively and powerfully of a traditional craft that met the needs of a neighbourhood. He described the demands it made, not only for high standards of workmanship, technical knowledge and experience of materials but also for familiarity with the district, the soil on which the timber grew, the type of farm a waggon would be supplied to, and the men involved. The work itself was interesting, requiring men to use their resources, and rewarding them with a sense of belonging to a guiding tradition, of co-operating with materials, of seeing something beautiful coming out of necessity. They worked in a non-competitive ethos. Finally Sturt noted the changes that came when the car began to supplant the waggon, skill yielded to machinery, the self-supporting workman became a wage-earning hand, and an autonomous community was devoured by a large-scale economy. His observation, 'That civilisation may flourish a less-civilised working-class must work', has been rephrased but neither faced nor answered.

Given better health Sturt would have written books on politics, art, folk culture, and perhaps literature. This is clear from his *Journals* (in the excellent selection by E. D. Mackerness), many pages of which amount to substantial essays. A socialist, he expected little of socialists: 'If they could attain their ends, they would find that as yet we are a people unfit for the improved order; that while learning to manage a State, men had not yet learned how to live.' It is difficult to see the makings of a politician in other equally prescient pages, such as that on the abuse of the world's resources: 'Civilisation has gone astray: instead of finding out How to Live, we have gone on pillaging – pillaging the earth's stores with violence, when we should be getting into close personal intimacy of friendship with her ways . . . England gets wealth and luxuries, but no happiness. We are too greedy to live well.' The same intelligence might have made him a good literary critic, and it certainly accounts for the sanity – especially in his day – of his views on current topics. He was refreshingly forthright on the glamour of war, noise and other aspects of progress, 'that abstraction' the State, and the armed forces – 'those disastrous burdens'. Thus one attends all the more closely to his main preoccupations, such as the relevance of the past to the present.

Flora Thompson (*Lark Rise to Candleford*) is another in whose writing people are at the centre, and like Sturt she wrote about what she knew from within. Covering similar ground at the same time in a different county, her book leaves one with markedly the same impression as *Change in the Village*. A peasantry with rights in the land had become a class of wage-earners, which though robbed of its holding still retained habits of thought and behaviour that were part of the peasant culture. Introducing her book, H. J. Massingham stresses that she records the end

of a self-sufficient country England living by the land, cultivating it by husbandry and associating liberty with the small property. It was not poverty that broke it – that was a secondary cause. It was not even imported cheap and foodless foods. It was that the Industrial Revolution and the Enclosures between them demolished the structure and the pattern of country life . . . now we plough and sow an empty land.

Though the English tradition of writing about the country may be said to have developed strongly in the eighteenth century, the contributors to it do not greatly concern us. There were the landscape poets, such as James Thomson (1700–48) with his popular *The Seasons* and Wordsworth in his earliest phase. Goldsmith's *The Deserted Village* (1770) is a most moving poem, but the village that is cleared by a wealthy owner is probably in Ireland. Gilbert White (1720–93) with his life-long study of natural history stands at the head of a long line of prose writers, but he had little time to take note of human beings. It was with Mary Russell Mitford that the cult of the village, now so flourishing, began; *Our Village* (1824) consists of sketches in which clichés abound and all is idealised. Characteristically, after allowing the Harvest Home to be 'a pleasant noise', she adds 'though for one's ears' sake, one makes some haste to get away from it'. This comment contrasts sharply with George Eliot's (1819–80) account in Ch. 53 of *Adam Bede*, and the response of Adam, to whom the distant chant was 'a sacred song'; 'It's wonderful how that sound goes to one's heart almost like a funeral bell, for all it tells one o' the joyfullest time of the year, and the time when men are mostly the thankfullest.' Her description of Adam as representative of pre-industrial civilisation vividly evokes the nature of that order: 'He was not an average man. Yet such men as he are reared here and there in every generation of our peasant artisans – with an inheritance of affections nurtured by a simple family life of common need and common industry, and an inheritance of faculties trained in skilful courageous labour.' The whole of the passage at the end of Ch. 19 is worth looking up.

Two other great novelists had their roots in the country. Jane Austen's (1775–1817) moral outlook is based on a rural custom of good husbandry: Squire Knightley in *Emma* for example is a farmer developing his inheritance of responsibility; *Mansfield Park* shows us a conflict between rural and urban values; and so on. Thomas Hardy (1840–1928) did not publish till after George Eliot's best work had appeared; and by his time the decay of 'a vanishing life' was clear and irremediable. In the preface to *Far From the Madding Crowd* he noted, as one of the results of supplanting stationary cottagers by migratory labourers, the break of continuity that was fatal to the development of qualities depending on attachment to the soil. Like Wordsworth too he deplored the disappearance of the old copyholders who were ousted from their little plots when the system of leasing large farms grew general. He described how the husbandman had the interest of long personal association with his farm. 'The fields were those he had ploughed and sowed from boyhood, and it was impossible for him, in such cases, to sink altogether the character of natural guardian in that of hireling' (*Thomas Hardy's Personal Writings* (1967), pp. 172, 181). He was explicit about features of the life he wanted to record: the Dorset language, for instance, with its 'delicate ability to express the doings, joys and jests, troubles, sorrows, needs, sickness of life in the rural world' (*ibid*, p. 79). Especially in *Far From the Madding Crowd* and *The Woodlanders* he records some qualities of the farming life in people who were dedicated to their work in the natural, the agricultural, order of things.

Characteristic figures in that order are described below by W. H. Hudson (1841–1922) and more recent authors. General accounts have been given by writers such as Cecil Torr (1857–1928), a quiet country gentleman of good education, whose observations add up to a valuable local history. Augustus Jessop deserves a mention in that his *Before the Great Pillage* (1901) reminds us that it was the people at large who built and furnished the churches with the work of mainly local craftsmen, and that the plundering of the parish gilds in the reign of Edward VI was the robbing of the poor by the rich. Two works ahead of their time in diagnosing the terminal illness of rural England were D. C. Pedder's *Where Men Decay* (1908), an analysis of conditions in the country, and C. F. G. Masterman's *The Condition of England* (1909), a brilliant and forgotten book that discerns 'the passing of a race of men' since 'a peasantry, unique in Europe in its complete divorce from the land, lacking ownership of cottage or tiniest plot of land, finds no longer any attraction in the cheerless toil of the agricultural labourer'. He quotes that able and perceptive priest, C. L. Marson, who, having set forth the new helplessness of the village, goes on to depict the future:

As things go on now we shall have empty fields, except for a few shepherds and herdsmen, in all the green of England. Nomadic herds will sweep over the country, sowing, shearing, grass-cutting, reaping and binding with machines: a system which does not make for health, peace, discipline, nobleness of life. . . . England is bleeding at her arteries, and it is her reddest blood which is flowing away.

More recent writers are H. J. Massingham, author of vigorous books on farming and country crafts (e.g. *Where Men Belong* (1946)), and George Ewart Evans. Characteristic works by the latter are *The Horse and the Furrow* (1960), a fresh and engaging account of horses and horsemen in farming, and *Where Beards Wag All* (1970), on another not overworked subject, the relevance of oral tradition, with some particularly valuable pages on the strengths of dialect.

The last group consists of farmers and farm workers. The earliest of these is Joseph Ashby of Tysoe in Warwickshire, whose life is ably recounted by M. K. Ashby. Her book provides evidence of a real community of peasants, degenerating eventually into landless, poverty-racked labourers; presents the enclosures as symbols of repression; and particularises the failure of Church and school. Fred Kitchen's *Brother to the Ox* (1940) is the autobiography of a farm worker with no special advantages, brought up in a hard school where as a 'day-lad' on a farm he was taught nothing, but had to learn ploughing, thatching and stacking by watching other people. At that time he lived a life that was medieval in its dirt and discomfort; his clothes were caked with byre splashings, his hands chapped and swollen, but – 'I was perfectly happy.' He delighted in his work and took pride in doing it well. 'Ploughing may be looked upon as a lowly occupation; but to me the smell of new-turned earth, the free life and fresh air, the undefinable understanding that exists between man and horse places it far above . . . making a roadway.'

The experience that lay behind Adrian Bell's 'English Tradition and Idiom' (in Part 1) was that of an apprentice and then a farmer, outstandingly well described in a series of novels – the best of their kind since Hardy – with a country setting.[2] Of the apprentice period he wrote:

I was amazed. Here they were speaking in a language I knew of, but had not heard, nor even imagined could still be heard. I'd just come from four years in a public school; but no one there had told me that the language that was the real glory of English literature was still being used in the field by unlettered men like these. About this time, when I first started as a farm apprentice, I had to go out horse-hoeing, taking a horse carefully between the rows of tender young plants; and this is how one of the farm-men instructed me: 'You lead that mare as slowly as ever foot can fall'.

And on this quotation George Ewart Evans comments:

That short sentence had the mark, rhythm, and substance of the old culture, as Adrian Bell recognized when he first heard it. It was tied firmly to the reality the farm-workers knew; it was concrete and clear because it was full of the ordinary images of everyday life made wonderfully alive; it was the language of Shakespeare. Indeed, the phrase as *softly as foot can fall* occurs in *As You Like It*; but the old horseman had probably not heard of Shakespeare.

Where Beards Wag All

Closely similar observations were made about the same time by Henry Williamson in Devon and H. J. Massingham in Gloucestershire:

Some of his phrases, the plain common phrases of the country, I wrote down in my notebook at the time, and later was astonished and delighted, to find the same phrases in Shakespeare. (He had not taken them from the book Shakespeare; but the living Shakespeare had taken them from common speech.)

Henry Williamson, *The Village Book* (1930)

Modern crofting in Western Scotland has been well described by crofters from outside, like Margaret Leigh in *Highland Homespun* (1936) and Raymond O'Malley in *One-Horse Farm* (1948). The latter writes of the independence, the variety, the beauty of the environment, the freedom from competition, and the measure of self-sufficiency enjoyed. Crofting was hard work, and it is only at this point that his emphasis differs from Margaret Leigh's, for she perhaps unintentionally gives the impression that there were many opportunities for taking it easy. O'Malley's reflections resemble Sturt's, and are as crucial:

[There] were four aspects of specialisation that had as yet hardly affected the Glen – the divorce of employer from worker, of producer from consumer, of leisure from work, and of responsibility from execution. What is disturbing is that all these effects are not incidental to machine technique, but intimately and essentially a part of specialisation, which is inseparable from machine technique. The main outcome, therefore, of our experience in the Glen was the strengthening of our doubt as to the possibility of a leisure civilisation. Where work is creative, leisure also is creatively employed . . . In the promised leisure of the future.

it is the spare-time activities that must be the source of self-respect and of personal fulfilment. To Keats it was, admittedly, his poetry that gave meaning to life, and that has always been the case for a favoured, intelligent minority; the undiscussed assumption made by those who look forward to a leisure civilisation based on the machine is that what was possible to Keats is possible to everyone. . . . All the evidence of history goes against that assumption.

Last of our farming examples, J. S. Collis took to being a farm worker in 1940 instead of being tied to an army desk. As well as being an articulate account of the experience, his books are one of the best records of what it felt like to work on a farm immediately before mechanisation. Like O'Malley, he plots the way we are going; here for example he comments on 'the cost of living':

It means that we must pay *money* to be alive, a definite fee for being in the world, with a heavy Entrance Fee. Everyone must make a living rather than make a life. What is he going to be? it is asked of boys, for it is understood that it is not sufficient that he shall be *himself* – only a girl is permitted to say that she already *is*. I was not making a living jogging along here, but I could not help feeling Alive, the freedom of the fields, the freedom of the sky, the freedom of movement gratui-tously bestowed on me.

The Worm Forgives the Plough (1973)

This account cannot mention all those who have written per-ceptively about country life, nor do justice to those included. Those quoted do not amount to a 'school' of writing, but they all write good prose, sometimes outstandingly so, and if from any-one stem from Cobbett. They share his concern for the plight of the worker, though the sapping by poverty has been replaced by the disadvantages of affluence; his enjoyment of landscape; and his instinctive defence of values associated with agriculture – that instinct that made him so rightly hate the 'feelosophers' who sought mechanically to apply an inept and inhuman political economy.

In addition however one writer and one book call for attention. Edward Thomas (1878–1917) does not fall readily into any slot. He drew more strength from the countryside than has any poet of stature since his day, but he is not a 'country poet'. He wrote a good life of Jefferies and many sensitively observed books on rural topics, but his achievement is his poetry, apparently slight and casual, with country scenes providing the opportunity or opening. Two of them, 'Lob' and 'Words' (quoted here), are especially close to the themes of this book. The former relates the poet's springtime search for people who might have known an old man he had once seen in Wiltshire; and when he is given a dozen different answers it is clear that the poem is about the archetypal rural Englishman, who gave wild flowers, birds and places their beautiful names, and has a wonderful vocabulary of concrete terms and a store of expressions for transmitting the traditional wisdom. A string of the names he was known by through the ages ends with:

> Robin Hood, Ragged Robin, lazy Bob,
> One of the lords of No Man's Land, good Lob –
> Although he was seen dying at Waterloo,
> Hastings, Agincourt, and Sedgemoor too –
> Lives yet.

The two poems leave one in no doubt about Thomas's sense of a successful human ordering of things, an adjustment to the environment, the rhythm of the seasons, and the quality of the people themselves. Ronald Blythe's *Akenfield* (1969) is a skilfully edited collection of interviews, accorded by villagers to an author who won their confidence. Blythe points to the void where once the old village culture existed. Most of the inhabitants are now suburbanites, with the new arrivals paying tribute of devotion to the national village cult, playing at village life, and arousing the contempt of truly local people by such activities as getting up entertainments. Outside the village the hedges are being slaughtered in the interest of prairie farming, and the wild birds killed off by pesticides. Farms and farming are an extension of the factory and its methods. For example the specialist pea-grower has to sow and harvest his peas precisely when the man from the factory tells him to; and the harvesting is done by gangs of men with machines, working round the clock. As for the animals: beef cattle are kept indoors, cows are stalled in herringbone sheds all their lives, imprisoned pigs are so bored that they bite each other's tails off while being fattened with chemical additives, and poultry are stored in batteries, sometimes 'debeaked' to stop them pecking each other. A factory farmer confesses, about his intensive use of pigs and poultry: 'It's not what I wanted to do [arable farming] . . . and I feel that the kind of farming I do now isn't quite "right". Certainly it isn't satisfying.' And although he feels conscience-stricken when he puts pigs inside for their whole lives, he defends the insertion of additives in animal food: 'But then we have all kinds of additives in our food. Take bread, it isn't natural bread, there are all sorts of things in it. It is bought all cut up in cellophane and is horrible, but we eat it because it is the food of our time.'

According to *Akenfield* farming as it was for hundreds of years has disappeared, at least over much of East Anglia, and the farm is now a station on the conveyor to the supermarket. East Anglia is not the whole of England, and there are still hill farms, mixed farms, crofts, marginal and other farms elsewhere. But it is practically all accountancy farming, tied to making profits by doses of chemicals for soil and animals, and treating both as parts of a machine. Some farmers have different and not less profitable ideas, and they produce food that is more palatable, more nourishing and probably healthier. The truth is hard to find, because all the pressure and all the heavily financed research is onesidedly in favour of industrial agriculture and massive investment in chemicals. Such considerations do not concern us here, except as the occasion to point out that there can be no more books of the kind we have been discussing. More *Akenfields* there may well be; and so long as farming continues on its present lines Rachel Carson's *Silent Spring* will need every now and then to be updated.

1

A HOME-MADE
CIVILISATION

INTRODUCTION

From two or three hundred years before the Conquest up to the middle of the eighteenth century, England was a predominantly peasant society. The word 'peasant' covers a good many variants over time and space; Lincolnshire for example included at one period four distinct types. The constant elements were: some sort of holding or ownership of land for vegetables, sometimes grain, poultry and later a pig, together with access to waste or common land; occasionally the peasant supplemented the work he did for himself by working for an employer. The common always supplied fuel, and grazing for cows and geese. In addition it sometimes yielded timber for building, heather for thatching and bedding animals, clay and sand for walling, and opportunities for bee-keeping, snaring animals and picking wild fruit. There was never a complete peasant economy, for there were always men with little or no land who had to work full-time for another. But as long as some form of it existed there were a number of men who managed to keep themselves and their families in independence. Important also were the freedom from total dependence on an employer, and the satisfactions of working for themselves and controlling a part of their own lives.

As one reads the histories, the story of the small-holder over a thousand years emerges clearly as one of reduction, from peasant to pauper. Before the Conquest, 'the general drift of English peasant life was undoubtedly from freedom towards servitude';

William made things worse – though E. P. Thompson disputes this; and the Peasants' Revolt won freedom for serfs at the price of divorce from the soil. The England of the manor became the England of the peasant cultivator, but the decline continued. In 1587 for example William Harrison[3] recorded the trend from the old self-sufficient community to larger farms that could meet urban demands for food: 'Some owners, still desirous to enlarge those grounds . . . for the breeding and feeding of cattle, do not let daily to take in more, not sparing the very commons whereupon many townships now and then do live.' In the eighteenth century the crime of the sixteenth became a virtue, as the agricultural enthusiasts had their way, and the enclosures brought more profit to big farmers and higher rents to landlords. Mary Palmer has summed it up:

Enclosures were not new in the eighteenth century, but the passion for improvement and the certain hope of gain in these years made the practice of such magnitude as to effect a systematic destruction of the old system, and, particularly in the richer counties, the extinction of middling and small holdings for large scale capitalist farming served by landless labourers. Acts of Parliament enclosed common fields and meadows and wastes in one district after another. The man who owned a strip or two would get his little patch in the award. He could no longer graze his pigs or geese on the waste, or gather fuel there, and he must fence his allotted patch, pay his share of the legal costs of the enclosure, and sometimes even share the expense of fencing the parson's acres. The cottager with proved rights of common title would get his compensating plot, but often he could show no title, only knowing that he had always kept a cow on the common like his father before him. In any case the law did not recognise that a cow and a few geese on the common was something towards a living, for which a few perches of land that you had to sell because you couldn't afford to fence was no compensation. The cottagers lost their cows and their fuel. With the coming of machines, the cottage industries whereby wife and children had added a few shillings to the weekly family income disappeared. Prices rose by 60 per cent in the second half of the 18th century, wages rose by 25 per cent. So the labourer could buy less now with a wage

that was his sole resource than he could before enclosures with a wage
he had supplemented with a cow and his wife's knitting. The labourer
could not live on his wages.

Writing and Action[4]

There was no real safeguard for the dispossessed, who were given
into the hands of the large owner as a pool of cheap forced labour.
'Enclosure was a plain enough case of class robbery . . . and the
social violence of enclosure consisted precisely in the drastic,
total imposition upon the village of capitalist property-definitions'
(E. P. Thompson, *The Making of the English Working Class*).

The enclosures increased agricultural productivity, but they
destroyed self-sufficient communities, responsible for, and managing, their own affairs, who did not share the results of improved
farming:

Starved, workless, indebted, browbeaten and miscalled, how could the
poor make their own lives tolerable . . ? The half-fed children whim-
pered, and exasperated parents repressed and belaboured them, so that
the second and third generations added a dull, inhibited appearance to
all else . . . Kathleen was amazed when she saw early eighteenth century
pictures of 'peasant' children – handsome, lively, adventurous! No
artist could have seen such cottage children in a village from the 1790s
to the moment at which she stood, pondering the question . . . It was
strange enough to have a 'system' of farming that starved the men who
sowed, harrowed and cut the corn; stranger that other workers in
industry, the farmers, should at the same time prosper.

M. K. Ashby, *Joseph Ashby of Tysoe*

What did members of the vanished community have in
common? Sturt (*Journals*, p. 730) answers the question:

The 'Spirit' of our time is less likely to be authentic or vividly strong
than the spirit of our grandfathers, because while that was local,
parochial, ours is more cosmopolitan. The local old 'Spirit' was an
understanding, common to all neighbours, of the neighbourhood and
its intimate personal demands. With us, we have in common – the

B

newspapers. And we don't have to adjust ourselves to our understanding of our wider environment anything like so exactly as our grandfathers had to adjust themselves to theirs.

So, as they understood the same things as one another, in pretty much the same way, they arrived (I think) at a more frequent unison of will, of conduct, than we do. The roads and lanes, the fields and woods, entered largely into their personality. They 'understood' the look of daylight, the weather, the cattle, the local industry.

The folk industries required this intimacy with the neighbourhood in order that their products might suit the needs of the locality. The sawyers for example were versed in a craft full of skill, 'rich in associations with English village, English woodland . . . the men were in many ways a sort of epitome of the indomitable adaptation of our breed to land and climate. As a wild animal species to its habitat, so these men had fitted themselves to the local conditions of life and death.'

This picture of peasant artisans can be supplemented by many writers. They tell us that the peasant was hardworking, independent, honest; he took pride in his work. He was charitable and co-operative, lacking ambition, often puritanical in morals – this last quality can be felt in some of the less pleasant folk customs. He was cheerful and patient, with a great capacity for endurance. These qualities led Sturt to point to the source of Wordsworth's eminence: 'that rural sympathy of his, that strong understanding, that brave tender insight, that calm outlook – out of what fine social atmosphere did he . . . absorb all this? Whatever it was, and wherever Wordsworth got it, it was part of England's spontaneous living – a part of folk-life' (*Journals*, p. 782). This is not the place to consider that suggestion at length, but it is clear that much of Wordsworth's best work comes from one who was conscious that behind him lay the tradition he described in the letter to Charles James Fox, quoted earlier.

Among the descendants of the real peasants, the memory of their former independence and prosperity lived on. More active, as Sturt said, were the traditions 'that so often guided the hand of the craftsman'. Walter Rose, a master carpenter, recalled in *The Village Carpenter* that 'we were never unconscious of our gratitude to men whom we had never known, who had passed away many years before we were born, leaving their good handiwork as their enduring memorial'. This debt is noted again and again: the best shape, the best design, the best method had been evolved by men ages before. Feelings too flowed in channels formed long ago:

The Christmas holly and ivy, the Easter yew, would tell the same tale that the seasons told, of the onward movement of man's life; would give it significance too; would seem to repeat what had been felt about it by English folk for many centuries, thereby dignifying the otherwise insignificant-seeming moments, and encouraging cheerfulness instead of provoking a sigh.

George Bourne, *William Smith, Potter and Farmer* (1919)

Oral tradition was the medium through which the understanding of past generations lived for a while in those who received it, and then was handed on. The total resources of the community were thus available to its members. Naturally in such societies originality was at a discount; the price of a supportive code that guided the whole of one's life was lack of space for individuality.

Tradition flowed as well in art and craft and ways of doing things, and peasant cultures have produced lovely work, treasured by museums, in embroidery, weaving, furniture, wood- and stone-working, carving and pottery. But not a great deal of all this has survived in England, except in so far as those who built and embellished the churches were peasants. The strength of English folk culture has been in music and speech, dialect speech. Many writers, such as Cecil Torr in Devon and Edwin Muir in the Orkneys, have agreed with Hardy that local 'varieties of English . . . are intrinsically as grammatical and worthy of the royal title as is the all-prevailing competitor which bears it; whose only fault was that they happened not to be central, therefore were worsted in the struggle for existence' (Hardy, introduction to *Select Poems of William Barnes* (1903)). As Adrian Bell puts it so clearly in his article below, rural speech was expressive, full of idiomatic life and – because people spoke of what they knew – ran to the concrete rather than the abstract. In the country there flourished the traditional art of speech, in F. R. Leavis's words 'the popular, generally cultivated art of speech that made the English language that made Shakespeare possible'. And George Ewart Evans, after noting that some of the speech of Chaucer, Spenser, Shakespeare, Tusser and Clare lived on in dialect into the twentieth century, adds:

Language does not exist in a vacuum . . . the old language or dialect in East Anglia has persisted because the material culture that was its matrix lasted in comparatively unchanged form until the first quarter of this century. It was based on the historical work of East Anglia – arable farming – and while animal- and man-power remained the chief motive force of that farming its structure and its cultural ambience remained intact. But once the character of the work changed, as it did with the coming of the tractor and the motor-car, the character of rural society (and it is not an exaggeration to say the *millennial* character) also changed in a revolutionary way within a couple of generations.

Where Beards Wag All

While farming remained basically unchanged, the language survived, but the peasant way of life had gone by the middle of the nineteenth century. Its extinction – we have often been told – was necessary in the interest of greater agricultural efficiency; but the connotations nowadays of that last word must give us pause. What sort of 'efficiency' was it that destroyed a coherent and satisfying way of life and produced a population of paupers? The writers, from Thomas More to Walter Rose, quoted below have given their impressions, but an historian's view of a specific case is of great interest. Joan Thirsk has shown how the draining of the Lincolnshire fens ruined the fenlanders for the benefit only of the large farmers and gentry. Before drainage: 'At the beginning of the seventeenth century . . . the fenland was a prosperous farming region whose economy had been shaped by a thousand years of tradition and experience. It gave a comfortable living to a large population. There was no immediate economic reason to justify a fundamental alteration in the routine of husbandry' (*English Peasant Farming*). The ineptness of the profit-for-some-equals-prosperity-for-all equation reminds one of the example, cited by Levi-Strauss in *The Savage Mind* (1966), of a desert region of South California, now supporting only a handful of white families. Where they manage to subsist, several thousand Indians had lived in a land of plenty without exhausting the natural resources, because they had an inexhaustible knowledge of the fauna and flora around them. Similarly the English peasant, as Sturt points out below, had so intimate and so necessary a knowledge of his environment that he was part of it, and it was part of him. Such a symbiosis was beyond the ken of earlier economists.

All that Sturt claimed for the home-made civilisation of the rural English is confirmed by other observers. In remote places where enclosure could profit little the peasant order endured almost to within living memory. Edwin Muir, for example, brought up among small farmers, bears out all the points on which Sturt had insisted; he tells us what was not replaced when the economy came to an end:

I cannot say how much my idea of a good life was influenced by my early upbringing, but it seems to me that the life of the little island of Wyre was a good one, and that its sins were mere sins of the flesh, which are excusable, and not sins of the spirit; they did not realise what competition was, though they lived at the end of Queen Victoria's reign; they helped one another with their work, when help was required, following the old usage; they had a culture made up of legend, folk-song, and the poetry and prose of the Bible; their life was an order, and a good order. So that when my father and mother left Orkney for Glasgow when I was fourteen, we were plunged out of order into chaos.

An Autobiography (1926)

VESTIGES

As a general rule the village character was genial, steadfast, self-respecting; one could not but recognize in it a great fund of strength, a great stability; nor could one help feeling that its main features – the limitations and the grimness, as well as the surprising virtues – were somehow closely related to that pleasant order of things suggested by the hay-making sounds, by the smell of the wood-smoke, by the children's May-day garlands. And, in fact, the relationship was essential. The temper and manners of the older people turned out to have been actually moulded by conditions of a true village kind, so that the same folk-quality that sounded in the little garland song reappeared more sternly in my neighbours' attitude towards their fate. Into this valley, it is true, much had never come that had flourished and been forgotten in English villages elsewhere. At no time had there been any of the more graceful folk arts here; at no time any comely social life, such as one reads of in Goldsmith's *Deserted Village* or Gray's *Elegy*; but, as I gradually learnt, the impoverished labouring people I talked to had been, in many cases, born in the more prosperous conditions of a self-supporting peasantry.

Bit by bit the truth came home to me, in the course of unconcerned gossip, when my informants had no idea of the significance of those stray scraps of information which they let fall. I was not alive to it myself for a long time. But when I had heard of the village cows, which used to be turned out to graze on the heaths, and had been told how fir-timber fit for cottage roof-joists could be cut on the common, as well as heath good enough for thatching and turf excellent for firing; and when to this was added the talk of bread-ovens at half the old cottages, and of little corn-crops in the gardens, and of brewing and wine-making and bee-keeping; I understood at last that my elderly neighbours had seen with their own eyes what I should never see – namely, the old rustic economy of the English peasantry. In that light all sorts of things showed a new meaning. I looked with rather changed sentiments, for example, upon the noisome pigsties – for were they not a survival of a venerable thrift? I viewed the old tools – hoes and spades and scythes and fag-hooks – with quickened interest; and I speculated with more intelligence upon those aged people of the parish whose curious habits were described to me with so much respect. But of all the details that now gained significance, most to be noted were the hints of the comparative prosperity of that earlier time. For now some old woman, half starving on her parish pay, would indicate this or that little cottage, and remark that her grandfather had built it for her mother to go into when she married. Or now, a decrepit man would explain that in such and such a puzzling nook in the hillside had once stood his father's cow-stall. Here, at the edge of the arable strip, a building divided into two poor cottages proved to have been originally somebody's little hop-kiln; there, on a warm slope given over to the pleasure-garden of some 'resident' like myself, a former villager used to grow enough wheat to keep him in flour half the winter; and there again, down a narrow by-way gone ruinous from long neglect, Master So-and-so, whose children to-day go in fear of the workhouse, was wont to drive his little waggon and pair of horses.

Particulars like these, pointing to a lost state of well-being, accounted very well for the attraction which, in spite of individual faults, I had felt towards the village folk in general. The people stood for something more than merely themselves. In their odd ways and talk and character I was affected, albeit unawares, by a robust tradition of the English countryside, surviving here when the circumstances which would have explained it had already largely disappeared. After too many years of undiscernment that truth was apparent to me. And even so, it was but a gradual enlightenment; even now it is unlikely that I appreciate the facts in their deepest significance. For the 'robust' tradition, as I have just called it, was something more than simply robust. It was older, by far, than this anomalous village. Imported into the valley – if my surmise is correct – by squatters two centuries ago, it was already old even then; it already had centuries of experience behind it; and though it very likely had lost much in that removal, still it was a genuine off-shoot of the home-made or 'folk' civilization of the South of England. No wonder that its survivals had struck me as venerable and pleasant, when there was so much vigorous English life behind them, derived perhaps from so many fair English counties.

George Bourne, Change in the Village

THE PEASANT SYSTEM

The persistence into the twentieth century – the scarcely realized persistence – not so much of any definite ideas, as of a general temper more proper to the eighteenth century, accounts for all sorts of anomalies in the village, and explains not only why other people do not understand the position of its inhabitants to-day, but why they themselves largely fail to understand it. They are not fully aware of being behind the times, and probably in many respects they no longer are so; only there is that queer mental attitude giving its bias to their view of life. Although very feebly now, still the momentum derived from a forgotten cult carries them on.

But, having noticed the persistence of the peasant traditions, we have next to notice how inadequate they are to present needs. Our subject swings round here. Inasmuch as the peasant outlook lingers on in the valley, it explains many of those peculiarities I have described in earlier chapters; but, inasmuch as it is a decayed and all but useless outlook, we shall see in its decay the significance of those changes in the village which have now to be traced out. The little that is left from the old days has an antiquarian or a gossipy sort of interest; but the lack of the great deal that has gone gives rise to some most serious problems.

For, as I hinted at the outset, the 'peasant' tradition in its vigour amounted to nothing less than a form of civilization – the home-made civilization of the rural English. To the exigent problems of life it furnished solutions of its own – different solutions, certainly, from those which modern civilization gives, but yet serviceable enough. People could find in it not only a method of getting a living, but also an encouragement and a help to live well. Besides employment there was an intense interest for them in the country customs. There was scope for modest ambition too. Best of all, those customs provided a rough guidance as to conduct – an unwritten code to which, though we forget it, England owes much. It seems singular to think of now; but the very labourer might reasonably hope for some satisfaction in life, nor trouble about 'raising' himself into some other class, so long as he could live on peasant lines. And it is in the virtual disappearance of this civilization that the main change in the village consists. Other changes are comparatively immaterial. The valley might have been invaded by the leisured classes; its old appearance might have been altered; all sorts of new-fangled things might have been introduced into it; and still under the surface it would have re-tained the essential village characteristics, had but the peasant tradition been preserved in its integrity amongst the lowlier people; but with that dying, the village, too, dies where it stands. And that is what has been happening here. A faint influence from out of the past still has its feeble effect; but, in this corner of England at least, what we used to think of as the rural English are, as it were, vanishing away – vanishing as in a slow transformation, not by death or emigration, not even by essential change of personnel, but by becoming somehow different in their outlook and habits. The old families continue in their old home; but they begin to be a new people.

It was of the essence of the old system that those living under it subsisted in the main upon what their own industry could produce out of the soil and materials of their own countryside. A few things, certainly, they might get from other neighbourhoods, such as iron for making their tools, and salt for curing their bacon; and some small interchange of commodities there was, accordingly, say between the various districts that yielded cheese, and wool, and hops, and charcoal; but as a general thing the parish where the peasant people lived was the source of the materials they used, and their wellbeing depended on their knowledge of its resources. Amongst themselves they would number a few special craftsmen – a smith, a carpenter or wheelwright, a shoemaker, a pair of sawyers, and so on; yet the trades of these specialists were only ancillary to the general handiness of the people, who with their own hands raised and harvested their crops, made their clothes, did much of the building of their homes, attended to their cattle, thatched their ricks, cut their firing, made their bread and wine or cider, pruned their fruit-trees and vines, looked after their bees, all for themselves. And some at least, and perhaps the most, of these economies were open to the poorest labourer. Though he owned no land, yet as the tenant, and probably the permanent tenant, of a cottage and garden he had the chance to occupy himself in many a craft that tended to his own comfort. A careful man and wife needed not to despair of becoming rich in the possession of a cow or a pig or two, and of good clothes and household utensils; and they might well expect to see their children grow up strong and prosperous in the peasant way.

Thus the claim that I have made for the peasant tradition – namely, that it permitted a man to hope for well-being without seeking to escape from his own class into some other – is justified, partially at least. I admit that the ambition was a modest one, but there were circumstances attending it to make it a truly comforting one too. Look once more at the conditions. The small owners of the parish might occupy more land than the labourers, and have the command of horses and waggons, and ploughs and barns, and so on; but they ate the same sort of food and wore the same sort of clothes as the poorer folk, and they thought the same thoughts too, and talked in the same dialect, so that the labourer working for them was not oppressed by any sense of personal inferiority. He might even excel in some directions, and be valued for his excellence. Hence, if his ambition was small, the need for it was not very great.

And then, this life of manifold industry was interesting to live. It is impossible to doubt it. Not one of the pursuits I have mentioned failed to make its pleasant demand on the labourer for skill and knowledge; so that after his day's wage-earning he turned to his wine-making or the management of his pigs with the zest that men put into their hobbies. Amateurs the people were of their homely crafts – very clever amateurs, too, some of them. I think it likely, also that normally even wage-earning labour went as it were to a peaceful tune. In the elaborate tile-work of old cottage roofs, in the decorated ironwork of decrepit farm-waggons, in the carefully fashioned field-gates – to name but a few relics of the sort – many a village of Surrey and Hampshire and Sussex has ample proofs that at least the artisans of old time went about their work placidly, unhurriedly, taking time to make their products comely. And probably the same peaceful conditions extended to the labouring folk. Of course, their ploughing and harvesting have left no traces; but there is much suggestiveness in some little things one may note, such as the friendly behaviour of carter-men to their horses, and the accomplished finish given to the thatch of ricks, and the endearing names which people in out-of-the-way places still bestow upon their cows. Quietly, but convincingly, such things tell their tale of tranquillity, for they cannot have originated amongst a people habitually unhappy and harassed. But whether the day's work went comfortably or no, certainly the people's own home-work – to turn to that again – must often have been agreeable, and sometimes delightful. The cottage crafts were not all strictly useful; some had simple aesthetic ends. If you doubt it, look merely at the clipped hedges of box and yew in the older gardens; they are the result of long and loving care, but they serve no particular end, save to please the eye. So, too, in general, if you think that the folk of old were inappreciative of beauty, you have but to listen to their names of flowers – sweet-william, hearts-ease, marigold, meadow-sweet, night-shade – for proof that English peasant-life had its graceful side.[5]

Still, their useful work must, after all, have been the mainstay of the villagers; and how thoroughly their spirits were immersed in it I suppose few living people will ever be able to realize. For my part, I dare not pretend to comprehend it; only at times I can vaguely feel what the peasant's attitude must have been. All the things of the countryside had an intimate bearing upon his own fate; he was not there to admire them, but to live by them – or, say, to wrest his living from them by familiar knowledge of their properties. From long experience – experience older than his own, and traditional amongst his people – he knew the soil of the fields and its variations almost foot by foot; he understood the springs and streams; hedgerow and ditch explained themselves to him; the coppices and woods, the water-meadows and the windy heaths, the local chalk and clay and stone, all had a place in his regard – reminded him of the crafts of his people, spoke to him of the economies of his own cottage life; so that the turfs or the faggots or the timber he handled when at home called his fancy, while he was handling them, to the landscape they came from. Of the intimacy of this knowledge, in minute details, it is impossible to give an idea. I am assured of its existence because I have come across surviving examples of it, but I may not begin to describe it. One may, however, imagine dimly what the cumulative effect of it must have been on the peasant's outlook; how attached he must have grown – I mean how closely linked – to his own countryside. He did not merely 'reside' in it; he was part of it, and it was part of him. He fitted into it as one of its native denizens, like the hedgehogs and the thrushes. All that happened to it mattered to him. He learnt to look with reverence upon its main features, and would not willingly interfere with their disposition. But I lose the best point in talking of the individual peasant; these things should rather be said of the tribe – the little group of folk – of which he was a member. As they, in their successive generations, were the denizens of their little patch of England – its human fauna – so it was with traditional feelings derived from their continuance in the land that the individual peasant man or woman looked at the fields and the woods.

Out of all these circumstances – the pride of skill in handicrafts, the detailed understanding of the soil and its materials, the general effect of the well-known landscape, and the faint sense of something venerable in its associations – out of all this there proceeded an influence which acted upon the village people as an unperceived guide to their conduct, so that they observed the seasons proper for their varied pursuits almost as if they were going through some ritual. Thus, for instance, in this parish, when, on an auspicious evening of spring, a man and wife went out far across the common to get rushes for the wife's hop-tying, of course it was a consideration of thrift that sent them off; but an idea of doing the right piece of country routine at the right time gave value to the little expedition. The moment, the evening, became enriched by suggestion of the seasons into which it fitted, and by memories of years gone by. Similarly in managing the garden crops: to be too late, to neglect the well-known signs which hinted at what should be done, was more than bad economy; it was dereliction of peasant duty. And thus the succession of recurring tasks, each one of which seemed to the villager almost characteristic of his own people in their native home, kept constantly alive a feeling that satisfied him and a usage that helped him. The feeling was that he belonged to a set of people rather apart from the rest of the world – a people necessarily different from others in their manners, and perhaps poorer and ruder than most, but yet fully entitled to respect and consideration. The usage was just the whole series or body of customs to which his own people conformed; or, more exactly, the accepted idea in the village of what ought to be done in any contingency, and of the proper way to do it. In short, it was that unwritten code I spoke of just now – a sort of *savoir vivre* – which became part of the rural labourer's outlook, and instructed him through his days and years. It was hardly reduced to thoughts in his consciousness, but it always swayed him. And it was consistent with – nay, it implied – many strong virtues: toughness to endure long labour, handiness, frugality, habits of early rising. It was consistent too – that must be admitted – with considerable hardness and 'coarseness' of feeling; a man might be avaricious, loose, dirty, quarrelsome, and not offend much against the essential peasant code. Nor was its influence very good upon his intellectual development, as I shall show later on. Yet whatever its defects, it had those qualities which I have tried to outline; and where it really flourished it ultimately led to gracefulness of living and love of what is comely and kind. You can detect as much still, in the flavour of many a mellow folk-saying, not to mention folk-song; you may divine it yet in all kinds of little popular traits, if once you know what to look for.

In this particular valley, where the barren soil challenged the people to a severer struggle for bare subsistence, the tradition could not put forth its fairer, its gentler, features; nevertheless the backbone of the village life was of the genuine peasant order. The cottagers had to 'rough it', to dispense with softness, to put up with ugliness; but by their own skill and knowledge they forced the main part of their living out of the soil and materials of their own neighbourhood. And in doing this they won at least the rougher consolations which that mode of life had to offer. Their local knowledge was intensely interesting to them; they took pride in their skill and hardihood; they felt that they belonged to a set of people not inferior to others, albeit perhaps poorer and ruder; and all the customs which their situation required them to follow sustained their belief in the ancestral notions of good and evil. In other words, they had a civilization to support them – a poor thing, perhaps, a poor kind of civilization, but their own, and entirely within the reach of them all. I have no hesitation in affirming all this; because, though I never saw the system in its completeness, I came here soon enough to find a few old people still partially living by it. These old people, fortunate in the possession of their own cottages and a little land, were keepers of pigs and donkeys, and even a few cows. They kept bees, too; they made wine; they often paid in kind for any services that neighbours did for them; and with the food they could grow, and the firing they could still obtain from the woods and heath, their living was half provided for. The one of them I knew best was not the most typical. Shrewd old man that he was, he had adapted himself so far as suited him to a more commercial economy, and had grown suspicious and avaricious; yet if he could have been translated suddenly back into the eighteenth century, he would scarce have needed to change any of his habits, or even his clothes. He wore an old-fashioned 'smock frock',[6] doubtless home-made; and in this he pottered about all day – pottered, at least, in his old age, when I knew him – not very spruce as to personal cleanliness, smelling of his cow-stall, saving money, wanting no holiday, independent of books and newspapers, indifferent to anything that happened farther off than the neighbouring town, liking his pipe and glass of beer, and never knowing what it was to feel dull. I speak of him because I knew him personally; but there were others of whom I used to hear, though I never became acquainted with them, who seem to have been hardly at all tainted with the commercial spirit, and were more in the position of labourers than this man, yet lived almost dignified lives of simple and self-supporting contentment. Of some of them the middle-aged people of to-day still talk, not without respect.

But in writing of such folk I have most emphatically to use the past tense; for although a sort of afterglow from the old civilization still rests upon the village character, it is fast fading out, and it has not much resemblance to the genuine thing of half a century ago. The direct light has gone out of the people's life – the light, the meaning, the guidance. They have no longer a civilization, but only some derelict habits left from that which has gone. And it is no wonder if some of those habits seem now stupid, ignorant, objectionable; for the fitness has departed from them, and left them naked. They were acquired under a different set of circumstances – a set of circumstances whose disappearance dates from, and was caused by, the enclosure of the common.

George Bourne, Change in the Village

THE 'ESTATESMEN'

Thus has been given a faithful description, the minuteness of which the reader will pardon, of the face of this country as it was, and had been through centuries, till within the last sixty years. Towards the head of these Dales was found a perfect Republic of Shepherds and Agriculturists, among whom the plough of each man was confined to the maintenance of his own family, or to the occasional accommodation of his neighbour.* Two orthree cows furnished each family with milk and cheese. The chapel was the only edifice that presided over these dwellings, the supreme head of this pure Commonwealth; the members of which existed in the midst of a powerful empire like an ideal society or an organized community, whose constitution had been imposed and regulated by the mountains which protected it. Neither high-born nobleman, knight, nor esquire was here; but many of these humble sons of the hills had a consciousness that the land, which they walked over and tilled, had for more than five hundred years been possessed by men of their name and blood; and venerable was the transition, when a curious traveller, descending from the heart of the mountains, had come to some ancient manorial residence in the more open part of the Vales, which, through the rights attached to its proprietor, connected the almost visionary mountain republic he had been contemplating with the substantial frame of society as existing in the laws and constitution of a mighty empire.

* One of the most pleasing characteristics of manners in secluded and thinly-peopled districts, is a sense of the degree in which human happiness and comfort are dependent on the contingency of neighbourhood. This is implied by a rhyming adage common here, 'Friends are far, when neighbours are nar' (near). This mutual helpfulness is not confined to out-of-doors work; but is ready upon all occasions. Formerly, if a person became sick, especially the mistress of a family, it was usual for those of the neighbours who were more particularly connected with the party by amicable offices, to visit the house, carrying a present; this practice, which is by no means obsolete, is called owning the family, and is regarded as a pledge of a disposition to be otherwise serviceable in a time of disability and distress.

William Wordsworth, Guide to the Lakes

Formerly, every household had nearly all that it wanted within itself. The people thought so little of wheaten bread, that wheat was hardly to be bought in the towns. Within the last few years, an old man of eighty-five was found of telling how, when a boy, he wanted to spend his penny on wheaten bread; and he searched through Carlisle from morning to evening before he could find a penny-roll. The cultivator among the hills divided his field into plots where he grew barley, oats, flax, and other produce to meet the needs of the household. His pigs, fed partly on acorns or beechmast, yielded good bacon and hams; and his sheep furnished wool for clothing. Of course he kept cows. The women spun and wove the wool and flax, and the lads made the wooden utensils, baskets, fishing tackle, &c. Whatever else was needed was obtained from the pedlars who came their rounds two or three times a year, dropping in among the little farms from over the hills. The first great change was from the opening of carriage-roads. There was a temptation then to carry stock and grain to fairs and markets. More grain was grown than the household needed, and offered for sale. In a little while the mountain-farmers were sure to fail in competition in the markets with dwellers in agricultural districts. The mountaineer had no agricultural science and little skill; and the decline of the fortunes of the 'statesmen', as they are locally called, has been regular, and mournful to witness. They haunt the fairs and markets, losing in proportion to the advance of improvement elsewhere. On their first losses, they began to mortgage their lands. After bearing the burden of these mortgages till they could bear it no longer, their children have sold the lands: and among the shop-boys, domestic servants, and labourers of the towns, we find the names of the former yeomanry of the district, who have parted with their lands to strangers. Much misery intervened during the process of transition. The farmer was tempted to lose the remembrance of his losses in drink when he attended the fairs and markets. . . .

To return to the former condition of the 'statesman'. The domestic manufactures he carried to town with him, – the linen and woollen webs woven by his wife and daughters, – would not sell, except at a loss, in the presence of the Yorkshire and Lancashire woollens and cottons made by machinery. He became unable to keep his children at home; and they went off to the manufacturing towns, leaving home yet more cheerless – with fewer busy hands and cheerful faces – less social spirit in the dales – greater certainty of continued loss, and more temptation to drink. Such is the process still going on.

Harriet Martineau, *A Complete Guide to the English Lakes*

PEASANT SURVIVORS

Old Sally's was a long, low, thatched cottage with diamond-paned windows winking under the eaves and a rustic porch smothered in honeysuckle. Excepting the inn, it was the largest house in the hamlet, and of the two downstair rooms one was used as a kind of kitchen-storeroom, with pots and pans and a big red crockery water vessel at one end, and potatoes in sacks and peas and beans spread out to dry at the other. The apple crop was stored on racks suspended beneath the ceiling and bunches of herbs dangled below. In one corner stood the big brewing copper in which Sally still brewed with good malt and hops once a quarter. The scent of the last brewing hung over the place till the next and mingled with apple and onion and dried thyme and sage smells, with a dash of soapsuds thrown in, to compound the aroma which remained in the children's memories for life and caused a whiff of any two of the component parts in any part of the world to be recognized with an appreciative sniff and a mental ejaculation of 'Old Sally's!'

The inner room – 'the house', as it was called – was a perfect snuggery, with walls two feet thick and outside shutters to close at night and a padding of rag rugs, red curtains and feather cushions within. There was a good oak, gate-legged table, a dresser with pewter and willow-pattern plates, and a grandfather's clock that not only told the time, but the day of the week as well. It had even once told the changes of the moon; but the works belonging to that part had stopped and only the fat, full face, painted with eyes, nose and mouth, looked out from the square where the four quarters should have rotated. The clock portion kept such good time that half the hamlet set its own clocks by it. The other half preferred to follow the hooter at the brewery in the market town, which could be heard when the wind was in the right quarter. So there were two times in the hamlet and people would say when asking the hour, 'Is that hooter time, or Old Sally's?'

The garden was a large one, tailing off at the bottom into a little field where Dick grew his corn crop. Nearer the cottage were fruit trees, then the yew hedge, close and solid as a wall, which sheltered the beehives and enclosed the flower garden. Sally had such flowers, and so many of them, and nearly all of them sweet-scented! Wallflowers and tulips, lavender and sweet william, and pinks and old-world roses with enchanting names – Seven Sisters, Maiden's Blush, moss rose, monthly rose, cabbage rose, blood rose, and, most thrilling of all to the children, a big bush of the York and Lancaster rose, in the blooms of which the rival roses mingled in a pied white and red. It seemed as though all the roses in Lark Rise had gathered together in that one garden. Most of the gardens had only one poor starveling bush or none; but, then, nobody else had so much of anything as Sally.

A continual subject for speculation was as to how Dick and Sally managed to live so comfortably with no visible means of support beyond their garden and beehives and the few shillings their two soldier sons might be supposed to send them, and Sally in her black silk on Sundays and Dick never without a few ha'- pence for garden seeds or to fill his tobacco pouch. 'Wish they'd tell me how 'tis done,' somebody would grumble. 'I could do wi' a leaf out o' their book.'

But Dick and Sally did not talk about their affairs. All that was known of them was that the house belonged to Sally, and that it had been built by her grandfather before the open heath had been cut up into fenced fields and the newer houses had been built to accommodate the labourers who came to work in them. It was only when Laura was old enough to write their letters for them that she learned more. They could both read and Dick could write well enough to exchange letters with their own children; but one day they received a business letter that puzzled them, and Laura was called in, sworn to secrecy, and consulted. It was one of the nicest things that happened to her as a child, to be chosen out of the whole hamlet for their confidence and to know that Dick and Sally liked her, though so few other people did. After that, at twelve years old, she became their little woman of business, writ- ing letters to seedsmen and fetching postal orders from the market town to put in them and helping Dick to calculate the interest due on their savings bank account. From them she learned a great deal about the past life of the hamlet.

Sally could just remember the Rise when it still stood in a wide expanse of open heath, with juniper bushes and furze thickets and close, springy, rabbit-bitten turf. There were only six houses then and they stood in a ring round an open green, all with large gardens and fruit trees and faggot piles. Laura could pick out most of the houses, still in a ring, but lost to sight of each other among the newer, meaner dwellings that had sprung up around and between them. Some of the houses had been built on and made into two, others had lost their lean-tos and outbuildings. Only Sally's remained the same, and Sally was eighty. Laura in her lifetime was to see a ploughed field where Sally's stood; but had she been told that she would not have believed it.

Country people had not been so poor when Sally was a girl, or their prospects so hopeless. Sally's father had kept a cow, geese, poultry, pigs, and a donkey-cart to carry his produce to the market town. He could do this because he had commoners' rights and could turn his animals out to graze, and cut furze for firing and even turf to make a lawn for one of his customers. Her mother made butter, for themselves and to sell, baked their own bread, and made candles for lighting. Not much of a light, Sally said, but it cost next to nothing, and, of course, they went to bed early.

Sometimes her father would do a day's work for wages, thatching a rick, cutting and laying a hedge, or helping with the shearing or the harvest. This provided them with ready money for boots and clothes; for food they relied almost entirely on home produce. Tea was a luxury seldom indulged in, for it cost five shillings a pound. But country people then had not acquired the taste for tea; they preferred home-brewed.

Everybody worked; the father and mother from daybreak to dark. Sally's job was to mind the cow and drive the geese to the best grass patches. It was strange to picture Sally, a little girl, running with her switch after the great hissing birds on the common, especially as both common and geese had vanished as completely as though they never had been.

Sally had never been to school, for, when she was a child, there was no dame school near enough for her to attend; but her brother had gone to a night school run by the vicar of an adjoining parish, walking the three miles each way after his day's work was done, and he had taught Sally to spell out a few words in her mother's Bible. After that, she had been left to tread the path of learning alone and had only managed to reach the point where she could write her own name and read the Bible or newspaper by skipping words of more than two syllables. Dick was a little more advanced, for he had had the benefit of the night-school education at first hand.

Flora Thompson, Lark Rise to Candleford

COTTAGES

To begin with the COTTAGES. They are scattered over the valleys, and under the hill-sides, and on the rocks; and, even to this day, in the more retired dales, without any intrusion of more assuming buildings:

> Cluster'd like stars some few, but single most,
> And lurking dimly in their shy retreats,
> Or glancing on each other cheerful looks,
> Like separated stars with clouds between.   M.S.

The dwelling houses, and contiguous outhouses, are, in many instances of the colour of the native rock, out of which they have been built; but, frequently, the Dwelling or Fire-house, as it is ordinarily called, has been distinguished from the barn or byre by rough-cast and whitewash, which, as the inhabitants are not hasty in renewing it, in a few years acquires, by the influence of weather, a tint at once sober and variegated. As these houses have been, from father to son, inhabited by persons engaged in the same occupations, yet necessarily with changes in their circumstances, they have received without incongruity additions and accommodations adapted to the needs of each successive occupant, who, being for the most part proprietor, was at liberty to follow his own fancy: so that these humble dwellings remind the contemplative spectator of a production of Nature, and may (using a strong expression) rather be said to have grown than to have been erected; – to have risen, by an instinct of their own, out of the native rock – so little is there in them of formality, such is their wildness and beauty. Among the numerous recesses and projections in the walls and in the different stages of their roofs, are seen bold and harmonious effects of contrasted sunshine and shadow. It is a favourable circumstance, that the strong winds, which sweep down the valleys, induced the inhabitants, at a time when the materials for building were easily procured, to furnish many of these dwellings with substantial porches; and such as have not this defence, are seldom unprovided with a projection of two large slates over their thresholds. Nor will the singular beauty of the chimneys escape the eye of the attentive traveller. Sometimes a low chimney, almost upon a level with the roof, is overlaid with a slate, supported upon four slender pillars, to prevent the wind from driving the smoke down the chimney. Others are of a quadrangular shape, rising one or two feet above the roof; which low square is often surmounted by a tall cylinder, giving to the cottage chimney the most beautiful shape in which it is ever seen. Nor will it be too fanciful or refined to remark, that there is a pleasing harmony between a tall chimney of this circular form, and the living column of smoke, ascending from it through the still air. These dwellings mostly built, as has been said, of rough unhewn stone, are roofed with slates, which were rudely taken from the quarry before the present art of splitting them was understood, and are, therefore, rough and uneven in their surface, so that both the coverings and sides of the houses have furnished places of rest for the seeds of lichens, mosses, ferns, and flowers. Hence buildings, which in their very form call to mind the processes of Nature, do thus, clothed in part with a vegetable garb, appear to be received into the bosom of the living principle of things, as it acts and exists among the woods and fields; and, by their colour and their shape, affectingly direct the thoughts to that tranquil course of Nature and simplicity, along which the humble-minded inhabitants have, through so many generations, been led. Add the little garden with its shed for bee-hives, its small bed of pot-herbs, and its borders and patches of flowers for Sunday posies, with sometimes a choice few too much prized to be plucked; an orchard of proportioned size; a cheese-press, often supported by some tree near the door; a cluster of embowering sycamores for summer shade; with a tall fir, through which the winds sing when other trees are leafless; the little rill or household spout murmuring in all seasons; – combine these incidents and images together, and you have the representative idea of a moun-tain-cottage in this country so beautifully formed in itself, and so richly adorned by the hand of Nature.

William Wordsworth, *Guide to the Lakes*

ENGLISH TRADITION AND IDIOM

'Hullo, here's a bit of long-meadow oak,' exclaimed one of the men who were helping to lay down the stage for our local play. That plank alone happened not to be of oak – but of poplar. His remark was a riddle to which all present held the clue (a favourite conversational method). It implied an intimate knowledge of local geography among his hearers. The interpretation is this. The im-mediate neighbourhood consists of arable land undulating in low ridges. Along each depression runs a brook taking the water from the fields, and along either side of these brooks lies almost the only pasturage in the district – a double chain of long narrow meadows. Oak trees are not characteristic of these long meadows, but poplars. Thus 'long-meadow oak' equals poplar. This is a random example of how closely the countryman's life and language run together; they are like flesh and bone. He only speaks when he feels, and feeling and humour choose always an expression which is a picture of life before the bare word. (Thus, too, one who 'looks as though

she's been a-stone-picking all her life' for 'a bent old woman'.)
The invention and multiplication of such phrases is never-ending
and can be guaranteed for the illiterate mind as long as one day
differs from another. The one straight line in the landscape is the
plough's furrow, obtained only with mental and muscular pre-
occupation. Even then (as standards of precision go) it is only the
roughest optical generalization, as it were, of straightness. Thus it
is that agriculture and its tradition have resisted so stubbornly the
age of the formula. Like an ash-pole hammered into the clay for a
fence, it still buds. In a sense the soil has been 'rationalized' for
centuries, but the bird that alights on it, the storm-cloud that im-
pends, are as incalculable as ever. It is the infinite variation of ex-
traneous circumstance, the guerrilla multitude of wild life that
man still only holds at bay, that is the genius alive in country
tradition. This genius now has its own battle to fight with modern
'awareness', for possession of the countryman's soul.

To be employed in agriculture is like living in the shadow of a
tidal wave. Rural 'timelessness' is an urban illusion – time flies
swifter to the farmer than to anyone. There is always urgency,
only the *tempo* of the life is so different, that to the modern citizen
the countryman's haste seems like leisure, and his phrases 'poetical'.
Demagogy has taken the latter ready-made and exploited them.
Platform politicians who have never wielded anything heavier
than their own fists are always putting their hands to the plough,
sowing and reaping and threshing and winnowing. Cartoonists
picture agriculture for their parables. Divorced from the earth-
life, the traditional processes thus become clichés and mental
symbols merely.

To understand how language is still reborn out of tradition in
the unlettered mind (I refer to the older men), it is necessary to be
immersed in the life till one *thinks* as well as talks, in local usage.
A thousand natural chances of the day come to provide jest, illustration, simile. It is something even to find oneself at liberty (talking to the countryman) to use the emphatic 'that do' for our

correct 'it does'; to say 'for everlasting of' instead of 'a great many'. This, possibly, is why rural speech is 'picturesque'. The countryman kindles as he speaks, assumes the authority of one rooted in his life, and that emotional quickening is the same in essence as the artist's – creative. In the glow of it he coins words. Linguistically there is a kind of half-light in his brain, and on the impulse of an emotion words get confused with one another and fused into something new – a new shade of meaning is expressed. 'I'm squaggled' or 'that squaggle me' (of a too-tight collar or a too-thick coat in hot weather). 'A spuffling sort of chap' is one who boasts and bustles about importantly. To be 'strandled' is to be both baffled and stranded. 'Rafty' is both raw and misty. These, I say, are not traditional words, but words born of momentary need out of tradition.

Traditional idiom is founded on the Bible, that having been (luckily) the one book read in farm and cottage for centuries. 'And she went and came and gleaned in the field after the reapers; and her hap was to light on a part of the field belonging to Boaz . . .' might have been spoken by any old countryman to-day. Thus to one whom I had passed in a car some way from home, I said, 'I saw you at – yesterday', and he replied, 'Yes, master, and I *had knowledge of you.*'

There is an associative naïveté in the application of words which is another reason for the freshness achieved by a limited vocabulary. A single illustration will serve. The same old man had been staying away from home, and it had been windy March weather. 'I had to get back,' he said, 'for I knew my mills would all be down.' This puzzled me for a minute, knowing that he was no miller, but a cottager, and knowing of only one mill in the parish, and that derelict. But when he added, 'And when I got home I found for everlasting of birds about the garden,' I realized he meant the revolving bird-scarers he had made, with four feathers for sails.

The countryman's speech is only roundabout to that superficial view which regards a poem as going a long way round to say what could be conveyed in a few words. Sustainedly, the emotional and muscular content of his idiom is almost equal to that of poetry, for he possesses that same instinct by which the poet places words in striking propinquity; the urgency of his feeling causing his mind to leap intermediate associations, coining many a 'quaint' phrase, imaginatively just, though superficially bizarre. Local idiom is actually terse, inventing ellipses of its own. 'They won't come to-day – DO (= but if they should) it won't be till late.' Water pours out of a pipe 'full-hole'. Another local peculiarity is the transposition of a physical sensation to the thing that causes it. A gardener will say that the smell of a hyacinth or lilac is 'faint', meaning, not that it is slight, but so pungent as to make him feel faint.

Comparatively, the illiterate man has few words; language is new to him; but a power within him insists on getting said what he has to say. He has to wrestle with his angel. He must feel the word almost physically, it must be born alive out of his lips. His metaphors are like flashes of lightning. 'Dark as iron.' He doesn't care a jot for grammar, but only that what needs must be said, gets said somehow. Words as such don't matter to him. He enjoys and uses quite ruthlessly his freedom from class or academic restrictions. 'Not a mucher' (not much good); 'Lessest' (least); 'Snew' (snowed). Pronunciation is altered to suit his convenience: 'Ellum' (elm); 'Flim' (film); 'Meece' (mice). His need is for emphasis, for his surroundings are his perpetual wonder. Fires, floods, freezings – spring in winter – winter in summer – there is always something prodigious to be told of. The dark source is very present to him just beyond the screen of visible phenomena. Nature to him is always a masked face. The mask changes; it is grim or gay, but the face behind it is always unseen. His very phrase 'in good heart' senses the being latent in the soil. And he has an infinite sensibility of the moods of the weather. His rain vocabulary alone is considerable; it may be merely 'smeary,' or again 'a tidy mizzle', or 'rain pourin', or 'heavens hard'.

What is the outlook to-day? We have been standing a long time

making up our minds to ford a river. Some started, others followed, and now that most are well in, it is found to be deeper and
more difficult than was at first realized. 'Just a little learning –
just a little acquisition of knowledge,' we said, 'and look, we shall
be across and standing at the gates of the celestial city.' But now,
finding ourselves in difficulties, we cry out to those still on the
bank, 'Don't attempt it – you are much better off where you are.'
Too late. We are all for it now. The country fathers are the only
relics of that illiterate class which (finding it almost extinct) we
realize now has ever been the source and renewal of our literature.
The educated person, if he comes in contact with an old man who
can neither read nor write, although his surface-mind feels superi-
or, feels in his heart an involuntary respect, sensing that the old
man has in his own personal way a knowledge and understanding
somehow outside his own. If he can get that old man to 'talk' he
rejoices in having touched life at a fresh aspect. Isn't it a boast
among 'intelligent' people that you got such and such an old
country fellow to 'talk'? He is one of those who had that ruthless-
faery way with the educated man's own terms, humanizing his
'polyanthus' into Polly Ann. Only the other day I heard one re-
ferring to a hard-drinking man as being afflicted with 'delirious
trembles'.

The young men have no such whimsies. The first taste of
education and standard English has had the effect of making them
acutely self-conscious. They realize (and agricultural depression
helps in this) not that they stand supreme in a fundamental way of
life, but that they are the last left on a sinking ship. No one decries
civilization who has not experienced it *ad nauseam*. Modernity
offers dim but infinite possibilities to the young countryman if
only he can rid his boots of this impeding clay. Pylons, petrol
pumps and other 'defacements' are to him symbols of a noble
power. The motor-bus, motor-bicycle, wireless, are that power's
beckonings. But he is late, he is held hapless in a ruining countryside, everyone else is laughing at him, he feels: at his heavy boots,

his rough ways. Doesn't the daily paper laugh at him, and the magazine? Look at the 'comic' country articles, the illustrated jokes. The old men had their defence. They knew what they knew. But he can't stay where they are. The contentment of it is gone. Naturally he seizes on the most obvious and spurious symbols of culture first; he wants to wear low shoes and get a job behind a counter.

Not but that, even to-day, with all the clichés of popular journalism, language just breathes of itself. We invest our machines with personalities. There are words such as 'wangle', 'stunt', coined by the times to express new shades of meaning, and old meanings resuscitated, such as 'stall' in regard to the aeroplane. But England still compromises between the old and new, choking the old source language, yet hanging on to clichés long unrelated to current life. We must go to America for a modern counterpart of the old idiomatic vigour of common speech. American slang may be ugly and unpleasant, but it has the fascination of abounding vitality, hectic and spurious though that may be. It presupposes knowledge of a thousand sophistications, of intimacy with the life of a modern city, just as the traditional idiom presupposed a familiarity with nature and the processes of agriculture. But no urban idiom, however ingenious, could ever be regarded as compensating for that founded on the traditional order. It must always be sharp, cerebrated and opportunist. It is an excitement that feeds on itself having no root in fundamentals.

In place of abstract knowledge, the illiterate countryman has a genius, an intuitive and associative consciousness similar to that of the child. At the other end of the scale, the poet (in the widest sense of the word), as an example of high culture, is nearer the illiterate labourer than all the grades that go between. Culture moves slowly, but in a circle. But modern conditions have put their spoke in the wheel. Elementary education's first effect is to supersede that genius. That sense of abundant satisfaction in *being* dies from our words. They are robots, purely functional; we

consciously make them out of bits of Latin and Greek. They serve
their one purpose, and suggest nothing. The mass of acquired
facts, imposed technicalities, cultural summaries, make a flutter on
the pool whose dark depth was our primitive genius. We are all
surface to-day; all being talked to like children by the few technical masters, or bawled at by industrial and newspaper magnates
attempting a psychological tyranny.

'Back to earth' is a trite enough phrase; but the implications of
it in the sense of a return, somewhere in the social scale, to a faith
in intuitive values are no such simple matter.

Adrian Bell, in *A Selection from 'Scrutiny'*

In the debate on the old and new translations of the Bible, it seems
to have been taken for granted that the new words are more un-
derstandable than the old. To me just the opposite is true. My
young impressionable years were spent among farm men whose
speech had the cadence of the Authorised version of the Bible,
which had been the one book in their heritage. The fact that the
centuries of 'literary' English had passed them by, meant that their
talk preserved a sharpness of definition derived from the experience of their five senses. It had a tone of moral force even when
describing the state of the soil.

When I had been re-educated in the spoken word, in the life of
the fields, and was made to see, hear and honestly to feel again, I
found the old Bible was speaking to me with a force and clarity
I had not realised before. By contrast a new translation when read
in church tends to run over me like water over a stone: I have to
make an effort to attend. The old words, 'He restoreth my soul'
sink deep.

The men I worked beside were talking all the time, to their
horses or to one another (there was no tractor din to drown the
voice). Memorable words of judgment and wit were exchanged
that presumed no gulf of 'archaism' between them and the scriptures. 'The crackling of thorns under a pot' occurred literally to

us every morning under our kettles in the back'us. It was all a common experience of daily living. As for those famous mistranslations – 'He saith among the trumpets Ha, Ha,' what could be more apt when the vast array of heavy horses paraded in the show ring while the band played and the flags fluttered? Excited by so many of his kind, certainly he did say 'Ha, ha' loudly and often, and his neck (those arching necks of the Suffolks) was indeed 'clothed with thunder'.

The old words were illumined to us daily, in the broadcasting of small seeds, in reaping and gleaning – in one of our tumbrils up to the axle in the mud of a gateway, like the chariots of Pharaoh stuck in the mire so that 'they drave them heavily'. Often I heard men use that word 'drave' when the going was bad.

If we allow that miracles enter into Christian belief, then I conceive that the Authorised version of the Bible could itself have been a miracle, to guide and hearten and console British folk for as long as they lived in the sweat of their brow and in quietness of purpose. Since that was then the life of the people I worked with on the farms, the old Bible has always spoken to me more plainly than the new.

Adrian Bell, A Countryman's Notebook

Words

Out of us all
That make rhymes,
Will you choose
Sometimes –
As the winds use
A crack in a wall
Or a drain,
Their joy or their pain
To whistle through –
Choose me,
You English words?

I know you:
You are light as dreams,
Tough as oak,
Precious as gold,
As poppies and corn,
Or an old cloak:
Sweet as our birds
To the ear,
As the burnet rose
In the heat
Of Midsummer:
Strange as the races
Of dead and unborn:
Strange and sweet
Equally,
And familiar,
To the eye,
As the dearest faces
That a man knows,
And as lost homes are:
But though older far
Than oldest yew –
As our hills are, old –
Worn new
Again and again:
Young as our streams
After rain;
And as dear
As the earth which you prove
That we love.

Make me content
With some sweetness
From Wales

Whose nightingales
Have no wings –
From Wiltshire and Kent
And Herefordshire,
And the villages there –
From the names, and the things
No less.
Let me sometimes dance
With you,
Or climb
Or stand perchance
In ecstasy,
Fixed and free
In a rhyme,
As poets do.

Edward Thomas

ASPECTS

The peasant life

With the peasant-life, most of the meaning has gone out of our English landscape, and, for me, half the charm. For a moment I was vividly aware of this today . . .

If the peasant life was narrow and void of aspirations, at least it clung to the country-side with a more faithful love than ours. Faithful, respectful, nay, almost venerating, that love was: the love of children for their fathers, of patriots for their fatherland. In that temper the peasantry nestled in their valleys; more at home there – tied, subservient as they were to the soil and the seasons amongst the hills – than we can conceive – keeping it to ourselves, or selling, without true understanding.

Narrow, even brutish, the peasant life may well have been; but again, there was something to be said for its security; much to be said for the absence of those contrasts of wealth that make modern

C

labouring-class life so horrifying. The peasant, settled in his village, with opportunity for the old self-supporting village pursuits, did at least know what he had to do and how to do it: his prospects he knew, and if they were never dazzling with hope, they need not often have been so bewildering with fear, as the modern labourer's. He was one of a people, with his share in what was going: his suffering was shared in times of famine, his struggles against oppression or bad government were shared by his fellow peasants. But now, the labourer is an individual, struggling alone, not with but against his fellows – against influences far less easy to understand and far less hopeful for him, than famine and bad weather or a bad lord of the manor. So the country is not comforting to think of, now-a-days.

Tradition

An ideal anticipates an end that has not previously been reached; considerable mental and imaginative activity is involved in it; it proceeds with authenticity out of the brain of each individual who gives himself to its guidance, so that he is an innovator, not an imitator. A tradition, on the contrary, imposes itself from outside upon the individual, who accepts it without question and allows its impetus to carry him along. By the influence of tradition, the past makes its impress upon the present; the impersonal collective good sense of many men flows into the actions of one. Hence something dignified and reposeful characterises the life of those who are living by a good tradition.

It is the peculiar unhappiness of the present time in England – at least in English country neighbourhoods – that the time-honoured traditions are disappearing and nobody knows what new ones are replacing them. We have lost touch with the land, and with the seasons of the year. The summer brings its crops; but it doesn't bring to their harvesting a skilled and prospering people who can look ahead with any certainty to the autumn and winter and spring. And though the land has all its old properties, of soil and water, and warm or chilly aspect, and there are the lanes and woods, the pastures and coppices, just as before, you will not find people conversant with all these particulars, and adapting their labours and economies to them, in the old way. This is even more true of the rich than of the poor. The rich in their country residences care nothing for the land and understand nothing either of it or of its people. They do but come to pass time in it, bringing into it their town outlook, the town pursuits, and careless what they spoil in making up their pleasure gardens or driving their motor-cars. Of any traditional rural life and rural knowledge they seem utterly bereft.

Of course I am writing of what I see here, in this 'growing residential neighbourhood'. Here the prevailing sordidness of living is oppressive. It is not that individual people are disagreeable, or base. It is that no tradition is present, to carry us forward from yesterday into tomorrow. Tomorrow we don't know what we shall be doing, or even where we shall be. Nor is there any reverence for the countryside, or any interest in the seasons, unless it be a greedy commercial one. Watch the people on the roads – the men with carts and vans, the rich with their motor-cars, the working class women, the trades-people – and look too at the uses the country is put to, the indifference about its comeliness, the readiness to sell or break up or cut down or level away or build over anything or any site: you will realise that there is no tradition alive worthy of the name, but that a commercial or else a pleasure-seeking spirit is the only thing that guides us. We are decent people, but we have arrived at a very sordid out-at-elbows period of our nation's history.

'Good old days'?

[*Part of a reply to a correspondent who had written in praise of the 'good old days'*]

The more I examine it, the more I grow sceptical of the well-being of the people, in these 'good old times'. I suspect that disease, squalor, poverty, oppression, were more plentiful than they are now. Bleak, harsh, painful, bitter – don't you think England may have been that, more often than not, to the comfortless peasants? . . . Yet I will take it at its best. I will concede the happy peasantry, their country's pride, and admit their fine skill in rural handicrafts, their delight in their folk lore, their pleasing genius for song, their merriment. Let it all be granted, in its immense contrast to the dreariness of our present villages, and still – I would not go back to it . . .

I think English men and women have it in them to be something better than peasants; and indeed, we are beginning to know it. That standard is too humble and narrow a one, for men of this fine breed (for we *are* a fine breed). I desire to be able to judge my fellow countrymen, and to approve them, not as good peasants, but as good well-developed human beings.

That, you know, is a view that hardly Milton himself was able to take. It had not dawned upon the world in his day. To the rest of society the peasantry seemed a body of useful creatures not to be regarded from an ideal standpoint. Think how many layers of society were imposed over them – squires, parsons, bishops, nobles, one above the other – and it was not until the top layer was reached that people dreamed of testing men and women by the highest standard. A Prince, an Earl, an Archbishop, a Courtier, might be thought of as a human being with varied faculties each one of which ought to be cultivated and made the best of; but that privilege of development was not conceded to the farmer, the sailor, the ploughman. These were expected to do their duty in that state of life etc. etc., and to leave it to their 'betters' to care about being swift clever many-sided human beings. Moreover the people themselves shared this lowly view of their own fate. They hardly claimed the right to be excellent, except in their narrow walk of life. The shepherd was willing to be a shepherd, and not much besides; and so with the carpenter, the blacksmith, and all the host of them. Separating them from a full existence lay those superimposed strata of society, under which they were buried miles deep – too deep for hope or ambition to reach them.

But today it is different. I claim, and many with me are claiming, a full varied development for the English. And the English are not many years distant from claiming something of the sort for themselves. Somehow the layers that were above them have worn thin. The unknown people are beginning to feel themselves near the surface, where, besides getting a living, they may live it worthily. Believe me, as I go about the roads and look at them, I feel that the release is very near indeed, and I am gladdened by the immense riches of character, legible in people's faces and manners. Just another generation or two of ambitious thought (thought ambitious for the true success of *Englishness*) and then there may be a magical change, the English coming to new life, after so many centuries.

George Sturt, *Journals*, pp. 559, 610–12 and 622–3

Attitudes

Before their fête the Rationals[7] had a dinner, and I went. A man opposite me was saying that he had given more benefit to the Society than the Society had given to him, for he was now past fifty and had never drawn sick-pay yet. I was able to say that I was past fifty also, and had never yet been ill enough to stay in bed all day. But a man lower down the table must have thought that we were getting proud, for he remarked very audibly just then, 'There be a sort that do go sudden, when they do go.' A few years afterwards I was ill enough to stay in bed for many weeks, but I managed to get out of doors for May Day. I noticed a group of people talking together and glancing at me now and then, and presently one of them came over and explained, 'What us be sayin', zir, be this: whatever shall us do for our May Day, when you be dead.'

They were ringing a knell at North Bovey one afternoon when I was out beyond there; and it sounded very weird, when the gusts of wind carried the wail of the bells across the hills. I met one of the Lustleigh ringers as I was coming back, and I asked him why they never did it here. He answered, 'But us do. Sometimes. Not for all folk like, though. But us'll ring'n for thee.'

When I was overhauling one of the old houses here, I made good some panelling that had been covered up with lath and plaster. After it was done, a man came over to tell me of some seasoned oak of extraordinary width, which I might buy. I said that it would make fine panels, but my panelling was done. And then he said, 'Well, and if you didn't use it for panellin', it might serve some other purpose. Why, th'old Mr ***** and his wife both had their coffins made from that same tree.'

One of the old inhabitants was talking to me about the War; and this was how it struck him, 'What be the sense of their contendin'? Why, us in Lustleigh don't wage war on they in Bovey, and wherefore should the nations fight?' Another one looked at it from another point of view, 'It be a terrible thing, this war: proper terrible it be. I never knowed bacon such a price.'

Life is never very strenuous here. People always fancy there is time to spare – 'the days be long'. That answers to the Spanish *mañana* – to-morrow – or the Arabic *ba'd bukra* – the day after to-morrow – and is almost worthy of Theodore and Luke. In the *Sayings of the Fathers* Palladius relates that they were discontented with their dwelling, and in the winter they said they would move in the summer, and in the summer they said they would move in the winter; and they went on saying that for the space of fifty years; and they both died in that place.

Things happened here in Wreyland manor which seem trivial now that we have only the bare facts, as set down on the record of the manor court; but in real life the facts may have aroused such animosities that they would seem momentous then – John More and Thomas Sachet have been cutting down trees on the

Lustleigh side of the Wrey, thereby choking the stream so that it
is overflowing on the Wreyland side and doing damage here.
Henry atte Slade has been catching pheasants and partridges inside
the manor bounds. (Slade is just outside.) Ralf Golde's pigs have
been eating Ralf Wilcokes' apples from the Feast of Saint Christina
unto the Feast of the Nativity of the Blessed Mary. (From 24 July
to 8 September.) Thomas Wollecote's pig has been eating Thomas
Ollesbrome's apples, and Ollesbrome has killed the pig, though
Wollecote has offered him twenty bushels of apples as compensation. In this case two issues were set down for trial: the offer of
the apples, and the killing of the pig. Wollecote failed on the first
issue, and did not proceed on the second – it may be that Ollesbrome had brought the pig into court, as his defence was that he
had not killed it.

That was the Fifteenth Century, and the Twentieth is not unlike
it. In this present Century there were two men living in Lustleigh
parish who have now gone away – men of assured position and
independent means. One man lived in a valley, and the other on a
hillside just above; and one man had a garden, and the other had
a dog. When the dog got busy with bones, it went off to the garden
and carried out its burials and exhumations there. At least, that is
what the owner of the garden said, and what the owner of the dog
denied; and the contention was so sharp between them that one of
them summoned the other before the magistrates at Newton to
be bound over to keep the peace.

In a humbler state of life there were two old ladies who kept
chicken; and whenever one of them fed her chicken, her neighbour's chicken came over in a mass and scrambled for the food.
It was a thing that chicken would naturally do; but she felt certain
that her neighbour egged them on. One day she seemed to be in
heavenly happiness, and she explained to me, 'I be a-thinkin' of
that woman there, when I shall see her in the torments.' I asked
where she was going to see that, and she answered with asperity,
'Where be I a-goin? Why, Abram's bosom, o' course.' Her

thoughts were on the parable of Lazarus and Dives.[8] People of her generation did not consider eternal life worth having without eternal punishment for everybody they disliked.

There is a House of Mercy at Bovey, and its inmates have been described to me as 'maidens as hath gotten babies without ever goin' nigh a church', in other words, unmarried mothers. They were taught laundry-work; and a worthy old washerwoman gave me her whole mind – not merely a bit of it – about 'they paltry gentry as took their washin' away from honest folk to give it to they hussies.'

Old people here would often speak of London as though it stood upon a hill. And they could give a reason, 'Folk always tell of going *up* to London.' When the railway came, it was perplexing. This portion of the line ascends about 400 feet in about six miles, with gradient of as much as 1 in 40. Yet up trains went down, and down trains up.

In talking to a very old inhabitant, I spoke of something out on Dartmoor, and he replied, 'Well, Dartymoor be a place I never were at.' I remarked that it was within a walk, and he replied, 'I never had no occasion to go there.' My own grandparents seldom stirred unless they had occasion. In a letter to my father, 16 May 1852, my grandfather says, 'I hope we shall have a fine day, as your mother never was at Torquay, and I not for near thirty years.' He was sixty-three then, and she was seventy. Torquay is fifteen miles from here, and neither of them had ever lived more than thirty miles away.

On a Sunday morning I met a Lustleigh damsel on her way to church, wearing a new dress and evidently wishing it to be observed. For want of anything better to say, I said, 'You don't go in for hobble skirts, I see.' She answered, 'No, not I: a proper fright I'd look in they.' And I inquired Why. The answer was, 'Why, mother says my thighs be like prize marrows at a show.'

Three old ladies, on their way to church, just caught the last remark, and passed on with averted eyes in consternation at our talk.

Cider used always to be made of apples, but I fear that it is very often made of other things now. However, the name does not imply that it is made of apples, but only means that it is strong. And in that sense Wyclif has 'wyn and sydir' in Luke, i. 15, where later versions say 'strong drink'. Non-alcoholic cider is a contradiction in terms.

Men can easily get drunk on cider; but they do not suffer for it next day, if they have had pure cider of fermented apple juice and nothing else. Unhappily, this wholesome drink has given way to other drinks that are less wholesome. A shrewd observer said to me, 'When each man had three pints of cider every day, there was not half this bickering and quarrelling that goes on now.' And that, I think, is true. They were always in the genial stage of drunkenness, and seldom had the means of going beyond that. A few, however, very often went a little way beyond; and they have been described to me as 'never proper drunk, nor proper sober neither, but always a-muddled and a-mazed.'

This failing was not confined to Devonshire. My father notes in his diary, 7 August 1847, at Dinan in Brittany, 'The apples thick beyond conception, and the priests already praying to avert the evil consequences they apprehend from the plenty and cheapness of cider.' He also writes to my grandmother from Dinan, 15 August, 'The apples are so abundant this year that the country will almost be drowned in cider. How they will consume it all, is a wonder, for they export none. The lower orders are drunk, it seems, a great deal of their time. The priests always pray for a bad apple crop as the only hope of saving the people from perpetual drunkenness.'

A former Rector of Lustleigh was remonstrating with a man one afternoon for reeling through the village very drunk. But the man had his reply, 'Ay, 'tbe all very fine for you to talk, but you goes home to dinner late, and us doesn't see you after.'

Speech

A man here said to me, 'Her went up 'xactly like an angel,' as if he often saw them go, and thought I must have seen them too. (He was speaking of the finish of a play he saw in town.) Another person here was very certain of what angels did or did not do. A stranger came to the back door one Sunday morning, and asked for a drink of cider to help him on his way. He was denied it by the maid who was in charge there, and thereupon he said to her, 'You know not what you do. You might be entertaining angels unawares.' To which she answered, 'Get thee 'long. Angels don't go drinkin' cider church-times.'

The well here, sunk in 1839, secured great praise, as I was told. 'Th'apothecary man come here and saith as he must anderize the well. And I saith, "Well, if you must, you must." And then he come again and saith, "I've anderized that well, and if you drink of that, you'll live for ever".' That was the substance of what he said, but not (I believe) the form in which he said it. People here are apt to put things in the form they would have used themselves. A lady of great dignity once noticed a donkey here, and remarked what a fine animal it was; and she was perturbed at hearing that the villagers were saying she had praised the animal in detail, ending up, 'and if there be one part of'n as I admire more than another, it be his rump.'

In the old letters and diaries here I find many words and phrases that have now gone out of use. The garden was 'very rude' when it was untidy. The stream was 'stiff' when it was high, and it 'landed' if it overflowed. A man was 'thoughtful' when he was cunning, and 'high-minded' when he was pretentious; and was a 'patriot' when he was a profiteer. People 'had a hoarse' just as they had a cough, and were 'confined' when they were kept indoors by any kind of illness – some invalid old ladies had three or four 'confinements' every year. They all 'used' exercise, and did not take it; nor did they ever take tea. 'We drank tea with Mrs ***** at Moreton, and Jane was on the carpet all the while: she has been to Exeter without a bonnet.' I do not know why people drag in scraps of French like 'chaperon' and 'sur le tapis', nor why they follow Anglo-Indians in saying 'pucka' for 'proper'.

Being of opinion that some fields near here would never yield enough to cover their rent, the farmer's wife approached the landlord in this way, ' "But, maister," saith I, "us cannot pluck feathers from a toad." And he saith, "so I've heard tell afore now, and I believe 't be true".' It is just the metaphor they use in France, 'Il est chargé d'argent comme un crapaud de plumes.' And when someone did a work of supererogation here, the comment was strangely like 'le Bon Dieu rit énormément'.

People habitually say You for Ye, yet snigger at the use of Us for We down here. Devonshire speech is not capricious, but has a syntax of its own. The classic phrase is 'her told she'. A pious person assured me that 'us didn't love He, 'twas Him loved we'. They never say 'we are', but 'us be' or else 'we am', contracted into 'we'm'. They say 'I be' as well as 'I'm', but never 'me'm' or 'me be', though invariably 'me and Jarge be', or 'me and Urn', or whatever the name is, and never 'Ernest and I' or 'George and I'. They say 'to' for 'at' – 'her liveth to Moreton' – and formerly said 'at' for 'to' – 'I be goin' at Bovey', but now it is the fashion to say 'as far as' Bovey.

Happily, the school has not taught them English that is truly up to date. They have not learned to say, 'The weather conditions being favourable, the psychological moment was indulged in.' They still say, 'As 'twere fine, us did'n.' And their pronunciation is unchanged: beetles are bittles, beans are banes, and Torquay is Tarkay.[9]

Old folk used to search the Scriptures very diligently and picked up words and phrases that they used in most embarrassing ways. One old lady told me in sorrow and in wrath, 'The Parson, he come here, and I spoke Scripture to'n. And "good mornin'," he saith, "good mornin'," and up he were and away over they steps 'fore I could say another word.' I found that she had used some words the Parson had to read in church but did not wish to hear elsewhere.

Even when ordinary words are used, they are not always used in the accepted way. A youth married one of his loves and went on flirting with the others, but was found out at last. And he was greeted with, 'Just come you here now, I've got something for you with your tea: your little secrecies is become the greatest of publicities.' In another household the wife gave force to her remarks by throwing plates and dishes at her husband's head. (She also had something for him with his tea.) He knew exactly how to dodge them; and, as his usual seat was in a line between his wife's seat and the door, the things came whizzing out across the lane, to the astonishment of passers-by who did not know her ways.

Time softens these asperities. A bereaved husband was speaking of his wife in her last illness. 'Her sat up sudden in the bed, and saith, "I be a-goin' up the Clave." [Lustleigh Cleave.] And I saith to her, "Thee canst not go up the Clave: thee be a-dyin'." And her saith to me, "Ye wicked, dommed, old mon." Poor dear soul, they was the very last words as ever her spoke.'

Hearing a good deal of laughter in the lane, I inquired what was going on. And the answer was brought back, 'Please, zir, it be little Freddie ***** a-tryin' to say swear-words, and he cannot form'n proper.' I once said a swear-word here – at least, they thought I did. A bee was pestering me persistently one afternoon, while I was sitting in the garden; and at last in a moment of irritation I called it a coleopterous creature. Some one heard me, and afterwards I heard him telling some one else, 'He were a-swearin' fine: called 'n bally-wopserous.'

A few years ago there was a child in the village who was so absurdly like the Flora in the *Primavera* that we always called her the little Botticelli. But this disquieted her mother, and she sent up to say that she would like to know the meaning of that word. More recently a Lustleigh boy was going to be a Roman Senator in some theatricals in town, and he wrote home to his mother to send him the materials for making up a Toga. Not knowing what a Toga was, she sent him the materials for making up a Toque. On first hearing of a Turkish bath, a farmer's child assumed it was a turkey's bath.

Down here a man remarked to me one day, as he was gazing across some fields, 'It be a wonder-workin' thing, that Consecrated Bone.' I began to think we had a relic here. But he spoke of concentrated bone manure.

A quantity of plants arrived here while I was away, and among them were some Kalmias and Andromedas. On my return I asked where they had all been put; and I was told that some of them were in the greenhouse, others were in various parts of the garden, and the Camels and Dromedaries were out in the orchards.

There was an old lady here who always said, 'If there be a flower that I do like, it be a Pertunium.' It was neither a petunia nor a geranium; but I never found out exactly what it was. Botanists might adopt the name, when they want one for a novelty, as it is better than most of theirs. It may be convenient to give things Greek or Latin names, and it certainly sounds better to say Archæopteryx and Deinotherium than Old Bird and Awful Beast. But it is absurd to take the ancient name for one thing, and give it to another; yet that is what Linnæus and his followers have very often done.

Besides their botanical names, many things have trade names now. There is a plant here of the sort that is described at Kew as Rhododendrum Ponticum Cheiranthifolium. But, when I wanted

to get another like it, I found the nurseryman did not know it by
that name. He called it Jeremiah J. Colman.

An old gardener once gave me his opinion that a laundry was
better than a garden, 'as garments had not got such mazin' names
as plants'. And the maze grows more intricate, when Berberis
Darwinii is Barbarous Darwin, and Nicotiana is Nicodemus, and
Irises are Irish, and they English Irish be braver than they Spanish
Irish.

Cecil Torr, Small Talk at Wreyland

Folk Tales

[*A man going home drunk fell into a ditch and went to sleep. When
pulled out by an 'enemy' of his, he crawled back again.*]
This tale of the man who crawled back into the ditch rather than
owe any benefit to an enemy seemed to me authentic enough
until I read the same tale, not from Farnborough, but from Ulster.
Then I recognised its nature. It is one of a number of provincial
or folk-tales, such as Englishmen have long loved to attach to
some neighbour or other, either in derision of him, or in picturesque illustration of a well-known foible. The tale of the doctor
whose pestle talked to his mortar is almost certainly another of the
series. To be sure, I never heard it elsewhere; yet plainly it could
be fitted to any country practitioner, and no less plainly a certain
sort of Englishman would enjoy fitting it. In short, these stories
have a quality hard to describe, perhaps, but very recognisable to
any truly provincial Englishman. Others may fail to see it; but a
native will feel it 'in his bones'.

Characteristic of all these is the tale of Cocker Nash (pronounced
Naish) – to give the West Surrey version. It is told that Cocker
Nash, a fish-hawker, being the worse for drink, lost his way in
the woods of Waverley one winter evening; and, growing frightened, began to call out 'Man lost! Man lost!' Pigeons said 'Coo-
oo, coo-oo.' Was it an answer? Again the man cried; and again
came the supposed answer. And now there could be no doubt:

it must be some voice asking 'Who? who?' Whereupon, almost frantic, the fishmonger screamed out, 'Cocker Nash, of Farnham.'

I think no other memory of Cocker Nash survives in Farnham, although it may be taken for granted that a simpleton of that name once lived there. Anyhow, the story is handy. My old friend Bettesworth once tried to fasten it on to a neighbour whose name must not be told; and indeed the narrative is a cap easily fitted. It is placed in Wessex by Mr. Hardy; some years ago a friend came upon it at Freshwater in the Isle of Wight, where the adventure was ascribed to a local worthy lost in the Undercliff. There is a version of it, again with a local name, at Dunstable; finally, I may mention a North-country variant, which tells, not of a man lost, but of a bachelor withdrawing to a wood to pray for a wife. 'Who? who?' the voice seemed to ask; and the answer was given, 'Any wife will do, Lord; any wife will do.'[10]

Pigeons figure in another story of this class; and with a voice nowise attributed to the Lord. A certain Taffy (I don't know why he was a Welshman, but Richard Jefferies gives it so) went to steal a cow from a stall. Near the door hung a cage containing a pigeon or dove, usually saying nothing but 'Coo-oo'. But when the thief opened the door to take the cow – what was that? A wicked, insinuating voice saying, 'Take two, take two-o-o.' Surely it was the devil, tempting the thief to double his crime? But Taffy, thoroughly frightened, fled without a cow at all.

In *The Scouring of the White Horse* Thomas Hughes told how one Job Cork, in great trouble, was enjoined by his wife to 'Ha' patience and think o' thy namesake,' but retorted with a groan, 'Ah, but he never had his breeches all cockled up' – for that was Job Cork's trouble. His chamois-leather breeches, wet through after game-beating, had been too quickly dried in the domestic oven, and proved unwearable in the morning. Precisely this was said to have happened to a neighbour of my own, in West Surrey. True, his name did not fit; but his wife did not fail, in the story, to bid him have patience and think of Job. I suspect that a certain yarn from Scotland (quite unprintable) is akin to this. The incident is different: Job is not mentioned; yet the old heartless rustic humour sounds clear in the wife's retort bidding her husband 'Have patience' amidst his wailings under ridiculous misfortune.

In this sort of folk-anecdote there is enough of John Smith's whimsical humour, and of the country he belonged to, to justify, I hope, collecting further examples here. Moreover, it should be noted, these tales are rapidly dying out. The schoolmaster, the railway, the week-end cottage, are wiping away many such traces of an older England – wiping them clean away. So that if they are worth saving at all, that task cannot be undertaken too soon.

Some of the tales must be very old indeed. One there was, of which I remember a variant in Grimm's *Fairy Tales*. The hero there was, I think, a Prince, while the villain was a giant. In the English version (which reached me from Farnborough, but had probably come from Yorkshire) the persons were a small boy named Jack, and a chimney-sweep who had kidnapped him and carried him away in a sack. Crossing a heath, the sweep sat down and went to sleep. Jack crept out of the sack and put stones in, to take his own place. But the sweep said, 'Jack, how heavy you be!' and got the little boy into the sack again. Next time, Jack, thinking to escape detection, put in bushes instead of stones; but it was no use. 'Jack, how you pricks!' said the sweep. So it came to a third occasion, when Jack put horse-droppings into the sack. Was this also a failure? I do not know. The story ends with the sweep complaining, 'Jack, how you stinks!'

There is an old story of a London cabman called out from a public-house he had entered, by a boy: 'Hi! mister! Your hoss is fell down!' To which the cabman replied, indignantly, 'Gahn! You pushed him down!' But Bettesworth knew this horse-driver by name. He was not a London cabman, but a West Surrey coal-hawker, and the horse was an ancient grey.

Many years ago a certain farmer in West Surrey had the reputation of being an atheist; of whom the following incident was told, with something of a shudder. It was a wet hay-making; the cut grass was spoiling in the meadows, and this impious man, taking some of it on a prong and holding it skywards, said contemptuously, 'There, God! What d'ye think o' that?'

An impecunious young gentleman of Farnham who liked to be taken for a keen hand and a sportsman was generally alleged to have gone shooting duck at Frensham Pond, when he found too late that, instead of wild duck, he had been killing tame ducks, the property of the landlord of the inn, and that he would have to pay dear for his sport.

Tales of moon-rakers should be collected, and the history of moon-raking villages should be investigated, as an interesting feature in English country life. But this is not quite the place for discussing that matter. The subject of provincial folk-tales should not be left, however, without drawing attention to a curious anecdote – not quite of the humorous rustic order, yet obviously of traditional value. It is the tale of a missing will, discovered to the interested parties just in the nick of time, by the ghost of somebody long dead. The odd thing is the use to which this tale has been put. Sir Oliver Lodge (in *The Survival of Man*) gives it, without suspicion, as an authentic German occurrence proving spirit-life after death. But readers of *The Antiquary* may recall that Sir Walter Scott had told practically the same tale long before, giving it only a different setting.

George Bourne, *A Farmer's Life*

LIVING EVIDENCE

i

The present inhabitants of the Laurel Country are the direct descendants of the original settlers who were emigrants from England and, I suspect, the lowlands of Scotland. I was able to ascertain with some degree of certainty that the settlement of this particular section began about three or four generations ago, i.e.

in the latter part of the eighteenth or early years of the nineteenth. How many years prior to this the original emigration from England had taken place, I am unable to say; but it is fairly safe, I think, to conclude that the present-day residents of this section of the mountains are the direct descendants of those who left the shores of Britain some time in the eighteenth century.

The region is from its inaccessibility a very secluded one. There are but few roads – most of them little but mountain tracks – and practically no railroads. Indeed, so remote and shut off from outside influence were, until quite recently, these sequestered mountain valleys that the inhabitants have for a hundred years or more been completely isolated and cut off from all traffic with the rest of the world. Their speech is English, not American, and from the number of expressions they use which have long been obsolete elsewhere, and the old-fashioned way in which they pronounce their words, it is clear that they are talking the language of a past day, though exactly of what period I am not competent to decide. One peculiarity is perhaps worth the noting, namely the pronunciation of the impersonal pronoun with an aspirate – 'hit' – a practice that seems to be universal.

Economically, they are independent. As there are practically no available markets, little or no surplus produce is grown, each family extracting from its holding just what is needed to support life and no more. They have very little money, barter in kind being the customary form of exchange.

Many set the standard of bodily and material comfort perilously low, in order, presumably, that they may have the more leisure and so extract the maximum enjoyment out of life. The majority live in log-cabins, more or less water-tight, usually, but not always, lighted with windows; but some have built larger and more comfortable homesteads.

They are a leisurely, cheery people in their quiet way, in whom the social instinct is very highly developed. They dispense hospitality with an open-handed generosity and are extremely interested in and friendly toward strangers, communicative and unsuspicious. 'But surely you will tarry with us for the night?' was said to us on more than one occasion when, after paying an afternoon's visit, we rose to say goodbye.

They have an easy unaffected bearing and the unselfconscious manners of the well-bred. I have received salutations upon introduction or on bidding farewell, dignified and restrained, such as a courtier might make to his Sovereign. Our work naturally led to the making of many acquaintances, and, in not a few cases, to the formation of friendships of a more intimate nature, but on no single occasion did we receive anything but courteous and friendly treatment. Strangers that we met in the course of our long walks would usually bow, doff the hat, and extend the hand, saying, 'My name is — ; what is yours?' an introduction which often led to a pleasant talk and sometimes to singing and the noting of interesting ballads. In their general characteristics they reminded me of the English peasant, with whom my work in England for the past fifteen years or more has brought me into close contact. There are differences, however. The mountaineer is freer in his manner, more alert, and less inarticulate than his British prototype, and bears no trace of the obsequiousness of manner, which, since the Enclosure Acts robbed him of his economic independence and made of him a hired labourer, has unhappily characterized the English villager. The difference is seen in the way the mountaineer, as I have already said, upon meeting a stranger, removes his hat, offers his hand and enters into conversation, where the English labourer would touch his cap, or pull his forelock and pass on.

A few of those we met were able to read and write, but the majority were illiterate. They are, however, good talkers, using an abundant vocabulary racily and often picturesquely. Although uneducated, in the sense in what that term is usually understood, they possess that elemental wisdom, abundant knowledge, and intuitive understanding which those only who live in constant touch with Nature and face to face with reality seem to be able to acquire . . .

Physically, they are strong and of good stature, though usually spare in figure. Their features are clean-cut and often handsome; while their complexions testify to wholesome, out-of-door habits. They carry themselves superbly, and it was a never-failing delight to note their swinging, easy gait and the sureness with which they would negotiate the foot-logs over the creeks, the crossing of which caused us many anxious moments. The children usually go about bare-footed, and on occasion their elders too, at any rate in the summer time. Like all primitive peoples, or those who live under primitive conditions, they attain to physical maturity at a very early age, especially the women, with whom marriage at thirteen, or even younger, is not unknown . . .

That the illiterate may nevertheless reach a high level of culture will surprise those only who imagine that education and cultivation are convertible terms. The reason, I take it, why these mountain people, albeit unlettered, have acquired so many of the essentials of culture is partly to be attributed to the large amount of leisure they enjoy, without which, of course, no cultural development is possible, but chiefly to the fact that they have one and all entered at birth into the full enjoyment of their racial heritage. Their language, wisdom, manners, and the many graces of life that are theirs, are merely racial attributes which have been gradually acquired and accumulated in past centuries and handed down generation by generation, each generation adding its quotum to that which it received. It must be remembered, also, that in their everyday lives they are immune from that continuous grinding, mental pressure, due to the attempt to 'make a living', from which nearly all of us in the modern world suffer. Here no one is 'on the make'; commercial competition and social rivalries are unknown. In this respect, at any rate, they have the advantage over those who habitually spend the greater part of every day in preparing to live, in acquiring the technique of life, rather than in its enjoyment . . .

My sole purpose in visiting this country was to collect the traditional songs and ballads which were still being sung there. I naturally expected to find conditions very similar to those which I had encountered in England when engaged on the same quest. But of this I was soon to be agreeably disillusioned. Instead, for instance, of having to confine my attention to the aged, as in England, where no one under the age of seventy ordinarily possesses the folk-song tradition, I discovered that I could get what I wanted from pretty nearly everyone I met, young and old. In fact, I found myself for the first time in my life in a community in which singing was as common and almost as universal a practice as speaking. With us, of course, singing is an entertainment, something done by others for our delectation, the cult and close preserve of a professional class of specialists. The fact has been forgotten that singing is the one form of artistic expression that can be practised without any preliminary study or special training; that every normal human being can sing just as everyone can talk; and that it is, consequently, just as ridiculous to restrict the practice of singing to a chosen few as it would be to limit the art of speaking to orators, professors of elocution, and other specialists. In an ideal society every child in his earliest years would as a matter of course develop this inborn capacity and learn to sing the songs of his forefathers in the same natural and unselfconscious way in which he now learns his mother tongue and the elementary literature of the nation to which he belongs.

And it was precisely this ideal state of things that I found existing in the mountain communities. So closely, indeed, is the practice of this particular art interwoven with the ordinary vocations of everyday life that singers, unable to recall a song I had asked for, would often make some such remark as, 'Oh, if only I were driving the cows home I could sing it at once!' On one occasion too I remember that a small boy tried to edge himself into my cabin in which a man was singing to me and, when I asked him what he wanted, he said, 'I always like to go where there is sweet music.' Of course, I let him in and, later on, when my singer failed to remember a song I had asked for, my little visitor came to the rescue and straightway sang the ballad from beginning to end in the true traditional manner, and in a way which would have shamed many a professional vocalist. I have no doubt but that this delightful habit of making beautiful music at all times and in all places largely compensates for any deficiencies in the matter of reading and writing.

But, of course, the cultural value of singing must depend upon the kind of songs that are sung. Happily, in this matter the hillsman is not called upon to exercise any choice, for the only music, or, at any rate, the only secular music that he hears . . . is that which his British forebears brought with them from their native country and has since survived by oral tradition.

Cecil Sharp, Preface to the first edition of 1917 of
English Folk-Songs from the Southern Appalachians

ii

I have talked with scores of old country people on this subject of folk-singing. They all repeat the same tale. Everyone sang in their young days, they will tell you; they went to their work in the mornings singing; they sang in the fields, and they trudged home in the evenings to the accompaniment of song. Talk to any old peasant and you will find that he has an intimate acquaintanceship with the old songs. Maybe, he will confess that he himself was 'never no zinger', but he will volunteer to 'tell' you a song, and own to the ability to join in when others are there to give him a lead. The evidence is overwhelming that, as recently as thirty or forty years ago, every country village in England was a nest of singing birds.

The old singers were proud of the large number of songs that they could sing. To prove their prowess they would often arrange singing matches, which would last for several evenings. Each night the competitors would meet and sing songs alternately, until one of them had exhausted his repertoire; when the loser paid for his defeat in being mulcted in the cost of all the refreshments that had been consumed during the contest. The unsuccessful competitor has often told me that the day after his discomfiture several songs came back to his mind, which, if he had remembered at the time, might have reversed the verdict. This, I have no doubt, is true enough; you never know when you have got to the bottom of a singer's memory . . .

The history of music and of language has been very much the same. Literature has been built upon the speech of the common people, as art-music has been founded upon their music. Peasant music is genuine music; peasant speech is genuine language; neither peasant music nor peasant speech is a corrupt form of the music or of the speech of cultivated people. . . .

Folk-songs and folk-dances, in days gone by, played an import-ant part in the social life of the English village. That life is now waning, and with it are passing away the old traditions and customs. It is happily still possible, here and there, and in out-of-the-way nooks and corners, to come upon peasant men and women old enough to remember the village life of sixty, seventy or even eighty years ago; and they will sing to you the songs and explain to you the dances that, in their young days, and on summer evenings, were sung and danced on the village greens.

Cecil Sharp, English Folk-Song: Some Conclusions

THE IMPACT OF ENCLOSURES

Sixteenth century

Note that in all those parts of the country where the finest and therefore the most expensive wool is produced the nobility and gentry and even some abbots – otherwise holy men – are not

satisfied with the returns and the annual income that their prede-
cessors had. They are not content by living in idleness and luxury
to do no good to their country; they must actually harm it. They
leave no ground for cultivating, but enclose everything for pasture;
they pull down houses and destroy towns, leaving only the church
for penning sheep in. And as if their coverts and game preserves
weren't already wasting enough of your land these good people
turn all the dwellings and every scrap of cultivated land into a
wilderness.

As a result tenants are evicted so that a single greedy glutton
and plague-spot to his country may join field to field and enclose
thousands of acres with one fence. Some of them are cheated by
deception, crushed by violence or worn down by ill-treatment
till they are forced to sell up. One way or another the wretched
people have to go – men and women, husbands and wives,
orphans and widows, parents with young children, and the whole
household – not a rich one, but numerous since farm work needs
many hands. As I said, out they go from the homes they're used
to and know so well; and they find nowhere to go. All their
household goods, which wouldn't fetch much even if they could
find a buyer, they sell for a trifle, since they've got to get out.

Even that trifle is used up after a spell of wandering about – and
then what is left for them but to steal, and be hanged (quite rightly
you may say), or to tramp about and beg. Even then they're
thrown into prison as vagrants, for wandering about in idleness –
though they are very anxious for work, there is no one to hire
them. For when there is no arable land left, there is no farm work
to be done – and that is what they have been trained for.

Thomas More, *Utopia*, Book I, translated by the editor

Eighteenth century

Byng   Has Meriden Common been long enclosed?
Woman Ah, lackaday, Sir, that was a bad job; and ruined all us
       poor volk; and those who then gave in to it, now repent it.

B   Why so?

W   Because, we had our garden, our bees, our share of a
         flock of sheep, and the feeding of our geese; and could
         cut turf for our fuel. Now all that is gone! Our cottage,
         as good a one as this, we gave but fifty shillings a year
         for; and for this we are obliged to pay £9 10s.; and
         without any ground; and coals are risen upon us from
         7d to 9d the hundred. My cottage with many others is
         pulled down; and the poor are sadly put to it to get a
         house to put their heads in! Heigh ho!

[*When Byng read this description to a lady, she described the charitable
help given to the poor by herself and her friends, and Byng went on:*]
That was highly commendable; but charities will not remove the
evil; the poor must have land allotted to them for their support;
else under their present oppression, they can have no hope but
from vice, and theft.

My opinion holds, that the labourer has quitted the country;
and that Enclosing Acts have in great measure been the cause. But
I shall be answer'd by 'Think you not that our population is as
great as formerly?' 'Why, in many counties where manufactures
flourish, I think it is, but they have sucked up the villages and single
cottages. Birmingham, Manchester and Sheffield swarm with inhabitants; but look at them, what a set of mean, drunken wretches!'

The business of agriculture is as permanent, and moves as regularly as the Globe. But is that the case with manufactures? May
not some event overturn them? And who is to maintain the
mechanic? The husbandman works regularly, is sober and industrious, and poorly paid, but the artisan will work (from high
wages) but four days in a week, and wallow in drink the other three,
and if unemployed, will be ripe for, and active in any mischief.
Then in gallop the dragoons, and ride over them!

John Byng (Lord Torrington) *A Tour in the Midlands* (1789)
from *The Torrington Diaries*

Nineteenth century

The village was a cluster of ancient homesteads, formerly the habitations of yeomen who had farmed the scattered acres of the parish. It was about a mile long, a straggle of houses and out-buildings without plan, alongside a small stream that had supplied its original settlers with water. These homesteads, by their size and capacity, showed the evolution of the ancient community. Some were much larger than others, and had ample yards with barns of several bays, sheds for cattle, and a pightle of pasture attached. These had been the homesteads of younger sons who had inherited their fathers' lands. The smaller houses, which were often comfortable thatched cottages, had been the homes of younger sons who had inherited what was left of the estate, and had taken up, cleaned and cultivated fresh acres from the sur-rounding belt of forest, so as to secure their position in the village. Most of the more ancient homes had buildings of some sort attached; cottages that had none were of a later date. The whole irregular group told the unwritten story of a developing com-munity, a group of pastoral folk, holding their lands under the ancient system of manorial tenure, a village that had continued to grow as long as a narrowing belt of forest remained from which acres could be taken for tillage by those who had no land.

The process went on until the whole three-thousand-odd acres that comprised the parish were taken up into cultivation. It fol-lowed then that those who could not get land of their own must needs work for others; and so eventually the system of permanent wage employment began. To the employer it was more conveni-ent than the occasional hire of those who also had their own plots to till. For those landless labourers the cottages without buildings were built. They paid weekly rents.

This was the order of village life before the Enclosure, and it illustrates the type of village into which I was born. The reclama-tion of fresh land had reached the boundary; the expansion of pastoral life and livelihood had found its limit; the problem of an increasing population had been acute. It was evident that the system that had served many generations had failed to meet the existing need. Besides, for one holder to cultivate separate acres in different parts of the parish was obviously wasteful and did not encourage improved methods of agriculture. Operations on a larger scale were beginning to take the place of individual efforts; as in craft work the drift was towards mass production; and it was clear that land in large blocks would give a larger yield – a need made more imperative by war.

To give effect to these changes, Parliament passed separate Acts for redistributing and enclosing the land of parishes. It was not a mere enclosing of waste commons; it was the compulsory enclosing of all land held in common by the people. Yet, although they were not blind to the advantages of enclosed land in one block, most of the holders dreaded a forced enclosure. They knew full well that it was by no means a simple redistribution, under which each holder would retain the same acreage in one block instead of in several. By the experiences of other parishes, already enclosed, they had learned what to expect. Commissioners, empowered by law, would arrive, and for the time being all land would be vested in them. The surveying and the new allocation of land would of necessity take time, during which no one would know which land to cultivate – the experience of the village was that a season's arable crop was lost. They knew, too, that the commissioners' fees, together with the cost of remaking the public roads, the planting of hedges, digging of ditches, and the erection of fences to protect the young growing quicks around the newly arranged fields, would all be chargeable on the land – not, as it is now, a debt spread over a period for payment, but to be paid forthwith. Also, instead of the Church tithe being collected in kind – as the tenth shock, cock of hay, bucket of milk, lamb, calf, or newly born pig – a block of land would be appropriated as the permanent property of the Church.

To the holders of one or two acres only, the enclosure offered no advantage; yet they were obliged to fall in line with the holders of many acres, and were subject to the same proportion of expense. Such men were poor, and if they were receiving parish relief, the land allotted to them after enclosure was entered in the award as the property of the parish officers. Others had small mortgages secured on their plots; these were suddenly faced with the need of money to pay for redemption and to meet the enclosure expenses. Unable to raise the money, many parted with their ancestral plots for what they could get.

Though I live on the same soil, and remember vividly the stories told by several who passed through this experience, I still find it difficult to conceive the revolution of village life that resulted. The yeoman no longer existed; in his place the farmer was established. The small cultivator of one or two acres, who had also worked for others in his spare time, now became a labourer working for a weekly wage. Those yeomen who held many acres, yet had not the spare capital with which to meet the expenses, had their acreage reduced accordingly. My great-grandfather's holding was reduced from 97 acres, with rights of grazing, to 40, yet many held that he came out of the ordeal fairly well. The operation threw a quantity of land on the market, much of which was bought by a capitalist, a stranger to the village, who was said to have come from the north of England. My own people left the land and turned instead to the building crafts; but my grandfather always used to regard this change as a mistake.

The village, as I knew it, in the days of my youth, still showed the effects of these experiences; the philosophy of its life had been changed but not remoulded by the settlement of the enclosure. The forty years since that event were to many natives but as a day; their hearts still clung to the semi-free life when, without fear of trespass, all were able to ramble from end to end of the long parish, along the lanes and over the baulks that separated the multitude of separate acres. They could not forget the soil, once

their own, and now for ever forfeited, the loss of which constituted their humiliation. Some, when boys, had run the tracks
through the long mowing grass [to mark the dividing lines],
when, in ceremonial form, the yeomen had assembled, each with
scythe, to cut the meads that lined the brooks on each side of the
parish. Others had helped to tend the common herd that left the
village daily to graze the portion of the parish left fallow, or the
meads after the hay was carried. The love of the soil bred by that
kind of life was not accidental, but an inborn spirit, a sentimental
trust bequeathed by many ancestors who had lived in a like way.

That love did not die, even though after the enclosure the
majority of the villagers had no rood of land to call their own,
nor even to cultivate by rental. In penury they tilled the land of
others, yet it continued to animate them with its subtle spirit; its
lore still found expression through their lives.

As carpenters to the village we had special opportunities to
know and observe our neighbours. Our place, halfway up the
tree of social status, put us in touch with farmers at the top and
labourers at the bottom. We kept their farmhouses and cottages
in good repair, and when they had done with them at last, we
sent them to their rest in good coffins. On the whole, our intercourse was happy: they accepted us as integral to the village life,
as we knew ourselves to be.

It would be unbelievable, if it were not true, that in the redistribution of the land at the enclosure of 1830, no provision was made
for allotments to be let to the poor. When all that can has been
said in defence of that revolution in ancient village life, the simple
bare fact stands out, a revelation of the callous disregard of the
landless labourer, and evidence of his utterly degraded condition.

It would have been simple for Parliament, when passing the
separate Acts of Enclosure, to insert a condition that lands made
over to the Church in lieu of tithes should be available for allotments for the poor at a just rental, if required. But such matters

were left to the discretion of those in authority in each parish. The consequence in my village was that, for some forty years after, the cottagers could not get even a plot on which to grow their own vegetables.

No special knowledge of the villagers is necessary to understand what a loss this must have been. But they patiently submitted; Botany Bay and Van Diemen's Land (if not the gallows) were then only too familiarly associated with rebellion.[11] It is well to remember that the daily work of these men was cultivating the land of others, on a large parish of over three thousand acres, yet never before or since was so much produced from the soil, and the producers so hungry.

Just about the time of my birth, however, one or two small fields were first subdivided into roods to be let, and these were all eagerly taken by the poor. Their characters were not demoralised by it; indeed their lives were more orderly and law-abiding. The notion that a plot of land would make them inconveniently independent was shaken; it was more than counterbalanced by the relief it afforded to a poverty that was painful to witness.

Walter Rose, *Good Neighbours*

Perhaps, indeed, its calamitous nature was veiled at first behind some small temporary advantages which sprang from it. True, I question if the benefits experienced here were equal to those which are said to have been realized in similar circumstances elsewhere. In other parishes, where the farmers have been impoverished and the labourers out of work, the latter, at the enclosure of a common, have sometimes found welcome employment in digging out or fencing in the boundaries of the new allotments, and in breaking up the fresh ground. So the landowners say. But here, where there were few men wanting constant labour, the opportunity of work to do was hardly called for, and the making of boundaries was in many cases neglected. In that one way, therefore, not many can have derived any profit from the enclosure. On the other hand, an advantage was really felt, I think, in the opening that arose for building cottages on the newly-acquired freeholds. Quite a number of cottages seem to date from that period; and I infer that the opportunity was seized by various men who wished to provide new house-room for themselves, or for a married son or daughter. They could still go to work almost on the old lines. Perhaps the recognized price – seventy pounds, it is said to have been, for building a cottage of three rooms – would have to be exceeded a little, when timbers for floor and roof could no longer be had for the cutting out of fir-trees on the common; and yet there, after all, were the trees, inexpensive to buy; and there was the peasant tradition, still unimpaired, to encourage and commend such enterprise.

There is really little need, however, for these explanations of the people's unconcern at the disaster which had, in fact, befallen them. The passing of the common seemed unimportant at the time, not so much because a few short-lived advantages concealed its meaning as because the real disadvantages were slow to appear. At first the enclosure was rather a nominal event than an actual one. It had been made in theory; in practice it was deferred. I have just said that in many cases the boundaries were left unmarked; I may add now that to this day they have not quite all been defined, although the few spots which remain unfenced are not worthy of notice. They are to be found only in places where building is impossible; elsewhere all is now closed in. For it is the recent building boom that has at last caused the enclosure to take its full effect. Before that began, not more than ten or twelve years ago, there were abundant patches of heath still left open; and on many a spot where nowadays the well-to-do have their tennis or their afternoon tea, of old I have seen donkeys peacefully grazing. The donkeys have had to go, their room being wanted, and not many cottagers can keep a donkey now; but kept they were, and in considerable numbers, until these late years, in spite of the enclosure. But if the end could be deferred so long, one may judge how slowly the change began – slowly and inconspicuously, so that those who saw the beginning could almost ignore it. Even the cows – once as numerous as the donkeys – were not given up quite immediately, though in a few years they were all gone, I am told. But long after them, heath for thatching and firing might still be cut in waste places; fern continued until six or seven years ago to yield litter for pig-sties; and since these things still seemed to go on almost as well after the enclosure as before it, how should the people have imagined that their ancient mode of life had been cut off at the roots, and that it had really begun to die where it stood, under their undiscerning eyes?

Nevertheless, that was the effect. To the enclosure of the common more than to any other cause may be traced all the changes that have subsequently passed over the village. It was like knocking the keystone out of an arch. The keystone is not the arch; but, once it is gone, all sorts of forces, previously resisted, begin to operate towards ruin, and gradually the whole structure crumbles down. This fairly illustrates what has happened to the village, in consequence of the loss of the common. The direct results have been perhaps the least important in themselves; but indirectly the enclosure mattered, because it left the people helpless against influences which have sapped away their interests, robbed them of security and peace, rendered their knowledge and skill of small value, and seriously affected their personal pride and their character. Observe it well. The enclosure itself, I say, was not actually the cause of all this; but it was the opening, so to speak, through which all this was let in. The other causes which have been at work could hardly have operated as they have done if the village life had not been weakened by the changes directly due to the loss of the common.

They consisted – those changes – in a radical alteration of the domestic economy of the cottagers. Not suddenly, but none the less inevitably, the old thrift – the peasant thrift – which the people understood thoroughly had to be abandoned in favour of a modern thrift – commercial thrift – which they understood but vaguely. That was the essential effect of the enclosure, the central change directly caused by it; and it struck at the very heart of the peasant system.

For note what it involved. By the peasant system, as I have already explained, people derived the necessaries of life from the materials and soil of their own countryside. Now, so long as they had the common, the inhabitants of the valley were in a large degree able to conform to this system, the common being, as it were, a supplement to the cottage gardens, and furnishing means of extending the scope of the little home industries. It encouraged the poorest labourer to practise, for instance, all those time-honoured crafts which Cobbett, in his little book on Cottage Economy,[12] had advocated as the one hope for labourers. The cow-keeping, the bread-making, the fattening of pigs and curing of bacon, were actually carried on here thirty years after Cobbett's time, besides other things not mentioned by him, such as turf-cutting on the heath and wheat-growing in the gardens. But it was the common that made all this possible. It was only by the spacious 'turn-out' which it afforded that the people were enabled to keep cows and get milk and butter; it was only with the turf-firing cut on the common that they could smoke their bacon, hanging it in the wide chimneys over those old open hearths where none but such fuel could be used; and, again, it was only because they could get furze from the common to heat their bread ovens that it was worth their while to grow a little wheat at home, and have it ground into flour for making bread. With the common, however, they could, and did, achieve all this. I am not dealing in supposition. I have mentioned nothing here that I have not learnt from men who remember the system still flourishing – men who in their boy-hood took part in it, and can tell how the turfs were harvested, and how the pig-litter was got home and stacked in ricks; men who, if you lead them on, will talk of the cows they themselves watched over on the heath – two from this cottage, three from

D

that one yonder, one more from Master Hack's, another couple from Trusler's, until they have numbered a score, perhaps, and have named a dozen old village names. It all actually happened. The whole system was 'in full swing' here, within living memory. But the very heart of it was the open common.

Accordingly, when the enclosure began to be a fact, when the cottager was left with nothing to depend upon save his garden alone, as a peasant he was a broken man – a peasant shut out from his countryside and cut off from his resources. True, he might still grow vegetables, and keep a pig or two, and provide himself with pork; but there was little else that he could do in the old way. It was out of the question to obtain most of his supplies by his own handiwork: they had to be procured, ready-made, from some other source. That source, I need hardly say, was a shop. So the once self-supporting cottager turned into a spender of money at the baker's, the coal-merchant's, the provision-dealer's; and, of course, needing to spend money, he needed first to get it.

The change was momentous, as events have sufficiently proved.

George Bourne, *Change in the Village*

2

MASTERS AND MEN: THE FARMING LIFE

INTRODUCTION

The nineteenth century saw the agricultural England consisting mainly of small units move towards the industrial one, in which farming became a branch of capitalism, running to large estates. The trend towards larger farms and production for urban and luxury consumption rather than local need had accelerated in the eighteenth century, and by about 1825 there were no peasants left. The protests of Wordsworth and others against the extinction of small farmers were unheeded, and pauperisation and production increased side by side. As the century advanced, goods for export were required to pay for cheap imported food, and the peasant of earlier days became the labourer depending on international trade rather than the weather. The depression of 1873 onwards hit agriculture hard, as free trade exposed farmers to competition from countries anxious to buy our industrial products. Much arable land went out of cultivation, and by 1901 the wheat acreage was barely half that of 1872. Hardy noted in particular the effect on the village, which used to contain 'an interesting and better-informed class' consisting of blacksmith, carpenter, shoemaker, small higgler and shop-keeper. Landowners who did not employ them rejected them as tenants, so 'the occupants who formed the backbone of village life have to seek refuge in the boroughs. This process, which is designated by statisticians as "the tendency of the rural population towards the larger towns", is really the tendency of water to flow uphill when forced' (*Personal*

Writings, p. 171). But it was not the village craftsman alone who wanted a stake in the land; the ordinary labourer continued to voice this aspiration for the rest of the century, and it was vestigial for many years of the twentieth.

For 150 years – till 1940 – the disinherited had the worst of 'this process'. Too often they endured miserable poverty and cruelty, whether employed, or workless in the poor-house, as Crabbe (in *The Village* onwards) so forcefully described. Later 'for many who had worked hard all their lives and had preserved their self-respect so far, the only refuge in old age was the Workhouse. There old couples were separated' (Flora Thompson). The wealth of farmers and landowners increased, but the farm workers were kept down to a level of animal subsistence. This was effected first by the enclosures, then by the counter-revolutionary tone of the first half of the century, and finally by the yielding of agriculture to industry. At times wages fell; widespread employment meant destitution. Cobbett's accounts of this are confirmed in every word by many dreadful descriptions of rural poverty. Sturt notes that even at best 'Liberty there was none . . . the old village life was hard and ugly and comfortless' (*Journals*, pp. 674–5).

Protest against poverty has often been met with suppression. At the trial of four men at the Lent Assizes in 1567, one of them said: 'We can get no work nor have we no money, and if we should steal we should be hanged, and if we should ask, no man would give us. But we will have a remedy one of these days, or else we will lose all, for the commons will rise, we know not how soon, for we look for it every hour.'[13] All were hanged. Things were no better 250 years later. In 1816 in the fens there was much hunger, caused mainly by the enclosures. While their children were starving, the unemployed had to watch grain being loaded for London by farmers, already wealthy. They rioted, and armed with hooks and scythes marched to Ely, whence after breaking some windows they returned home. Eventually eighty men were arrested and taken to Ely to be made an example of. The trial

judges were chosen by the Bishop of Ely; five were hanged, five
were transported for life, and the rest imprisoned.[14] No wonder
Cobbett, writing up his ride down the Avon valley in *Rural Rides*,
claimed: 'This is the worst used labouring people upon the face
of the earth'; there is abundant evidence to support him. For instance the rural life of East Anglia after 1870 was largely one of
sluggish and sunken poverty; in Suffolk 'prosperity was for the
farmers and landowners, not for the workers on the land . . .
labourers were paid a very meagre wage, housing conditions were
deplorably bad' (Rev. J. G. Cornish, *Reminiscences of Country Life*
(1939)).

For most of this misery farmers were responsible, and from
Cobbett's time it is difficult to find a good word spoken for them,
except in fiction. He detested jumped-up farmers and their style
of living:

worst of all, there was a *parlour*. Aye, and a *carpet* and *bell-pull* too!
One end of the front of this once plain and substantial house had been
moulded into a parlour, and there was the mahogany table, and the fine
chairs and the fine glass, and all as bare-faced upstart as any stock-jobber
in the kingdom can boast of. And there were the decanters, the glasses,
the 'dinner-set' of crockery ware, and all just in the true stock-jobber
style. And I dare say it has been '*Squire* Charington and the *Miss*
Charingtons'; and not just plain Master Charington, and his son
Hodge, and his daughter Betty Charington, all of whom this accursed
system has transmuted into a species of mock gentlefolks, while it has
ground the labourers into real slaves.

Rural Rides (19 October 1825)

The 'bondage' system that operated in the north of England and
in southern Scotland was also denounced as serfdom by Cobbett.
He inveighed against the 'hellish system' that made large profits
for the farmers and left those who grew the food nothing but
'skin and bone and nakedness'. He saw in the 'English country
gentleman' something superlatively base; 'they are . . . the most
cruel, the most unfeeling, the most brutally insolent of all

creatures'. Cecil Torr records that his grandfather also disapproved of farmers who 'aped the gentleman', while their labourers were pinched and begrudged; but he only paid the current wage himself – 10s. 6d. a week, in 1840 – and looked forward to reducing even that.

All this is borne out by Hardy, who wrote that the labourer was greatly wronged by bad wages from farmers who could afford more, and notes that 'it was once common enough on inferior farms to hear a farmer address a field of workers with a contemptuousness which could not have been greatly exceeded' – had they been serfs (*Personal Writings*, p. 183). Flora Thompson's father 'used to say that the farmer paid his men starvation wages all the year and thought he made it up to them by giving that one good meal' – the harvest supper. Ninety years after Cobbett, Col. Pedder also attacked absentee landlords and farmers who paid their men irregularly and did nothing to improve rotten cottages.[15] Throughout of course the farmers hated the union: 'You were right under and you could not move; and there was no one to protect you. If a farmer knew you had joined the union you'd get the sack' (Evans, *Where Beards Wag All*).

The peasant had now to be an earner and spender of money. Cobbett disapproved of the change, noting that whereas previously farmers had boarded their men, they now paid them because they could not keep them on so little as they gave them in wages. 'The labourers retreated to hovels, called cottages; and instead of board and lodging, they got money; so little of it as to enable the employer to drink wine; but then, that he might not reduce them to *quite starvation*, they were enabled to come to him, in the king's name, and demand food as paupers.' In manufacturing towns the new money-economy imposed the periodicity of a twenty-four-hour factory day upon the rhythms of day and night and the seasons – as Wordsworth observed (*Excursion* VIII, 153). But in the country too the employers did their best to extend the discipline of factory into leisure time by attacking fairs and other occasions for jollity. In non-monetary systems of exchange the thing bartered had had some symbolic meaning; it was a form of giving oneself. But when money is the medium the symbolic element disappears, for it is merely a sign, a calculation.

While civilised money tends to alienate man from his labour by transforming his labour into an abstract commodity, by detaching it from him and by transferring considerations of 'worth' and 'value' from a human to a marketing context, primitive exchange has the contrary effect; social value and social effort are always directly expressed and understood; they strengthen the sense of community.

Stanley Diamond[16]

Sturt was acutely aware of the change to money. For instance, commenting on the astonishing efficiency of the old village men and women, he notes that the younger men are now less thorough than in the past:

In the case of the labourers, the reason for the change may be found in the rewards of labour, which are now estimated in money. If a man can get his three shillings a day, that is the most he can hope for: he is no better off, perhaps he is worse off, if he puts into his work much care and knowledge. His master will not thank him for any finish: will rather grumble at him for being too slow.

But with the older men, as the master was – necessity: the necessity of the weather and the crops and horses and cattle, so the reward to the efficient man was in the excellence of the crops, the welfare of the animals. Hence it was worth while to be efficient; and there was a real penalty, never to be escaped, for being slipshod or a sham.

Journals, p. 674

W. G. Hoskins has shown that the significance of the final enclosures lay in the abolition of common rights and the sudden plunging of the peasant into a money-economy that he did not understand. 'It was not simply the substitution of one system of farming by another, which on balance was perhaps more productive for the country as a whole (though even this is questionable); but the destruction of an entire society with its own economy and traditions, its own way of living and its own culture' (*The Midland Peasant* (1957)).

The needs of a people thus dispossessed were great, but they were never met. The Church did nothing about a problem of which it was unaware; in Joseph Ashby's Tysoe for example the vicar led the effort to make the labourer creep and cringe. The inadequacy of education was also total. At the beginning of the century popular education was dreaded, as providing the means 'of corresponding and continuing schemes of sedition and insurrection' (quoted by Torr in *Small Talk at Wreyland*); and when it became free and compulsory, the form it took was narrowly vocational, seeking to turn out clerks and workmen. As Sturt saw it, education 'is not an aid to the English to become something they instinctively desire to become; it does not come to them as a welcome offer of help; but it is an influence foisted upon them from outside: a constraining agency; an artificial environment, within which the natural genius of the people is in danger of distortion' (*Journals*, p. 394). That is certainly how it was felt; 'school did not exist for the children' (M. K. Ashby) and 'at school they worked unwillingly, upon compulsion, and the life of the schoolmistress was a hard one' (Flora Thompson). Hardy too disliked education, because it reduced rural speech to uniformity. Sturt saw one need with especial clarity – the lack of emotional education and the neglect of the imagination (in a training college): 'I call it a systematic waste of youth, of Life, of one's best parts and best years, this Education. It's a denial of the most vital portion, of the living spirit itself: a sort of blasphemy against the holy ghost.' Since the aim of true education is to produce not wealth and apparatus but perfect human beings, it should bring the individual into closer harmony with his environment and in touch with the living traditions of his day. It is difficult to detect any effective improvement since Sturt's day.

Many witnesses have praised the courage and endurance of the men who suffered the starvation and near-starvation that was the lot of so many in the nineteenth century. Joseph Ashby believed that 'the Tysoe labourer kept to the straight way because the village had once been a true community'; and Sturt often noted that villagers were supported by vestiges of their peasant code. History agrees. W. G. Hoskins, who acknowledges his debt to Sturt, writes of the peasant economy, 'made up of trifles':

It was this economy, which lived almost entirely off its own resources, that enabled the peasantry of all classes from the yeoman down to the cottager and labourer not only to stand up to the catastrophic rise in prices of the later sixteenth century but even, for many of them (labourers included), to improve their position; and it was this same economy which enabled the village to withstand for so long the dis-integrating effect of parliamentary enclosure and not to collapse at the first blow. The tenacious cement that bound it together, compounded of local resources, of traditional knowledge of those resources and skill in making use of them, of living in a place which had meaning and significance for its inhabitants, of work that still, for the great majority, completely satisfied their creative impulses, of governing themselves through their fellows – such a cement was not likely to give way at one blow, however formidable.

The Midland Peasant

Thus the continuity that Wordsworth and Hardy thought so conducive to the development of sound character lasted a genera-tion or two after the end of the peasantry, owing not only to the toughness of peasant fibre, but also to the persistence of farming methods. George Ewart Evans recalls that within living memory farm workers recognised fourteenth-century agricultural terms, and crafts such as the wheelwright's still met local needs. Farm work did not cease to require a variety of skills, and the craftsmen went on enjoying their work; Walter Rose tells us again and again that the carpenters relished using their skill and 'cherished' their job. The less skilled also took great pride in their work: the horse-man in the condition of his horses and in a smart turn-out (they and not the farmer seemed to buy the horse-brasses), the carter in his carved and decorated vehicle, the ploughmen in their furrows.

The latter would walk many miles to inspect each other's work; and Fred Kitchen on many pages of *Brother to the Ox* expresses his happiness in doing a variety of jobs on the farm – one gets the same impression from Flora Thompson. However, as machines took over, there was less scope for skill and pride in the exercise of it.

Other elements from earlier days lasted through the nineteenth century. Some of the labourers had cottages that were fit to live in.

One has only to look at the villages [writes W. G. Hoskins] of almost any county in England, above all perhaps in the counties of the stone belt, to see how many of them were rebuilt in the years between 1580 and 1640, and see how well they were built, with what profound assurance and serenity of mind; and to see that the builders were part of a home-made rural civilisation that was to them eternal, satisfying and unquestionable.

There still survive dwellings and small farms that seem to have grown out of a beautiful landscape, in the way that Wordsworth described in his *Guide to the Lakes*, which we quoted earlier. But far too many existed in poky hovels made of dried mud, as we gather from Dorothy Wordsworth, writing up her journal in Dorset: 'The peasants are miserably poor; their cottages are shapeless structures (I may almost say) of wood and clay – indeed they are not all beyond what might be expected in savage life.'[17] Very few farmers seem to have done anything to improve unhealthy and squalid housing.

Before mechanisation, hay-making and harvesting were joyous family occasions for those in work. Gleaning also was enjoyable and profitable, for an energetic family could collect enough grain to provide flour for half the winter. Machines ended gleaning because of their efficiency, though some harvesters nowadays seem to leave behind more grain than any other form of reaping. The fairs, which were so important in the lives of the poor, continued till late in the nineteenth century. The folk songs that Cecil Sharp and others collected, just in time, survived into the first decade or two of the present century. So, almost to within living memory, there were pockets of England in which organic communities persisted: nearly self-sufficient villages, in which people lived in harmony with their environment, and in which wage-earning had not removed enjoyment from life. The passage, included below, from *Far From the Madding Crowd* sums up: 'So the barn was natural to the shearers, and the shearers were in harmony with the barn.' If one seeks an example from life, Walter Rose supplies a good one, in his description of a not especially outstanding craft that met the needs of a district, as well as giving scope to the creative instinct to produce things of beauty and good workmanship. Zest colours every page of his account of 'the natural life of the hedge-carpenter', whose work was in tune with, and part of, the beauty of the countryside.

This beauty, a largely man-made one, probably attained its maximum about the middle of the century. This was when the planted trees, on which the landscape depended for utility as well as for appearance, reached their maturity. The rural loveliness of England then is more convincingly evoked by Richard Jefferies than by any other writer – he felt it so keenly in all its aspects. Since then, decay has set in. At first natural, it has been accelerated by human neglect and misuse, by wire and metal, by prairie farming, and by universal suburbanisation. Thus have been created large areas of the scruffy nor-town-nor-country deplored by Clough Williams-Ellis fifty years ago, and since then merely aggravated and extended.[18] The future of the English countryside is now that of a garden for the refreshment and re-creation of town-dwellers – by no means an ignoble one, but not one in which agriculture is likely to do much for its beauty.

It is sad that amid all this loveliness the farm worker here and there was degraded to utter wretchedness. Of course there were good farms, good employers and good times, so that farm workers could not only lead full and happy lives, like Fred Kitchen, but

also rise in the world materially, like Joseph Arch of Warwickshire and Isaac Mead[19] in Essex, and others. But despite all that can
be said, Sturt, the most sensitive and precise of all observers, felt
that there was something wrong, manifesting itself in a 'want of
peace and harmony' in himself. This, he wrote,

springs from our distracted 'times', and from a breach of continuity in
the traditions of English country life. To me – I feel it more and more
– there is no country now; at least about here there is none. There are
trees and fields and hedge-rows and so on; but all the old meaning has
departed from them with the ancient peasant life that created them.

Journals, p. 563

I got to a little hamlet, where I breakfasted; but could get no corn for my horse, and no bacon for myself! All was corn around me. Barns, I should think, two hundred feet long; ricks of enormous size and most numerous; crops of wheat, five quarters to an acre, on the average; and a public-house without either bacon or corn! The labourers' houses, all along through this island, beggarly in the extreme. The people dirty, poor-looking; ragged, but particularly *dirty*. The men and boys with dirty faces, and dirty smock-frocks, and dirty shirts; and, good God! what a difference between the wife of a labouring man here, and the wife of a labouring man in the forests and woodlands of Hampshire and Sussex! Invariably have I observed, that the richer the soil, and the more destitute of woods; that is to say, the more purely a corn country, the more miserable the labourers. The cause is this, the great, the big bull frog grasps all. In this beautiful island every inch of land is appropriated by the rich. No hedges, no ditches, no commons, no grassy lanes: a country divided into great farms; a few trees surround the great farm-house. All the rest is bare of trees; and the wretched labourer has not a stick of wood, and has no place for a pig or cow to graze, or even to lie down upon. The rabbit countries are the countries for labouring men. There the ground is not so valuable. There it is not so easily appropriated by the few. Here, in this island, the work is almost all done by the horses. The horses plough the ground; they sow the ground; they hoe the ground; they carry the corn home; they thresh it out; and they carry it to market: nay, in this island, they *rake* the ground; they rake up the straggling straws and ears; so that they do the whole, except the reaping and the mowing . . .

At about four miles from Petersfield we passed through a village called Rogate. Just before we came to it I asked a man who was hedging on the side of the road how much he got a day. He said, 1s. 6d.: and he told me that the *allowed* wages was 7d. a day for the man *and a gallon loaf a week for the rest of his family*; that is to say, one pound and two and a quarter ounces of bread for each of them; and nothing more! And this, observe, is one-third short of the bread allowance of gaols, to say nothing of the meat and clothing and lodging of the inhabitants of gaols. If the man have full work; if he get his eighteen-pence a day, the whole nine shillings does not purchase a gallon loaf each for a wife and three children, and two gallon loaves for himself. In the gaols the convicted felons have a pound and a half each of bread a day to begin with: they have some meat generally, and it has been found absolutely necessary to allow them meat when they work at the tread-mill. It is impossible to make them work at the tread-mill without it. However, let us take the bare allowance of bread allowed in the gaols. This allowance is, for five people, fifty-two pounds and a half in the week; whereas the man's nine shillings will buy but fifty-two pounds of bread; and this, observe, is a vast deal better than the state of things in the north of Hampshire, where the day-labourer gets but eight shillings a week. I asked this man how much a day they gave to a young able man who had no family, and who was compelled to come to the parish-officers for work. Observe that there are a great many young men in this situation, because the farmers will not employ single men *at full wages*, these full wages being wanted for the married man's family, just to keep them alive according to the calculation that we have just seen. About the borders of the north of Hampshire they give to these single men two gallon loaves a week, or, in money, two shillings and eight-pence, and nothing more. Here, in this part of Sussex, they give the single man seven-pence a day, that is to say, enough to buy two pounds and a quarter of bread for six days in the week, and as he does not work on the Sunday there is no seven-pence allowed for the Sunday, and of course nothing to eat: and this is the allowance, settled by the magistrates, for a young, hearty, labouring man; and that, too, in the part of England where, I believe, they live better than in any other part of it. The poor creature here has seven-pence a day for six days in the week to find him food, clothes, washing, and lodging! It is just seven-pence, less than one half of what the meanest foot soldier in the standing army receives; besides that the latter has clothing, candle, fire, and lodging into the bargain! Well may we call our happy state of things the 'envy of surrounding nations, and the admiration of the world!'

I have never been able clearly to comprehend what the beastly Scotch *feelosofers* mean by their 'national wealth'; but, as far as I can understand them, this is their meaning: that national wealth means that which is *left* of the products of the country over and above what is *consumed*, or *used*, by those whose labour causes the products to be. This being the notion, it follows, of course that the *fewer* poor devils you can screw the products out of, the *richer* the nation is.

This is, too, the notion of Burdett as expressed in his silly and most nasty, musty aristocratic speech of last session. What, then, is to be done with this *over-produce*? Who is to have it? Is it to go to pensioners, placemen, tax-gatherers, dead-weight people, soldiers, gendarmerie, police-people, and, in short, to whole millions *who do no work at all*? Is this a cause of 'national wealth'? Is a nation made *rich* by taking the food and clothing from those who create them, and giving them to those who do nothing of any use? Aye, but this over-produce may be given to *manufacturers*, and to those who supply the food-raisers with what they want besides food. Oh! but this is merely an *exchange* of one valuable thing for another valuable thing; it is an exchange of labour in Wiltshire for labour in Lancashire; and, upon the whole, here is no *over-production*. If the produce be exported, it is the same thing: it is an exchange of one sort of labour for another. But *our course* is, that there is not an exchange; that those who labour, no matter in what way, have a large part of the fruit of their labour taken away, and receive nothing in exchange. If the over-produce of this Valley of Avon were given, by the farmers, to the weavers in

Lancashire, to the iron and steel chaps of Warwickshire, and to other makers or sellers of useful things, there would come an abundance of all these useful things into this valley from Lancashire and other parts: but if, as is the case, the over-produce goes to the fund-holders, the dead-weight, the soldiers, the lord and lady and master and miss pensioners and sinecure people; if the over-produce go to them, as a very great part of it does, nothing, not even the parings of one's nails, can come back to the valley in exchange. And, can this operation, then, add to the 'national wealth'? It adds to the 'wealth' of those who carry on the affairs of state; it fills their pockets, those of their relatives and dependents; it fattens all tax-eaters; but it can give no wealth to the 'nation', which means the whole of the people. National Wealth means the Commonwealth or Commonweal; and these mean, the general good, or happiness, of the people, and the safety and honour of the state; and these are not to be secured by robbing those who labour, in order to support a large part of the community in idleness. Devizes is the market-town to which the corn goes from the greater part of this Valley. If, when a wagon-load of wheat goes off in the morning, the wagon came back at night loaded with cloth, salt, or something or other, equal in value to the wheat, except what might be necessary to leave with the shopkeeper as his profit; then, indeed, the people might see the wagon go off without tears in their eyes. But now they see it go to carry away, and to bring next to nothing in return.

What a *twist* a head must have before it can come to the conclusion that the nation gains in wealth by the government being able to cause the work to be done by those who have hardly any share in the fruit of the labour! What a *twist* such a head must have! The Scotch *feelosofers*, who seem all to have been, by nature, formed for negro-drivers, have an insuperable objection to all those establishments and customs which occasion *holidays*. They call them a great hindrance, a great bar to industry, a great drawback from 'national wealth'. I wish each of these unfeeling fellows

had a spade put into his hand for ten days, only ten days, and that
he were compelled to dig only just as much as one of the common
labourers at Fulham. The metaphysical gentlemen would, I believe,
soon discover the *use of holidays*! But *why* should men, why should
any men, work hard? Why, I ask, should they work incessantly,
if working part of the days of the week be sufficient? Why should
the people at Milton, for instance, work incessantly, when they
now raise food and clothing and fuel and every necessary to maintain well five times their number? Why should they not have
some holidays? And, pray, say, thou conceited Scotch feelosofer,
how the 'national wealth' can be increased by making these people
work incessantly, that they may raise food and clothing, to go to
feed and clothe people who do not work at all?

The state of this Valley seems to illustrate the infamous and
really diabolical assertion of Malthus, which is, that the human
kind have a natural tendency *to increase beyond the means of sustenance for them*.[20] Hence, all the schemes of this and the other Scotch
writers for what they call checking population. Now, look at this
Valley of Avon. Here the people raise nearly twenty times as much
food and clothing as they consume. They raise five times as much,
even according to my scale of living. They have been doing this
for many, many years. They have been doing it for several
generations. Where, then, is their natural tendency to increase
beyond the means of sustenance for them? Beyond, indeed, the
means of that sustenance which a system like this will leave them.
Say that, Sawneys, and I agree with you. Far beyond the means
that the taxing and monopolizing system will leave in their hands:
that is very true; for it leaves them nothing but the scale of the
poor-book; they must cease to breed at all, or they must exceed
this mark; but the *earth*, give them their fair share of its products,
will always give sustenance in sufficiency to those who apply to it
by skilful and diligent labour.

William Cobbett, *Rural Rides* (4 September 1823, 12 November
1825)

[By the year 1830,] as the working people went on getting poorer and poorer, they became more and more immoral, in innumerable instances men committed crimes for the purpose of getting into jail; because the felons in jail were better fed and better clad than the honest working people. As the working people became poor, the laws relating to them were made more and more severe; and the Poor-Law, that famous law of Elizabeth,[21] which was the greatest glory of England for ages, had by degrees been so much mutilated and nullified, that, at last, it was so far from being a protection for the working people, that it had, by its perversions, been made the means of reducing them to a state of wretchedness not to be described. The sole food of the greater part of them had been, for many years, bread, or potatoes, and not half enough of these. They had eaten sheep or cattle that had died from illness; children had been seen stealing food out of hog-troughs; men were found dead, [in] May [of that] year, lying under a hedge, and when opened by the surgeons nothing but sour sorrel was found in their stomachs. The spot on which these poor creatures expired was surrounded with villas of Jews, and fund-jobbers, living in luxury, and in the midst of pleasure-gardens, all the means of which living they had derived from the burdens laid on the working people.

Besides suffering from want, the working people were made to endure insults and indignities such as even Negroes were never exposed to. They were harnessed like horses or asses and made to draw carts and wagons; they were shut up in pounds made to hold stray cattle; they were made to work with bells round their necks; and they had drivers set over them, just as if they had been galley slaves; they were sold by auction for certain times, as the Negroes were sold in the West Indies; the married men were kept separated from their wives, by force, to prevent them from breeding; and, in short, no human beings were ever before treated so unjustly, with so much insolence, and with such damnable barbarity, as the working people of England had been. Such were the fruits of public debts and funds! Without them, this industrious and moral and brave nation never could have been brought into this degraded state.

[For some years,] I had seen the cause of Reform fast gaining ground; but, it was not until the month of October, 1830, when the chopsticks set about the work, that I really expected it to come in any reasonable time. Every event must have a beginning; and the greatest events have frequently had their beginnings in trifling causes. I had often used to tell [my] friends, in Long Island and at New York, that no change would ever take place, unless it were begun amongst the hedgers and ditchers and the ploughmen and the thrashers; how often had I told them that people were not formidable when assembled together in great towns. What, then, was it not the meetings and petitions of the great towns that produced Parliamentary Reform? They did good, particularly by the speeches they brought forth, but, the great and efficient case was, the movements of the chopsticks. I had had my eye upon all the movements of the great bodies. I had, in the two preceding years, been about lecturing in person over the far greater part of England; [but, until I found] the working people in almost all of the counties of England in a state of commotion [my hopes did not grow fixed].

All across the South, from Kent to Cornwall, and from Sussex to Lincolnshire, the commotion extended. It began by the labourers in Kent entering the buildings of the great farmers and breaking their thrashing machines; for, please to observe, one effect of heavy taxation was the invention of machinery. The farmer or manufacturer was so pressed for money by the government, that he resorted to all possible means of saving the expense of labour; and as machines would work cheaper than men, the machines were preferred. The labourers saw, at any rate, that the thrashing machines robbed them of the wages that they should have received. They, therefore, began by demolishing these machines. This was a crime; the magistrates and jailers were ready with punishments; soldiers, well fed and well clothed out of the taxes, were ready to shoot or cut down the offenders. Unable to resist these united forces, the labourers resorted to the use *of fire*, secretly put to the barns and stacks of those who had the machines, or whom they deemed the cause of their poverty and misery. The mischief and alarm that they caused by this means were beyond all calculation. They went in bands of from 100 to 1000, and summoned the farmers to come forth, and then they demanded that they should agree to pay them such wages as they thought right.

The farmers, in their defence, said that they could not pay the wages, that were demanded, because they had so much to pay in rent, taxes, and in tithes. The labourers, therefore, in many instances, went to the parsons; and in one parish, in Sussex, they ordered the collector of the taxes not to take the money out of the parish, as it was, they said, wanted there. These proceedings would have been put an end to had it not been for the fires. The military forces, backed by all the great farmers, the land-owners, and especially the parsons, would have subdued these half-starved machine-breakers; but the Fires! No power on earth could have prevented them, if the millions of labourers resolved to resort to them.

The fires, after spreading westward along the county of Kent, soon stretched through Sussex, and thence through Hampshire, Wiltshire, Dorsetshire, Berkshire, and all the most fertile corn-growing counties. A Special Commission, sent into the West and Southwest, transported about four hundred men, and left a fearful number for execution. This mass of punishment did not, however, destroy the effects of these risings of the labourers. The trials, the publications making observations of the trials, the endless discussions, in all shapes and sizes, relative to the poor-laws; and, I may say, my 'Protestant Reformation' and 'Poor Man's Friend', made the *Swing* men, these thrashers, hedgers, ditchers, plough-men, mowers, and reapers understand [a great deal].

Such was the state of England. Here you saw a people, inhabiting the most productive land in the world, a people to whom God had given a large portion of all his choicest blessings, safety from foreign foes, climate, soil, mines, woods, downs, flocks and herds, and, above all, *industry* perfectly unparalleled; a people, too, whose forefathers gave them the best laws that ever existed in the world; here you saw this people, who were famed for their willing obedience to the laws, and whose forefathers had scorned the thought of maintaining even a single soldier except in case of war; here you saw this people, whose laws said that no man should be taxed without his own consent; first reduced to a state of half-starvation; next setting the laws at defiance; and then attacked by a standing army sent against them to capture them and put them in prison. Such were the effects of heavy taxes, and particularly when raised for the purpose of upholding a funding system, which was a system of usury and monopoly added to that of grinding taxation.

William Cobbett, *Political Register*

CHILDHOOD

In Scotland, 1820

My mother was not less remarkable, as a woman, for the labour she encountered and overcame, in domestic toil to keep our clothes mended – no easy task in such a family, where all the earnings might have gone on food without our having too much – and to add by out-field labour to the income. At the time I was born all the family were at home, consisting then of eight children. The eldest, Margaret, now no more, mother of those five excellent young men, the Doughtys (all rising in the world, and some of them risen as regards social station), she was then as she was to her dying day (and I helped to lay her in her grave, when her sons, mere children, all wept around us and their bereaved father); she was always a helpful creature to everybody who needed help. She

sacrificed her life by going from her own house in a delicate condition, to help an afflicted family to bake and wash, and to wash
and nurse the dying father of that family. This she did from pure
charity, and died herself in the effort. When I was born, Margaret
was the only daughter able to work. She worked daily in the fields
and the barns, and morning and night in the house. She was my
first tailor, and the first clothes which she made for me were made
from the old corduroys of my brother William. When we lived
in Springfield, the house rent was paid by finding one shearer for
the harvest, no matter how long the harvest might be; also an
outfield worker winter and summer for the farmer; and in addition to the latter a 'stack carrier', whenever the threshing mill was
going. This last might happen thirty or forty days in the year,
and usually in the winter months. For the shearer in harvest, and
for the carrying of stacks into the barn, no wages were paid; but
the shearer was allowed breakfast and dinner in harvest time, and
a bushel of grain called 'supper barley'. The other worker, called
the 'bondager', was paid ten-pence per day, the hours being usually
ten, but later whenever the farmer chose.

The carrying of the sheaves from the stackyard into the barn,
which was a part of the house rent, was heavy work. My mother
did that all the winter before I was born and the winter after,
besides shearing in the harvest time – the hours being in harvest
between sun and sun. The stack carrying was done thus; two
women had a barrow made of two poles, with canvas stretched
between the poles; upon which canvas were laid ten or twelve
sheaves. The two women then carried that load through the yard
and up a gangway to the upper floor of the barn, meeting another
couple going down empty. They laid down their barrow, and
rolled the sheaves out of it on the floor, where another woman
was 'loosing out' and laying the loosened sheaves upon a table,
where the man who fed into the mill stood. One woman stood
on the stack outside and forked down the sheaves to the ground;
while another on the ground assisted to load the women who

carried the barrows. At this work and in the harvest field did my mother bear the burden of heavy labour and of me. After I was born I was carried to her on such occasions to be suckled. My brother James has told me that the duty of carrying me devolved chiefly on him.

Should you ever be in Scotland and see Springfield, you will find a row of shabby looking tiled sheds, such as they continued to be when I was there last, the centre one of which is about twelve feet by fourteen, and not so high in the walls as will allow a man to get in without stooping. That place without ceiling, or anything beneath the bare tiles of the roof; without a floor save the common clay; without a cupboard or recess of any kind; with no grate but the iron bars which the tenants carried to it, built up and took away when they left it; with no partition of any kind save what the beds made; with no window save four small panes on one side – it was this house, still a hind's house at Springfield, for which, to obtain leave to live in, my mother sheared the harvest and carried the stacks.

How eight children and father and mother were huddled in that place is not easily told. The worst of it was, that food was so very dear, clothes were so very dear, as to us not to be obtainable, and national glory was so very dear – that glory which Europe was mad about at that time, and for which we, like others, had to pay, that even those bare walls, for which so much of my mother's labour had to be paid in rent, were less comfortable than they might have been.

Next to Margaret was your uncle William, who from boyhood to this present year of his age always contributed to, and never detracted from, the assistance and comfort of our parents, and such others of the family as needed his brotherly aid, and who has prospered in everything to which he has put his hand. He was a stripling when I was born, and worked for such wages as a youth could obtain in that part of the country. When he came home at night, my father has told me, he stripped off his coat, took off his hat, put on his night cap, got down the 'elshen box', with awls, hemp, rosin, scraps of leather, lasts, tackets, and hammer; and taking all the children, one by one, as if he had been the father of the family, examined their feet to see which of them had shoes most in need of mending – for all needed repairs, new shoes being in those dear years out of the question. He would then sit down and cobble the shoes by the light of the fire until near midnight, while our mother would mend the other clothes of those in bed, or spin lint to make yarn for the weaver to weave shirting, or card and spin wool for stockings that were daily decaying. William would then end the day with his private prayer, and go to bed. He would rise at four o'clock in the mornings, and do the heaviest part of James's work amongst the farmer's cows and other cattle, before going to his own day's work two or three miles distant. James was too young for the heavy task of cleaning the cowhouses every morning, which had to be done; but as he could make shift, with the assistance of one or two of the other children nearest him in age, to carry straw and turnips to the cattle, and give them water; and as the payment of the few pence per day was an object of importance to the family, William got up every morning to do part of the work to keep James in the employment.

Alexander Somerville, *The Autobiography of a Working Man*[22]

In the Fens, 1850–1860

In the very short schooling that I obtained, I learnt neither grammar nor writing. On the day that I was eight years of age, I left school, and began to work fourteen hours a day in the fields, with from forty to fifty other children of whom, even at that early age, I was the eldest. We were followed all day long by an old man carrying a long whip in his hand which he did not forget to use. A great many of the children were only five years of age. You will think that I am exaggerating, but I am *not*; it is as true as the Gospel. Thirty-five years ago is the time I speak of, and the place, Croyland in Lincolnshire, nine miles from Peterborough. I could

even now name several of the children who began at the age of
five to work in the gangs, and also the name of the ganger.

We always left the town, summer and winter, the moment the
old Abbey clock struck six. Anyone who has read *Hereward the
Wake*, by Charles Kingsley, will have read a good description of
this Abbey. We had to walk a very long way to our work, never
much less than two miles each way, and very often five miles each
way. The large farms all lay a good distance from the town, and
it was on those farms that we worked. In the winter, by the time
we reached our work, it was light enough to begin, and of course
we worked until it was dark and then had our long walk home.
I never remember to have reached home sooner than six and more
often seven, even in winter. In the summer, we did not leave the
fields in the evening until the clock had struck six, and then of
course we must walk home, and this walk was no easy task for us
children who had worked hard all day on the ploughed fields.

In all the four years I worked in the fields, I never worked one
hour under cover of a barn, and only once did we have a meal in
a house. And I shall never forget that one meal or the woman who
gave us it. It was a most terrible day. The cold east wind (I suppose
it was an east wind, for surely no wind ever blew colder), the sleet
and snow which came every now and then in showers seemed
almost to cut us to pieces. We were working upon a large farm
that lay half-way between Croyland and Peterborough. Had the
snow and sleet come continuously we should have been allowed
to come home, but because it only came at intervals, of course we
had to stay. I have been out in all sorts of weather but never remember a colder day. Well, the morning passed along somehow.
The ganger did his best for us by letting us have a run in our turns,
but that did not help us very much because we were too numbed
with the cold to be able to run much. Dinner-time came, and we
were preparing to sit down under a hedge and eat our cold dinner
and drink our cold tea, when we saw the shepherd's wife coming
towards us, and she said to our ganger, 'Bring these children into

my house and let them eat their dinner there.' We went into that
very small two-roomed cottage, and when we got into the largest
room there was not standing room for us all, but this woman's
heart was large, even if her house was small, and so she put her few
chairs and table out into the garden, and then we all sat down in a
ring upon the floor. She then placed in our midst a very large sauce-
pan of hot boiled potatoes, and bade us help ourselves. Truly,
although I have attended scores of grand parties and banquets
since that time, not one of them has seemed half as good to me as
that meal did. I well remember that woman. She was one of the
plainest women I ever knew; in fact she was what the world
would call quite ugly, and yet I can't think of her even now
without thinking of that verse in one of our hymns, where it
says,

> 'No, Earth has angels though their forms are moulded
> But of such clay as fashions all below,
> Though harps are wanting, and bright pinions folded,
> We know them by the love-light on their brow.'

Had I time I could write how our gang of children, one winter's
night, had to wade for half a mile through the flood. These floods
occur nearly every winter, when the Wash overflows her banks.
In harvest-time we left home at four o'clock in the morning, and
stayed in the fields until it was dark, about nine o'clock. As a rule
the gangs were disbanded during the harvest, each child going to
work with with its own friends, and when the corn was cut, the
whole families would go gleaning the corn left in the fields, this
being, of course, the gleaners' own property. A great many
families gleaned sufficient to keep them in bread for the whole
of the winter.

For four years, summer and winter, I worked in these gangs –
no holidays of any sort, with the exception of very wet days and
Sundays – and at the end of that time it felt like Heaven to me
when I was taken to the town of Leeds, and put to work in the

factory. Talk about White Slaves, the Fen districts at that time was the place to look for them.

Mrs Burrows in *Life as We Have Known It*
by Co-operative working women, ed. M. L. Davies

In Warwickshire, 1835–1840

I was a youngster of nine when I began to earn money. My first job was crow-scaring, and for this I received fourpence a day. This day was a twelve hours one, so it sometimes happened that I got more than was in the bargain, and that was a smart taste of the farmer's stick when he ran across me outside the field I had been set to watch. I can remember how he would come into the field suddenly, and walk quietly up behind me; and, if he caught me idling, I used to catch it hot. There was no sparing the stick and spoiling the child then! This crow-scaring was very monotonous work, and many a time I proved the truth of the old adage about Satan finding mischief, for idle hands. My idle hands found a good deal to do, what with bird-nesting, trespassing, and other boyish tricks and diversions. But if those days spent in the fields were rather monotonous, they were at any rate wholesome, and I throve apace. I had fresh air to breathe, plenty of room to stretch my young limbs in, and just enough plain food to nourish a growing boy.

From crow-scarer to ploughboy was my next step, with an accompanying increase in wage of twopence a day. Three shillings a week was that amount better than nothing, but it was a small contribution to the common family fund; it was not sufficient to keep me, let alone buy clothes. We should have been in a very bad way if my mother, by her laundry earnings, had not subsidized my father's wage. My clothing was of the coarsest. I had to go to school in a smock-frock and old hobnailed boots, and my work-a-day garb was the same.

When I was between twelve and thirteen years of age I could

drive a pair of horses and plough my own piece. It was a proud day for me when I drove my first pair and got eightpence a day wage. This kind of work is generally called 'gee-oh-ing'.

I quickly became an efficient geeoher, and proved then, as I have often done since, the truth of the old saying, 'Where there's a will there's a way'. I geeohed with a will, so the way of promotion was not long in being reached. There was a wealthy banker and Justice of the Peace in the village, a great hunting man, who kept six or seven horses. I began to drive a pair of horses at plough for him; and after a bit, thinking I suppose that I was a smart, likely lad, he took me into his stables, made me a sort of stable-boy, and gave me eight shillings a week to start with. Here was a rise for a lad, who was set on rising as fast and as much as he could. In time my wages went up to nine shillings a week, and I was able to be a real help to our little household, and lighten somewhat the burden of care resting on my mother's shoulders. But this was the high-water mark; and if my wages were higher than they had been, my working-day was a longer one. I had to give my money's worth, and I gave it, good measure, as I have always done. I would stick like a limpet to my books of an evening. 'Not an idle minute' was my rule. There were no slack half-hours for me, no taking it easy with the other lads. To make more money, to do more, to know more, to be a somebody in my little world was my ambition, and I toiled strenuously to attain it.

I went on working in the stables until I was about sixteen, and then I started mowing for the same banker. He used to pay me eighteenpence a day for what he would have had to pay another man half-a-crown. I knew this well enough, and the thought of the extra shilling which should have been in my pocket and was not, rankled and continued to rankle, though I kept pretty quiet about it at the time. In the succeeding summer I joined a gang of mowers all in the banker's employ; we worked from five o'clock until seven, but not a farthing's increase on my wage did I get, though I was now as expert with the scythe as the best mower among them. I felt the injustice of this treatment more and more keenly, but I dared not speak out – the time for *that* had not come and I could not risk the loss of my earnings, for my father was in receipt of only eight shillings a week just then. We had to practise the strictest economy in order to keep the wolf of hunger at bay. That wolf is the poor man's familiar; he would be on the prowl round the labourer's humble home from Monday morning until Saturday night – ay, and on Sunday too. He was a ravenous, profane beast, having no respect for the Sabbath day to keep it holy. He was always snapping, and snarling, and growling round the corner. Because we had no rent to pay we fared better than many, but manage as my mother might, we seldom got a taste of fresh meat more than once in the seven days.

It was at this period that a crushing blow fell upon our little family: my mother died. It was an irretrievable loss, a terrible grief to me. Mother, teacher, councillor, guide, and familiar friend – she was all that to me, and more. Oh, if only she could have lived to see me in Parliament, what a proud and joyful day it would have been for her! This sad event took place in 1842.

I stayed on in the old home for a while and took care of my father, but I was more than ever bent on improving my condition and earning a better wage. A man from another part of the kingdom introduced a new style of hedge-cutting into our county. I very soon found out that he could make a tidy bit of money by it, so I set to work at once and learned how to do it. The banker in whose employ I still was let me try my prentice hand, and I practised this new style on his hedges, improving steadily year by year. Then hedge-cutting matches were instituted – 'hedging matches' they called them. The first time I competed I gained a prize; the second time I again won a prize; and the third time I carried off the first prize. Then a championship match was arranged, all the head prizemen for many miles round being asked to compete. I entered the lists and won the first prize of two pounds, a medal, and the proud title of 'Champion Hedgecutter

of England'. I had made up my mind that I would master everything I took up, and I was determined to take up everything which
would further the one aim and object I had in life then – i.e., the
bettering of my own position by every honest means in my
power. The winning of this championship is an instance of how I
succeeded. Soon after this 'glorious victory', I went into different
English counties, and also into Wales, hedge-cutting. I got good
jobs and very good money, and was in great request. Not only
was I a master of this branch of my craft, with men working under
me, but, as I had taken to mowing when sixteen years of age, I
had now become a master hand at that also, and had almost invariably a gang of from twenty to twenty-five men under me in the
field. This was my reward for having caught slippery old Father
Time by his fore-lock. I made some very good mowing contracts
with large graziers; they would give me six and seven shillings an
acre. The farmers were not so liberal by half, as they seldom paid
more than three shillings an acre. Still, taking one contract with
another, I did well and could put more money into my pocket
that I had ever done yet.

I now worked my way back to Barford, and at last found myself once more in the old cottage. I had gained both money and
experience, I had travelled over large tracts of my native land, I
had been tried as a labourer and had not been found wanting;
as a mower, as a hedger and ditcher, I had more than held my own
with the best. Wherever I had worked I had given proof that I was
not one of the hopeless, helpless nobodies. I was conscious of
increased strength and vigour of mind and body; I had learned
where I stood among my fellow-workers, and consequently I was
more than ever determined to carve out an upward path for
myself, and be a somebody in the world of working men.

The Autobiography of Joseph Arch[23]

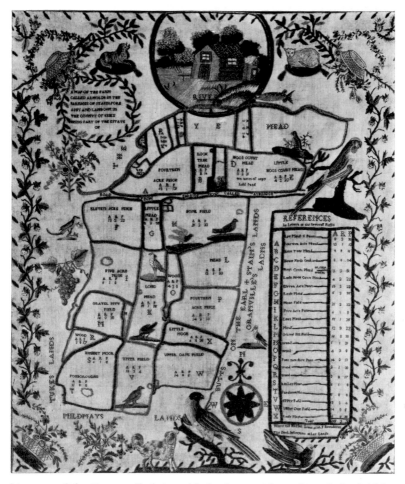

'A Map of the Farm called Arnolds in the parishes of Stapleford Abby and Lambourn in the County of Essex being part of the estate of . . .' (the name of the farm's owner has not been included). Late eighteenth century, worked in coloured silks on woollen canvas.

Private charity comes to the help of the starving cottager. Illustration from *The Children's Friend*, 1866.

Workforce at Long's, Aston, near Bampton, Oxon. *c.* 1898. Left to right, Ernest Long, Henry Glenister, Rich Long, Will Johnson.

Harvest team in a North Essex village, early twentieth century

'Out of the parish!' A *Punch* cartoon of 1865 showing a landowner ordering an aged labourer out of the parish so that he will not have to be supported by the local poor rates.

Late Victorian lacemaker from Olney, Buckinghamshire

Interior of a Dorsetshire labourer's cottage, 1846

McCormick's reaping machine

Dancing monkey and one-man band at Taplow, Buckinghamshire,
in the late nineteenth century

Dorsetshire peasantry

Children at Ovington, Hampshire, with May Day garlands, *c.* 1893

Pontrilas sawpit, 1933

Hay-harvest. Drawn by Duncan, 1846

Newton Abbot Agricultural Society's ploughing match, March 1847

A wheelwright's shop at Stratton, near Bude in Cornwall, in about 1910

'Fitness to environment'. Kettlewell, Yorkshire

'Risen out of the native rock'. Higher Pudnes, Devonshire

Craft into art (i). Drystone walling, Yorkshire

Craft into art (ii). Laid hedge

Harvesting near Whiteleaf Cross in about 1910

Craft into art (iii). Thatching

Craft into art (iv). Smocking

THE FARM AS IT WAS

The carter and the stable

Horses have not ceased to be the most valuable servants of many farmers, and so the carter's duties need not be very elaborately particularised here. In the morning he must clean and groom the horses and 'set the stable fair', he must feed and look after them during the day, and late in the evening 'make up for the night'. The cleaner the stable is kept the better, and the fresher the horses will be; but some carters have strange notions about this. There is an old idea to the effect that if the cobwebs, which in some stables hang like dingy stalactites from the rafters, are swept away the horses will catch cold.

In old stables there is an oak corn-bin or 'ark', with divisions for bran and oats, and a wooden peck measure. It seems difficult now to get the large black oats which were such a valuable part of the horses' food. Carters of the old sort would sooner starve themselves than their teams and by some farmers were given a bad name for pilfering corn to pamper them. For drinking, horses prefer soft water to hard, though now they often get the latter, since most farms have the Company's water 'laid on'. Some country places, however, are still dependent on ponds for their supplies and when these go dry in a hot summer the farmer may have to send his water-cart for miles. A Kentish farmer complained that when the rain came again the horses would not go back to the pond-water and so he had to 'bring them to it gradual', by adding a little muddy water every day to the clean.

Where the horses' tails are allowed to grow long, they are sometimes plaited with straws and ribbons, and to do this well is no fool's job. Both carters and farmers have often decided views as to how exactly it should be done. The old loose hairs are pulled from time to time and fresh ones take their place. An old farmer near Rhayader made all the rope which was used on his farm with

E

the pullings of the horses' tails, and most extraordinarily tough rope it must have been.

Carters are less employed now as such, for with the increase of motor transport road-waggons are no longer used for long journeys, except in a few flat parts of the country – in Cambridgeshire, Lincolnshire and parts of Kent and Sussex. But wherever horses are kept for ploughing and other farm work, there is a man whose job is to look after them; sometimes, though not so often as formerly, a head carter with a second and third under him. When the waggon was taken on the roads, the carter walked beside on the 'near side' in his smock and with his breeches tied up with whipcord, carrying his whip with its brass-ringed handle and accompanied by a boy or under-carter, for an assistant was necessary to adjust the skidpan or 'drag-shoe' on hills, or perhaps where other traffic was encountered. Often a journey had to be made to the mill with a load of corn to be ground, perhaps at a distance of five or six miles, and for this the carter had to be up at two in the morning, in order to be back in time for the regular day's work. Five quarters was about the capacity of a Kent or Sussex waggon, and the journey had to be made once a week. Sometimes the distance was more considerable; in parts of Wales lime was carted for fifteen miles, and elsewhere farmers sent to towns over twenty miles distant for 'night-soil' or even farther to attend markets or buy cattle. From the latter it might not be necessary to be back so early, but they might have to start at midnight in order to be there in good time in the morning. In making these expeditions the carter would wake himself at the right hour, and though he had nothing but the stars to tell him the time the position of the Plough would tell him exactly when he must set out.

It was the carter's duty to keep an eye on the waggon and point out necessary repairs before it was too late, and also to see to the state of the shoes and harness. Some farms of middling size kept a forge and a man who could act as farrier, but except on large estates this is very rare now. The occupation of carter was often hereditary, and the horse-bells and brasses were handed down from father to son.

At fairs and festivals the waggons as well as the horses were often decorated; the former with ears of corn tied in bunches to the lades and ladders, the latter with bells and brasses, and their manes and tails 'ridged up' or braided with straw and ribbons. It was no rare thing for the carter to be up by four o'clock on a week-day morning, or late on Sunday night, polishing the brasses in preparation for such an event or simply because the team was to be taken out on the roads the next day.

The ornaments, as has been said, are as a rule the carter's property. There are large and small horse-bells. The former, called latten-bells, are of the size of hand-bells, three or four to each horse, the set making up a full, rich scale. They are fixed to the names by a hooped rod, and being protected at top and sides by leathern flaps studded with small brass plates are known also as box-bells. Their old use was to warn on-coming traffic at night or in narrow winding lanes where it was difficult for meeting vehicles to back; they are to be found in the southern and western counties more than in the north.

The small bells, fastened on an upright ornament on the horses' heads or singly at the sides, make a constant slight tinkling or all jingle suddenly whenever a horse shakes his head. These are the head-bells; and though latten-bells are hardly ever to be seen in use at present, small bells and brasses are kept by a good many carters who take a pride in their teams – fewer now, it must be owned, in the country than in London and other large towns.

Sometimes a swinger takes the place of the head-bells, a small round plate of polished brass suspended in a brass ring, which glitters like a mirror as it swings. But what are generally called the 'brasses', or amulets, are irregular plates or discs about three inches across, in the form of some device, fastened either singly at the forehead or in a series to the broad piece of leather between the collar and the girth-strap, known as the martingale or breast-strap. These ornaments are said by antiquarians to be of very ancient origin; some supposing them to be referred to in the Bible (Judges viii. 21, 26), others considering them to have been charms against the evil eye. Among the commonest forms are the sun, moon and stars; the lotus and ox's head, and many trefoil and other shapes derived therefrom; roses, thistles, wheels, knots, trees, horsemen, horses, beasts, cocks, windmills, monograms and crests. There are brass studs and sometimes larger ornaments such as hearts, diamonds or stars, on the hame rein, and brass plates of more or less richness on the loin straps (which are purely fancy additions to the harness) and sometimes on the blinkers, though these used often to be embossed with raised or moulded shapes worked in leather – cockle-shells and such like. The edges of these pieces, and of the box-bells' covering, were often ornamentally incised or stitched.

For the comfort of those amateurs who collect horse-amulets, it may be added that these are still cast, at Wolverhampton, from old moulds and sold by saddlers in several parts of the country; as also are some inferior stamped brasses of later invention and others inset with knobs of coloured porcelain. Besides these, small head-bells, swingers and coloured brushes or plumes may be had new, but not many young horsemen will afford five shillings for these extravagances, although, it may be remarked, they can quite often pay for a seat at the cinema.

'Pride in horses! why, that's a thing o' the past.'

Bullock-teams

In early times oxen were almost universally employed for plough-ing, heavy horses, the ancestors of our shire-horses, being fewer, it is supposed, than at present and being kept as chargers for the use of the nobility.

In 1760, as Young records, bullocks were still about as common-ly used as horses on the farms of England. After this time, with

the improvement in the breeds of horses and the general introduction of lighter ploughs which could be drawn by two horses, the
old teams of eight or twelve oxen were generally abandoned,
though in a few districts, such as the Sussex and Berkshire Downs
and in parts of Wiltshire and Gloucestershire, they continued to
be in fairly common if not general use.

In Sussex many farms kept a score of oxen and used them for
drawing carts on the roads, as well as for work on the land. Such
carts are still sometimes to be seen; they were adaptable to shafts
for a horse or to a pole, called a neb, which could be fixed to the
yoke by which the two oxen drew it. When taken on the roads
it was necessary to have them shod; the shoes consisting of two
plates, one for each part of the hoof, sometimes with a flange inwards. The cost of shoeing was a halfpenny for each shoe – that
is fourpence for each beast. Many of these bullocks were sent from
Wales to Sussex and to London; and as they travelled by road a
smith accompanied them to mend or replace shoes which had been
broken or lost on the journey. The same thing was done when
Aberdeen Angus cattle were sent to London, a distance of three
hundred miles, which they accomplished by road in three weeks.

Up to 1914 there were a dozen or more teams at work on the
Sussex farms; by 1931 there were none, the last team belonging
to Major Harding at East Dean having been given up in 1929. But
it is not impossible that their use might be revived if arable farming
should again become profitable in that district, for they are said
to suit the land better than horses. They have several advantages:
though slower than horses, they pull with a steadier draught,
they are cheaper to feed, they are much less nervous, and will
work close under hedges and in places where horses will not go.
They would sometimes bolt, plough and all, when 'terrified' by
flies; but to prevent this a dressing can be easily and effectually
applied. When they had been worked for ten or a dozen years
(they are three or four years old when they begin), they were
fattened for beef, which was sold in Sussex at fourpence a pound.

The only team left in England in 1931 was the celebrated one of six Hereford cattle which belonged to Earl Bathurst at Cirencester. These Herefords are in constant work between 8 a.m. and 4 p.m. and yet are always fat and well-looking. At seven o'clock in the morning, before starting, they are fed with hay, which will stay by them for the rest of the working day. At half-past eight or nine, on reaching the ploughland, they rest for a while, and again at midday, when they ruminate their hay; at four o'clock they are watered and then turned out to grass and need no more attention until the next morning. During one day they can plough an acre of ground with a double-furrow plough, with no unusual exertion.

This team and others that were lately used in Gloucestershire are not harnessed with yokes, but collars; a practice which has been adopted by Rhodesian farmers. Instead of bits to the bridles the mullens, as they are called, have a chain under the jaw and a rein on the left-hand side only; to turn them to the right a verbal command must be given. The hames and cart-saddles are made of wood, as light as possible. The harness becomes very soft and supple with use, from the natural grease of the oxen; not dry and cracking as with horses.

Many farmers in Devon and other counties hang up in their halls the ox-yokes which were used in their grandfathers' times; these are generally made of oak carefully carved into shape and often blackened and polished. The 'bows' by which they were fixed to the necks of the oxen were made of ash, steamed and bent into shape and passed through two holes in each curve of the yoke. . . .

The ox-man had three or four songs, which he sang continually over and over again; and when he stopped singing, the oxen stood still in their tracks.

Waggons and carts

'Horse, oxen, plough, tumbrel, cart, waggon and waine,
    The lighter and stronger, the greater they gain:

The soile and the seed, with the sheafe and the purse,
The lighter in substance, for profit the worse.'

Thomas Tusser[24]

To make waggons as light and strong as possible was and is the
great concern of country wheelwrights. This practical object is
the primary reason for most of the chamfered ornament on the
older types, for no superfluous ounce of weight must be left, and
the joints and corners must therefore be thicker and stouter than
the intermediate parts and those on which the strain is slight. Oak
is the timber most used for the framework of the waggon, elm
planks for the sides and floor, elm logs for the naves of the wheels,
ash for the spokes and fellies and also for the shafts.

It is scarcely an exaggeration to say that there is a different style
of waggon to each county; for though certain of the old types are
to be found in several counties and are not restricted to a single
one, there was some distinctive peculiarity in the work of almost
every individual waggon-builder in the country. The harvest- and
road-waggons are the central types of the old county patterns, but
besides these there are among the older sorts timber-waggons,
millers' and brewers' waggons, and many other varieties; double-
shafted and pole-waggons, hermaphrodites, bavin-trucks, flat bed-
waggons; and many species of two-wheeled carts, tumbrils, butts
and the like. Apart from the work which is now done by lorries
and engines, the old types have in many districts given place to
what are called trollies and boat-waggons, and in many more the
traditional county pattern is altered and debased and shorn of all
curious elaboration.

Four-wheeled waggons are named according to the amount of
turning which is possible to the front wheels: quarter-lock, in
which the movement of the wheels is limited by the straight sides
of the waggon-floor; half-lock, in which a section is taken out of
each side, forming a 'waist' in which the wheels can turn further;
three-quarter lock, in which only the pole of the waggon impedes

their movement; and full-lock waggons, in which the wheels are made small and can turn under the floor of the waggon. The last sort are generally made now, their front wheels being about three feet high; but formerly all four wheels had to be large, so that the axles might clear the ground when the waggon went in the ruts, which in many country roads were, within the last fifty years, nearly two feet deep.

The differences between the traditional types can be realised better from illustrations than from description. It is a striking fact that some parts of the country are fifty years or more behind the fashion elsewhere; for example, straked wheels, which have been abandoned for many years in North-east Somerset, are still made sometimes in the south-west part of the county; and they are also used in parts of Sussex, Kent, Essex, Suffolk and Hereford. In Radnorshire one may even see wooden-armed axles made still, though in most parts of the country iron arms have been in use for the past seventy years or even longer.

Sowing

It is almost inevitable to think of a sower as one who scatters the seed broadcast on the furrows, like the sower in the parable. This must be an art as old as husbandry, but it is not now so familiar a sight as formerly. The sower marks the breadth of his cast with a stick at the headland, at the correct distance on his left side, and walks towards another one set up at the opposite side of the field; on reaching this he moves it to mark a new strip of the same width and returns to the first one. If the field is on a hill he will set up an intermediate stick on the rising ground in the middle. The seed is generally carried in a large kidney-shaped basket or box slung at the left side of the sower, while he throws it with his right hand as he paces across the field; as he returns, he pushes the seed-lip round to his right side and sows with his left hand. This seed-lip, otherwise called a seed-cot, hopper or scuttle, was made of thin wooden boards, bent to the required shape, like the old gallon and peck measures, but it is not common to meet with a wooden one now; galvanised iron vessels have taken their place. A sowing-sheet or looped-up bag was sometimes used instead.

In most of the eastern counties broadcast sowing has been abandoned, and wheat is now put in with a drill, but it is in quite common use in the West and North. Scotch farmers make their men sow with both hands alternately, so as to cover twice the ground in the time. The cast is made inwards; if with the right hand, the seed is thrown from right to left, descending in a curve with surprising evenness. Each cast is made in time with the step, with a steady and deliberate swing, and the experienced sower can regulate the amount with great nicety, so as to distribute exactly a given quantity, whether large or small, to every acre.

There is a tool for broadcast sowing called a fiddle, which has been known in the West of England for seventy or eighty years and is to be seen on some farms in Gloucestershire, Somerset and Dorset. It has a hopper from which the seed flows into some cups or paddles which can be whirled round; they turn on a spindle round which a bowstring is looped, and as the bow is drawn backwards and forwards (like a fiddle-bow) the seed is flung out with a centrifugal impulse. There seems to be little to recommend this tool beyond the fact that it sows on both sides and needs less skill to use; it can scarcely be easier to judge the quantity sown by it than by hand.

It was a universal custom to sow according to the calendar, not only in this country, but in all ancient civilisations. Winter wheat was sown in the 'darks of November' or, in some places, of October, to grow with the moon. It was usual to sow either when there was no moon or at a new moon, or at least when the moon was on the wax; and Arthur Young mentions as exceptional a successful farmer who sowed spring wheat 'in the wane of April'. The East Anglian farmers seem to be the only ones who now take notice of the moon in sowing; most farmers are inclined to ridicule the notion, yet there are signs that modern science may revive it. The faith of some old Welsh farmers knew no bounds: rams were put to ewes, settings of eggs put under the hen, and pigs killed, on the increase of the moon; if the last were duly done, the meat would swell, but if the beast were slaughtered in the wane, it would dwindle. There is a saying that it is 'no good looking for mushrooms after full moon, they don't grow except with the moon'. On the other hand an old countryman in Kent used to declare, of ferreting for rabbits, that 'they will bolt from their holes when the moon is wasting, for then they have the sign in their heels; but when she is making they have the sign in their heads, and then they will sit fast'.

'When you hear the first chapter of Genesis in church, put in your oats': that is, at Septuagesima. In Essex, if all the drilling were finished by Good Friday, the farmer's wife gave the men a seed-cake tea; and in Lincolnshire the end of sowing (about the second week of October) was celebrated with a 'frummity supper'. By many people, potatoes are planted on Good Friday afternoon; in South Devon it was said, 'We sow our potatoes at the foot of the Cross'.

When the seed is sown on the furrow, as it is with broadcast sowing, it must with all speed be harrowed in and otherwise protected from the rooks and other birds, which are nearly as mischievous coming after the sower as they are useful when they follow the plough. Bird-scaring – in Kent it is called 'bird-minding' by the old people – was the labourer's earliest task; boys of seven or eight used to do it for a shilling a week, though in some places they got as much as fourpence or fivepence a day. They were seldom provided with rattles; they might have some pebbles to shake in a tin, but often they had simply to shout. The board-schools have done away with much of this wholesome employment; even in the holidays such labour commands a higher price. The occasional report of a decrepit firelock may now startle the echoes, but science has otherwise made little change in this department of agriculture. The withered corpses of rooks are hung on sticks about the fields; and near towns, where old clothes are plentiful, there is generally a goodly population of scarecrows: 'dudmen', as they were once called. Pigeons attack the peas especially and will almost clear a field of them if given a chance. An old trick of Kentish farmers was to string one or two peas on long threads, with bits of paper tied to the ends like the tail of a kite. The unlucky bird which swallowed a tethered pea would fly off with the train of paper following it, furiously pursued by the rest of the flock, which for a long time would be wary of entering that field again.

There are worse enemies than birds in the field, and these not so easily dealt with, since they work in secret; that is to say wireworms, slugs and grubs. To protect the seed against these and against blight, the old method was to steep it in strong brine or chamber-lye, to skim off and reject the grains which floated, and to dry the rest by mixing them with lime or wood-ashes; but this excellent plan is seldom followed now. Rolling does much to destroy wireworms; soot keeps off slugs and earthworms.

For sowing grass and clover seed there is a seed-barrow, with a large narrow-rimmed wheel, and carrying a box or trough fifteen feet long. This is divided into sections which are filled with seed, and as the barrow is pushed, a gear from the axle turns a spindle which runs from end to end of the box; and on this are mounted brushes which, as they revolve, sprinkle the seed regularly out of small holes in the bottom of the trough. This is an old invention and is used on many farms; it is sometimes pushed by one man, sometimes with another man in front to share the weight. But there is an older invention still, which consists of the box only; a man had to carry it up and down the field shaking it as he went. There is one of these at a farm near Taunton, but it exists as a curiosity only.

Broadcast sowing is the only kind for which the ground is prepared by ploughed furrows, so that the seed falls into the hollows and is covered by raking the crests over it. For the other methods of sowing . . . – dibbling and drilling – the ploughed land is first harrowed and then lightly rolled.

Harvesting in the old style

In most parts of England reaping with sickles has been given up since about 1870, but this work is still to be seen in some parts of Scotland and Ireland. The sickle is a distinct tool from the broad and smooth-edged fagging-hook, which is still used for many jobs and for a time took its place in the harvest-fields of most parts of England before reaping-machines became common. Its blade is in the form of a continuous curve, ending in a point several inches beyond the line of the handle; this point is not sharpened and serves to divide the straws of the standing corn. An inch or so from the point the edge is sharp and serrated, nicks being filed along the under side of the blade (which is somewhat concave), in such a way that they radiate, as it were, from the 'heel' of the blade. About half a dozen patterns of sickle are still made, or at any rate listed by the large firms of tool-makers in Sheffield; those which still survive are mostly coarser-toothed and rather smaller than the sickles which were formerly used in England. It may be added that the sickle is used in May on the coast of Kerry, and perhaps by crofters and islanders on other rocky shores, for cutting the kelp or seaweed harvest, which is then at its best for turning into manure.

In reaping corn, the reaper stoops to his work or kneels on one knee, and leaning forward grasps in his left hand the straw near the ground, pushes the blade of the sickle round it and draws it towards him, pushing his left hand over it at the same time, to avoid the cut. After each cut he raises his left hand to clear the ears from those of the next handful to be reaped; and when he can hold no more he lays out the bunch to his side, lifting it high over the standing corn with the ears supported in the curve of his sickle. As he works across the field he clears a strip about six feet wide (or less perhaps if the crop is heavy), reaping across the end of the strip from the outside to the inside and laying out his handfuls together in sheaves, ready for the binder.

A woman or girl generally does the binding. She must first shake out all grass and weeds from the straw and then, pulling out a handful from the bottom of the sheaf, she first twists it below the heads, turning it over so that they are held against the sheaf under the twist; and then dividing the bond she passes the two ends of it round the sheaf, again twisting them together and pushing them tightly under the bond. This, at any rate, is a common way of binding sheaves, but there are other sheaf-knots . . .

Towards the end of the day the reapers put down their sickles and assist the binders in setting up the sheaves to dry in stooks or shocks. One binder is sufficient for three reapers, sometimes for more; and it used to be customary in some places for the children also to follow the reapers, making 'lock-bonds' and laying the sheaves in them ready to be tied.

Nowadays reaping with sickles is almost entirely confined to small holdings, or small farms in districts which are full of large immovable stones, which make the use of machines impracticable. In such places two or three reapers, or a labourer and his family, are as many as will be seen working together; but when the sickle was the only means of harvesting all the corn that was grown, the farmer who had a large crop had to employ as many reapers as possible, in order to get the work finished before the corn was over-ripe. Where labour was cheap, the work was sometimes done with surprising speed. An old farmer in Ireland remembered seeing a wheat-field of fifty-five acres, in which no fewer than forty men were reaping with sickles, and women binding. On his going to look at the work, which was being beautifully done, he found two of the women fighting tooth and nail, tearing out one another's hair; the owner of the field was for letting them fight it out, but being a man of authority he intervened and stopped the battle.

In different districts there were various ways of arranging for the reaping to be done, and in some places it was customary for a band of harvesters to consist of a fixed number of men. In Northumberland six reapers were called a bandwin; in Yorkshire three shearers went out with one binder and the four were spoken of as a yan; but these terms are long since obsolete. In Cambridgeshire reapers worked in twos, the first making a lock-bond and laying in half the 'shoof', the second filling it and tying it. The leader was generally called the lord or headman. In some counties it was his duty to call the others up by blowing a horn in the morning, and he would blow it again as a signal to cease work for meals and at the end of the day. In parts of Essex the custom of sounding the harvest-horn was kept up till 1914.

Sometimes the harvesters worked in families, and the farmer would then apportion each family's work by tying a knot at intervals in the standing corn.

The Irish reapers cut the straw close by the ground, and very little is wasted. This, though a slow process, leaves the field very neat and tidy; the ground is untrampled, the sheaves free from weeds and the straw straight and unbroken for the thatcher's use. But in England the stubble was left eight or ten inches long; and later in the year it was burnt to manure the land or 'hammered off' with a scythe to use as litter for cattle. In Essex the stubble was generally left till after Christmas as cover for the partridges; then it was cut off and used for making lambing-pens or for fuel.

A skilful and laborious man may reap a half-acre in a day. Formerly men worked for long hours throughout the harvest; and there are labourers still working in Somerset and Gloucestershire who have many times been up all night reaping by moonlight. One of them affirms that he and another man between them in one season mowed and reaped, of hay and corn, not less than two hundred acres of land. To sustain them in their Herculean labours a vast deal of fuel was needed. A gallon of cider to each man, and often ale in addition, was the regular daily allowance while this work lasted. The drink was carried in a wooden bottle

like a little tub, slung at the belt; with a cork and an air stop which
had to be removed before drinking from it. Every morning these
were filled up by the farmer's wife and stood in a row outside the
kitchen one for each man. A farm near Bishop's Lydeard still
continues the custom; perhaps others do also, but the farm labourer
of to-day drinks very much less than his forefathers, for his work
is no longer so constant and severe as to make it necessary.

Many farmers gave their men a meat dinner once a week, sometimes twice. The other meals during harvest were breakfast,
elevenses, dinner and fourses – in some places elevenses was called
'beaver' or 'cheesing' – but there was a good deal of difference in
the local significations of these terms and the times at which the
meals were eaten. Meals at harvesting were generally somewhat
different from those at other times. The school children had a
holiday at harvest-time; in Norfolk the girls went out 'carrying
elevenses' and 'carrying fourses', and the boys, whose duty it was
to lead the horses which drew the harvest-waggons were said to
be busied in 'hollering holdyer'; this was a signal to the men on
top of the load to hold tight when the waggon moved on, and
was yelled so loudly as to be heard, if possible, not only in the next
parish, but in the next county too!

In different counties there were many ways of setting up shocks
or stooks to dry before they were ready to carry to the stack or
the barn. In wet districts, as soon as may be, the stooks are put
into larger heaps called mows, the better to protect the corn from
the wet.

The number of sheaves in the shock varies in different districts;
formerly it was regularly fixed, but nowadays the terms shock or
stook are loosely used by most farmers, and probably not many
harvesters trouble themselves in the least about how many sheaves
they set up, beyond the fact that too few are liable to be blown
down, and too many will not dry easily. The stooks are made in
straight lines down the field; the harvester holding a couple of
sheaves by the heads, one under each arm, and dropping their

butts on the ground at either side of his feet: so that the two rest upright against one another. More pairs of sheaves are generally added behind and before, so that the finished stook contains six, eight, ten or even twelve sheaves. It is a mistake to place an odd sheaf at the end, for this prevents the air from circulating through the corn and drying it. Formerly a 'shock' was generally understood to contain six sheaves and a stook, stowk or hattock, twelve sheaves; in the northern counties (Derbyshire, Yorkshire, Cheshire, and Westmorland), twenty-four sheaves, that is, four shocks or two stooks, made up a threave, which was a convenient measure in those districts. In Cumberland, however, ten sheaves were reckoned to a hattock, or twelve to a stook. The term threave, thrave or trace was a pretty general one in several of the southern counties also, though it has now dropped out of common use. Where the land was ploughed in ten-foot stitches in Essex, the sheaves were set up in every alternate furrow, so that the rows of stooks, or 'traves' as they were there called, stood at the breadth of two ridges apart from one another.

In the south-western counties, except Cornwall, stooks were made to contain ten sheaves, originally, it is said, for convenience in paying tithes when they were collected in kind; hence they are sometimes called tethins or teddings. The collecting of tithes in kind was commuted for money payment by Act of Parliament in 1826, and it is somewhat startling to find that it may still be no further off than a second-hand tradition. Last haymaking season an old Wiltshire labourer, who is still hard at work at eighty-four, beguiled the dinner-hour by telling stories which he had heard when a boy from an old man with whom he then worked. This man had explained to him how at harvest-time it had been his duty to carry round green boughs and lay one on every tenth stook, which was thus set apart for the parson. The farmer first carried his own sheaves, then the rector's waggon would follow and pick up all his, carrying them off to the tithe barn. This old labourer had several stories about tithing, always at the expense of the parson. A certain very mean and grasping rector called on one of his parishioners, a poor widow with a large family, having heard that her sow had farrowed and intending to claim the tenth pig of the litter. For some time she argued the point, but he was firm and not to be put to shame. At last she said, 'Well zur, if you do have the tenth pig then you do take the tenth child too, for I've got eleven o' they!' Whether the rector agreed to these terms is not related. The same parson had an argument with another of his parishioners on the subject of bees, claiming the tenth swarm of the season. In the end the bee-keeper entered his study one day with a skep in his hand, turned it upside down and shook out all the bees, exclaiming, 'Here you be sir, the bees is yourn and the hive's mine!' He made good his retreat before the rector could collect his wits, let alone the bees.

In harvesting other crops than wheat, different methods had sometimes to be employed. When barley was bound in sheaves, on account of the shortness of its straw, it had to be tied with double or lock-bonds, the binder fastening two small handfuls together by the ears and tying the tails the other side. In Essex and parts of Norfolk, and elsewhere, it was not bound at all, but being mown with scythe and cradle, was laid out in rows; and when the sun had been on these for some time, they were turned over with long three-pronged pitchforks, called barley-forks, so that the other sides should be dried also, and then carried loose in the waggon. It was a good plan, despite its seeming awkwardness, for barley is more easily injured by rain at harvest than any other crop, and it dries much more quickly loose than in sheaves.

In Kent barley used to be made into mows, and this was called haling. Four sheaves were placed together two against two, their ears all together and butts outward, then four more on these with their butts somewhat off the ground; a third tier likewise, and finally three sheaves fastened together, with ears downwards so as to make a covering over the top. Thus the whole mow contained fifteen sheaves. Something much like this is done in Cardiganshire,

where the stooks consist of four sheaves only. The mows are made
by setting about fifteen more sheaves round a stook, their butts
also on the ground; then another fifteen (or perhaps fewer) in a
second and third tier; lastly three or four sheaves are tied close together at the top to keep out the wet. In Pembrokeshire wheat is
sometimes thus made into mows, but not oats. In Co. Galway,
where a good deal of reaping is done with sickles and the sheaves
are very small, they are laid into 'barts', which contain thirty
sheaves of wheat or twenty of oats. In other parts of the country,
on account of the frequent rains at harvesting-time, the stooks are
often made into mows as soon as the corn is dry enough to allow
this.

Farmers used to leave their corn longer to dry in stooks than
they commonly do now. Sometimes the reaping took a month,
and when the corn was all stooked and finished – it might be on a
Wednesday or Thursday – they would take another day or so to
lay the rick foundations; and then on Saturday the farmer would
very likely give his men a holiday and not begin stacking till
Monday. But now corn may be cut, stacked, threshed and sent to
the mill, all in a fortnight.

There were several old customs at harvesting, some local, others
widespread, but all more or less of a ritualistic nature. In Devonshire, before a field was reaped, the farmer's wife was known to
step in, before she would allow the reapers to begin, and cut the
first few handfuls with her own hand, 'for the church'; these she
would afterwards make into little sheaves and lay upon the altar.
This was perhaps a pretty fancy of her own; but the other customs
were possibly of pagan origin and had to do with the last sheaves
cut. One of these was the bringing in of the 'neck', which was
made of the last handful cut, the man who cut it standing between
two sickles laid edge to edge on the ground and crying 'I have a
neck!' There were sometimes set responses from the other reapers
and in the end a race to take it into the barn. The last load to be
brought in, called the 'horkey load', was the centre of great

rejoicing; it was crowned with a green bough and sometimes with a 'harvest-home sheaf' of great size, and the men, women and children rode home on it shouting and cheering. The great sheaf had to go at the bottom or in the middle of the rick and the bough was sometimes set on the top.

In Essex they went round to the farm or manor and 'hollered largess', which the master gave them in kind; one giving a barrel of beer or cider, another giving meat or bacon, and so on. In some places they levied contributions from the shopkeepers of the nearest market-town or hamlet. Then they would join forces and have the horkey or harvest-supper, it might be in a public-house, but more often in a barn. This giving of largess was gradually replaced by gifts of money, and in some places the harvest supper was paid for by the farmer, especially if he were a well-to-do man. This was of course besides the two or three meat dinners a week which many farmers gave their harvesters. At the horkeys a few old songs, and probably more new ones, were sung, and in former years one or two old men would perform country-dances on a board. But since the passing of the Agricultural Wages Bill, the horkey has been generally abandoned, though one or two landowners in the eastern counties are still generous enough to give a supper each year.

Gleaning

From time immemorial the poorer people had a right to glean in the harvest-fields after the farmer had carried his sheaves, and by this means many families managed to keep themselves in bread throughout the winter. The custom survives in a very few parts of the country; ten or fifteen years ago it was much more common, but from several causes it is quickly becoming extinct. The chief reason is that there is no longer an urgent necessity for it; the labourer's wages are higher, it is no longer common for him to be in actual want, and so there is much less incentive to thrift. With the increase of his pay he has forfeited or relinquished his right to many of the perquisites which he had traditionally assumed for centuries in the past. There is also a very strong kind of pride – false pride perhaps – or a sense of social position, which deters many from claiming rights which are theirs by inheritance; and when some give them up, the rest soon follow for fear of being thought paupers. Besides, gleaning was work for the women and girls, and 'you can't go gleaning in silk stockings!' But the introduction of reaping machines is the chief reason why there are no gleaners now. Reaping with fagging-hooks and scythes left more for the gleaners, if anything, than did sickles; but the earlier reaping-machines and horse-rakes left less behind them, the side-delivery reaper and the self-binder successively less and less, till there was not enough to be worth the toil of gleaning, and so the custom entirely died out.

After the field was raked one of the church bells was rung, at about eight in the morning and again at six in the evening, as a signal to the gleaners that they might be in the fields between those hours; and the women and children were up early and would wait by the gate till the bell was rung. In 1910 the gleaning bell was still rung in twenty or thirty parishes in Essex; in 1931, though there is still a little gleaning in several parishes, this old custom survives only at Farnham in Essex. A man was chosen to ring the bell and his name posted on the church door; each family of gleaners paid him a fee of twopence or sixpence for his services.

A stook or thrave of corn, called the 'guard-sheaf', was left near the gate until the farmer was ready to admit the gleaners; when it was removed they might enter and begin work. In Norfolk three sheaves, set up together and known as the 'policeman', answered the same purpose; in Lincolnshire there was a contrary custom of setting a white flag in the stubble as a signal that the gleaners might enter. People who were known to be honest and respectable had sometimes, by favour of the farmer, the privilege of gleaning between the thraves; much as Ruth had in the fields of Boaz.[25] But before the majority could enter the stubble was hand-raked by men and boys, and these rakings made into little sheaves and put with the thraves. After these were carted the ground on which they had stood was likewise raked for the farmer, and even then the gleaners found more than they would find after the machine now. Where the parish boundary crossed a field, there was sometimes no little dissension between the gleaners of the two parishes. Each family reckoned to gather so many handfuls a day, if possible, before they went home. Sometimes they had a use for the straw, but more often they cut it off about six inches below the ears and left it in the field. They carried home the gleanings in large head-bundles, or in sacks or perambulators.

What little gleanings are gathered now, mostly between Saffron Walden, Dunmow and Braintree, are used to feed chickens; the old windmills which ground the corn and dressed the flour being done away with, and little or no bread baked at home.

An Essex labourer described how a man who had a hand-threshing machine used to thresh out the corn for them at night, but sometimes it would be beaten out at home with flails. A miller, Metson of Sible Hedingham, used to grind the gleaners' corn, but it was necessary to wait for a wind. The usual arrangement was that he kept the bran as payment for the trouble of grinding, the cost of grinding and dressing being alternatively eightpence a bushel. The miller, to avoid confusion, numbered each family's gleanings in a separate bag.

The mother of each family used to bake once a week in the summer and once a fortnight in winter; and the bread, though rather dark, was better after ten days than white baker's-bread after two. Sometimes she would be up early and make 'apple-cake' or 'huffers' for the children's breakfast.

At that time every labourer's cottage had its own oven, and the wheat stubble or 'harme' was often the men's perquisite after the shooting season. The farmer lent his cart for carrying it, and it was made into stacks for heating the baking ovens, being pulled out from the stack with a 'harme-hook', or barbed spear such as is still used in Wales. Though wages were low, there were in most districts after-perquisites which made it possible for a family to get enough food and fuel to live within their earnings. The rent for a cottage might be only ninepence or a shilling a week, milk threepence a quart, butter tenpence a pound; cider, cabbages and white turnips (where the farms produced them) were often given for nothing.

Stacking and rick-making

Haystacks and cornricks have an almost endless variety of form and fashion; in almost every place there is some local peculiarity. Much depends, of course, on the conditions under which the crop is harvested. In wet and mountainous places there is generally more difficulty in bringing it in safely and special care must be taken to shape it so as best to resist the constant soakings of mist and winter rain. In windy places the thatch must have special strength and tightness, in fertile and sheltered places the ricks must be large and capacious to save unnecessary thatching; sometimes stacks are even built on to one another like a row of houses in a street, but this makes them all the more liable to damage and is very doubtful economy. If the hay is at all damp, it is of course better to put it into small than large stacks.

Another reason for variety is that there are many different materials which can be used for thatching. Wheat-straw is most usual, but oat-straw, river-reed, meadow-rush, rye, and fern are used also, the choice depending on what is most economical in each district. The foundations of the rick are determined in the same way. If it is of hay, anything will do which will keep the damp from under it; faggots are best, but brushwood, hurdles, or old harrows and cart-wheels are very often used. In Romney Marsh the willow-shoots which are cut out of the dykes every year are made into bundles for this purpose; after they have remained there for a year they make excellent firing.

As is well known, haystacks are liable to catch fire or 'mow-burn' if the hay is stacked before it is properly dry. An old way of preventing this was to build it round a sack filled with straw and to draw up the sack by degrees, so as to leave a flue or vent in the middle of the haystack. But there are two objections to this: if there were no ventilation underneath the stack also, the hay round the hole would turn mouldy, and if there were, the draught through the stack might make it more liable still to burn. Some farmers thrust a long stick into the middle of each rick; which primitive thermometer is now and then taken out and felt at the inward end to see whether the heat is becoming dangerous. On the other hand some farmers when stacking very dry and withered hay which has been cut too late would sprinkle a few thin layers of green mowings in the stack, to heat it somewhat and 'give it a flavour'. This is a questionable practice, but many farmers think that hay which is rather brown contains more nourishment.

In stacking corn, it is most important to preserve it from rats, mice and birds. Cornricks are nearly always round or rounded at the ends, the sheaves being laid with their heads inwards; but even so the sparrows will sometimes manage to pull out single straws, one at a time, and so one sees occasionally a sort of entanglement fixed round the rick to deter them.

The old way is to build them on staddles, that is, stone mushroom-shaped piers, with baulks of timber laid across them, so that the rats shall not climb up. But nowadays, when the corn does not remain so long in the rick and the threshing-machine finishes all its work in a day or two, this is not so necessary; and staddles have several drawbacks. The space they occupy from the ground up is equivalent to a load, or a load and a half, and it is much more difficult to lay the bed of a rick on the platform than near the ground and to balance it securely. For these reasons staddles are now to be seen on very few farms, and their use is almost unknown.

There were other inventions for the same purpose, but less effective. In many stone-wall countries, solid walled foundations were made, like large flat cheeses, and there were also inventions like low wooden tables or like the seats which used to be made round the trunks of old trees in gardens.

It may be worth while to describe some of the local styles of stacking and thatching, since with the greatly increasing use of iron haybarns these arts are becoming unnecessary and in some districts quite extinct. Moreover, good thatchers are not very common and few of them take pride enough in their work to add the ornamental finishes which were locally distinctive.

The shape and style of ricks is one of the most obviously noticeable features in each district to anyone who travels through the country. If one stops to examine them attentively the most surprising differences of principle become apparent. In Middlesex and most of the eastern counties the haystacks are oblong, high and gable-ended. In Kent the ends are generally sloped back to the ridge from a short distance down, in other southern counties rather more so, often from a point nearly as low as the side eaves. In Wiltshire the stacks incline to be squarer in plan, with only a short ridge, the eaves level all round; in Devon and parts of Somerset there is no ridge at all, but all four sides are alike and the thatch comes to a point. Elsewhere in Somerset, especially on the road from Bath to Chewton Mendip, small round haystacks are seen, very neatly shaped and raked; and for a distance of three feet from the ground they are closely sheared with a hayknife. This clipping would be likely to let the rain soak in and rot the hay at the bottom, were it not that it is sloped downwards and outwards from the middle of the stack and is overhung by that above, the circumference at the eaves being greater by several feet than that at the base.

There is a quite distinct system of thatching in Wales; here the thatch is fastened into position by a network of straw- or haybonds, the ricks being both round and oblong and varying greatly in proportions. On long ricks, double straw-bonds are often made to span the rick from side to side, while single bonds, sometimes of hay (which was the old method) but more often of straw or twine, are run through these, parallel to one another and from end to end of the rick. Some of the prettiest work of this kind is done in Anglesey. Thatching proceeds, as in England, from one end to the other of the rick, and as it does so the double bond is stretched over the thatch by a wooden pin which is moved down as the thatch progresses; at either side, near the base of the rick, the double bonds are tied to the hay. The thatch is made secure by the horizontal bonds, which are passed between the two strands of the straw-rope or else twisted round them. The way of tying the straw-rope to the haystack is simple and secure. The sides of the rick must have been carefully raked so that the hay holds firmly together; a larger bunch of it is then seized in one hand, while with the other the end of the straw-bond is stretched over it, the two are twisted together, and their end pushed under the stretched part. Thus the whole thatch is made fast without the use of any spars or wood save the short spike which is used as a tool in stretching the cross-bonds.

It should be added that while the typical shape of ricks in Anglesey is oblong in plan and rounded at shoulders and ends, the number and disposition of the bonds varies much, according to the defence which is needed against the prevailing wind. Few ricks are finished in the same way at both ends.

In other parts of North Wales the ricks are made on the same lines, though with less fancy. They are often longer in shape, rounded at the ends, and with the ridge bowed; the thatch does not come down to the end of the slope, where the eaves would otherwise be, and may cover no more than the ridge and two or three feet at either side. The long bonds are twisted and secured together on a stout wooden spike driven in at either end of the rick, pretty low down. The cross-bonds are usually fixed to single spars driven into the sides with points directed upwards, their heads pressing the loop of the bond into the rick. These ridge-thatches are most often seen in mountainous places and are of oaten straw or rushes.

In Cheshire and Lancashire the style of thatching is somewhat like the Welsh, though twine seems to have quite superseded hay for the horizontal bonds, while for the stouter cross-bonds rope is often used instead of straw. But in these counties the ricks still have an English look, from their sharp ridges and general square-ness of proportion.

In the poorer parts of Scotland and Ireland, and other wet mountainous districts where the hay is harvested with difficulty, the stack is generally made like a large round haycock, with a curved outline continuing from peak to base. The thatch is often at the top only, held on there by crossed bonds, weighted at both ends with stones, or with circumferent bonds added to form a net at the summit. On many there is no thatch; crofters by the sea use an old fishing-net, others ram the hay into position with stakes or baulks of timber. But these are the meanest sort of haystack, and since it is seldom worth their owners' while to put up hay-barns, the species is in no danger of dying out.

It used to be a fairly general custom to decorate ricks and stacks, or at least one of them in every rickyard, by way of completing the work of thatching with something of a flourish. One of the prettiest and probably oldest customs in Norfolk was to set an unthreshed sheaf of wheat on the top of the rick for the birds.

The very graceful finish which was called 'crowning the rick' was generally done on the largest and finest wheatrick, but now only the simplest and slightest forms of ornament are seen, and even they are being gradually abandoned. Sometimes a rick is surmounted by a handful of threshed-out ears made fast with a straw-plait, and in districts where reed-thatching is practised a little sheaf or fascia of reeds answers the same purpose. In the West of England haystacks, too, were often surmounted by a boat, an apple or a turnip, which the Somerset folk call a 'dolly'. In Devon a cock was often set at each end of the rick.

The thatchers in Hertfordshire were experts in straw-plaiting and often spent the midday hour in weaving a bird round a piece of board, cut to the required shape, and sometimes as much as three feet across, or on more elaborate fancies, such as toy wind-mills or pigeon-cotes. Sometimes they would make a working weather-cock, mounted on a stick which would revolve in the neck of a pint bottle embedded in the summit of the rick.

In Wales there are endless varieties of ornament. In Cardigan-shire especially neighbouring farmers seem to vie with one another in inventing them and in combining them with different forms of thatch-fastening; now tying the thatch down, now holding it with pegs, now weighting it with stones. Some of the ricks are crested with a thin straw-bond twisted round a stick, some with a knob of thatch tied up at intervals, others with a twist of straw round a straight bundle, and occasionally even with a slice of turf, cut to fit beneath the topmost tying-bond. The ridges of long ricks are now and then finished with a double straw-rope, between the strands of which the ridge-ends of the thatch are pushed up in alternate handfuls; and in Radnorshire ricks were even made with a crenellation of doubled and twisted handfuls of thatch continu-ing from end to end.

This generation is so accustomed to ready-made ornaments, of no beauty whatever, that hand-made things begin to be objects of curiosity and the most trifling of them becomes worthy of serious notice. Our national schools undertake to teach children 'hand-crafts' of one sort or another; but the old traditions of needlework embroidery, weaving and plaiting have, despite some spirited revivalists, long since ceased to be a part of common life.

An object which used to be seen quite often in cottages was a long sheaf or bundle of corn, with an ornamental twisted cover-ing; it was sometimes called a 'neck'. This may at one time have had a religious significance,* but it has for long been made only, as country people say, 'for a hobby'; either as a decoration for the harvest festival or to be hung up and admired in the village ale-house. Whether it was originally the 'kern baby' or 'neck of corn', made from the last sheaf reaped and kept till the following year to ensure the continuance of crops and seasons, is a matter for curious speculation. There are still a few people in Essex who can make them, and specimens are to be met with in Cambridgeshire, Northamptonshire, Bedfordshire and Hertfordshire and probably elsewhere, though the skill of making them is now nearly lost.

In these counties it is still common for small bits of straw, braided in twos or fives, to be stuck in boys' buttonholes or hats, but this class of home-made ornament has come to be disdained and with the march of education will no doubt soon be quite forgotten.

* 'Herodotus relates how sacred objects bound up in wheaten straw were brought from the Hyperboreans (of the Baltic) to the Scythians (of the lower Danube and South Russia), the latter forwarding them westward to the Adriatic.' – British Museum Guide, *Early Iron Age*, p. 9.

Thomas Hennell, *Change in the Farm*

THE GREAT BARN AND THE SHEEP-SHEARERS

It was the first day of June, and the sheep-shearing season culmin-ated, the landscape, even to the leanest pasture, being all health and colour. Every green was young, every pore was open, and every stalk was swollen with racing currents of juice. God was palpably present in the country, and the devil had gone with the world to town. Flossy catkins of the later kinds, fern-sprouts like bishops' croziers, the square-headed moschatel, the odd cuckoo-pint, – like an apoplectic saint in a niche of malachite, – snow-white ladies'-smocks, the toothwort, approximating to human flesh, the enchanter's nightshade, and the black-petalled doleful-bells, were among the quainter objects of the vegetable world in and about Weatherbury at this teeming time; and of the animal, the meta-morphosed figures of Mr. Jan Coggan, the master-shearer; the second and third shearers, who travelled in the exercise of their calling, and do not require definition by name; Henery Fray the fourth shearer, Susan Tall's husband the fifth, Joseph Poorgrass the sixth, young Cain Ball as assistant-shearer, and Gabriel Oak as general supervisor. None of these were clothed to any extent worth mentioning, each appearing to have hit in the manner of raiment the decent mean between a high and low cast Hindoo. An angularity of lineament, and a fixity of facial machinery in general, proclaimed that serious work was the order of the day.

They sheared in the great barn, called for the nonce the Shearing-barn, which on ground-plan resembled a church with transepts. It not only emulated the form of the neighbouring church of the parish, but vied with it in antiquity. Whether the barn had ever formed one of a group of conventual buildings nobody seemed to be aware; no trace of such surroundings remained. The vast porches at the sides, lofty enough to admit a waggon laden to its highest with corn in the sheaf, were spanned by heavy-pointed arches of stone, broadly and boldly cut, whose very simplicity was the origin of a grandeur not apparent in erections where more ornament has been attempted. The dusky, filmed, chestnut roof, braced and tied in by huge collars, curves, and diagonals, was far nobler in design, because more wealthy in material, than nine-tenths of those in our modern churches. Along each side wall was a range of striding buttresses, throwing deep shadows on the spaces between them, which were perforated by lancet openings, combining in their proportions the precise requirements both of beauty and ventilation.

One could say about this barn, what could hardly be said of either the church or the castle, akin to it in age and style, that the purpose which had dictated its original erection was the same with that to which it was still applied. Unlike and superior to either of those two typical remnants of mediævalism, the old barn embodied practices which had suffered no mutilation at the hands of time. Here at least the spirit of the ancient builders was at one with the spirit of the modern beholder. Standing before this abraded pile, the eye regarded its present usage, the mind dwelt upon its past history, with a satisfied sense of functional continuity throughout – a feeling almost of gratitude, and quite of pride, at the permanence of the idea which had heaped it up. The fact that four centuries had neither proved it to be founded on a mistake, inspired any hatred of its purpose, nor given rise to any reaction that had battered it down, invested this simple grey effort of old minds with a repose, if not a grandeur, which a too curious reflection was apt to disturb in its ecclesiastical and military compeers. For once mediævalism and modernism had a common standpoint. The lanceolate windows, the time-eaten arch-stones and chamfers, the orientation of the axis, the misty chestnut work of the rafters, referred to no exploded fortifying art or worn-out religious creed. The defence and salvation of the body by daily bread is still a study, a religion, and a desire.

To-day the large side doors were thrown open towards the sun to admit a bountiful light to the immediate spot of the shearers' operations, which was the wood threshing-floor in the centre, formed of thick oak, black with age and polished by the beating of flails for many generations, till it had grown as slippery and as rich in hue as the state-room floors of an Elizabethan mansion. Here the shearers knelt, the sun slanting in upon their bleached shirts, tanned arms, and the polished shears they flourished, causing these to bristle with a thousand rays strong enough to blind a weak-eyed man. Beneath them a captive sheep lay panting, quickening its pants as misgiving merged in terror, till it quivered like the hot landscape outside.

This picture of to-day in its frame of four hundred years ago did not produce that marked contrast between ancient and modern which is implied by the contrast of date. In comparison with cities, Weatherbury was immutable. The citizen's *Then* is the rustic's *Now*. In London, twenty or thirty years ago are old times; in Paris ten years, or five; in Weatherbury three or four score years were included in the mere present, and nothing less than a century set a mark on its face or tone. Five decades hardly modified the cut of a gaiter, the embroidery of a smock-frock, by the breadth of a hair. Ten generations failed to alter the turn of a single phrase. In these Wessex nooks the busy outsider's ancient times are only old; his old times are still new; his present is futurity.

So the barn was natural to the shearers, and the shearers were in harmony with the barn.

Thomas Hardy, *Far from the Madding Crowd*

SUMMER

All the procession of living and growing things passes. The grass stands up taller and still taller, the sheaths open, and the stalk arises, the pollen clings till the breeze sweeps it. The bees rush past, and the resolute wasps; the humble-bees, whose weight swings them along. About the oaks and maples the brown chafers swarm, and the fern-owls at dusk, and the blackbirds and jays by day, cannot reduce their legions while they last. Yellow butterflies, and white, broad red admirals, and sweet blues; think of the kingdom of flowers which is theirs! Heavy moths burring at the edge of the copse; green, and red, and gold flies: gnats, like smoke, around the tree-tops; midges so thick over the brook, as if you could haul a netful; tiny leaping creatures in the grass; bronze beetles across the path; blue dragonflies pondering on cool leaves of water-plaintain. Blue jays flitting, a magpie drooping across from elm to elm; young rooks that have escaped the hostile shot blundering up into the branches; missel thrushes leading their fledglings, already strong on the wing, from field to field. An egg here on the sward dropped by a starling; a red ladybird creeping, tortoise-like, up a green fern frond. Finches undulating through the air, shooting themselves with closed wings, and linnets happy with their young.

Golden dandelion discs – gold and orange – of a hue more beautiful, I think, than the higher and more visible buttercup. A blackbird, gleaming, so black is he, splashing in the runlet of water across the gateway. A ruddy kingfisher swiftly drawing himself, as you might draw a stroke with a pencil, over the surface of the yellow buttercups, and away above the hedge. Hart's-tongue fern, thick with green, so green as to be thick with its colour, deep in the ditch under the shady hazel boughs. White meadow-sweet lifting its tiny florets, and black-flowered sedges. You must push through the reed grass to find the sword-flags; the stout willow-herbs will not be trampled down, but resist the foot like under-wood. Pink lychnis flowers behind the withy stoles, and little black moorhens swim away, as you gather it, after their mother, who has dived under the water-grass, and broken the smooth sur-face of the duckweed. Yellow loose-strife is rising, thick comfrey stands at the very edge; the sandpipers run where the shore is free from bushes. Back by the underwood the prickly and repellent brambles will presently present us with fruit. For the squirrels the nuts are forming, green beechmast is there – green wedges under the spray; up in the oaks the small knots, like bark rolled up in a dot, will be acorns. Purple vetches along the mounds, yellow lotus where the grass is shorter, and orchis succeeds to orchis. As I write them, so these things come – not set in gradation, but like the broadcast flowers in the mowing-grass.

Now follows the gorse, and the pink rest-harrow and the sweet lady's-bedstraw, set as it were in the midst of a little thorn-bush. The broad repetition of the yellow clover is not to be written; acre upon acre, and not one spot of green, as if all the green had been planed away, leaving only the flowers to which the bees come by the thousand from far and near. But one white campion stands in the midst of the lake of yellow. The field is scented as though a hundred hives of honey had been emptied on it. Along

the mound by it the bluebells are seeding, the hedge has been cut
and the ground is strewn with twigs. Among those seeding blue-
bells and dry twigs and mosses I think a titlark has his nest, as he
stays all day there and in the oak over. The pale clear yellow of
charlock, sharp and clear, promises the finches bushels of seed for
their young. Under the scarlet of the poppies the larks run, and
then for change of colour soar into the blue. Creamy honeysuckle
on the hedge around the cornfield, buds of wild rose everywhere,
but no sweet petal yet. Yonder, where the wheat can climb no
higher up the slope, are the purple heath-bells, thyme and flitting
stonechats.

The lone barn shut off by acres of barley is noisy with sparrows.
It is their city, and there is a nest in every crevice, almost under
every tile. Sometimes the partridges run between the ricks, and
when the bats come out of the roof, leverets play in the waggon-
track. At even a fern-owl beats by, passing close to the eaves whence
the moths issue. On the narrow waggon-track which descends
along a coombe and is worn in chalk, the heat pours down by day
as if an invisible lens in the atmosphere focused the sun's rays,
Strong woody knapweed endures it, so does toadflax and pale
blue scabious, and wild mignonette. The very sun of Spain burns
and burns and ripens the wheat on the edge of the coombe, and
will only let the spring moisten a yard or two around it; but there
a few rushes have sprung, and in the water itself brooklime with
blue flowers grows so thickly that nothing but a bird could find
space to drink. So down again from this sun of Spain to woody
coverts where the wild hops are blocking every avenue, and green-
flowered bryony would fain climb to the trees; where grey-flecked
ivy winds spirally about the red rugged bark of pines, where bur-
docks fight for the footpath, and teazle-heads look over the low
hedges. Brake-fern rises five feet high; in some way woodpeckers
are associated with brake, and there seem more of them where it
flourishes. If you count the depth and strength of its roots in the
loamy sand, add the thickness of its flattened stem, and the width

F

of its branching fronds, you may say that it comes near to be a little tree. Beneath where the ponds are bushy mare's-tails grow, and on the moist banks jointed pewterwort; some of the broad bronze leaves of water-weeds seem to try and conquer the pond and cover it so firmly that a wagtail may run on them. A white butterfly follows along the waggon-road, the pheasants slip away as quietly as the butterfly flies, but a jay screeches loudly and flutters in high rage to see us. Under an ancient garden wall among matted bines of trumpet convolvulus, there is a hedge-sparrow's nest overhung with ivy on which even now the last black berries cling.

There are minute white flowers on the top of the wall, out of reach, and lichen grows against it dried by the sun till it looks ready to crumble. By the gateway grows a thick bunch of meadow geranium, soon to flower; over the gate is the dusty highway road, quiet but dusty, dotted with the innumerable footmarks of a flock of sheep that has passed. The sound of their bleating still comes back, and the bees driven up by their feet have hardly had time to settle again on the white clover beginning to flower on the short roadside sward. All the hawthorn leaves and briar and bramble, the honeysuckle, too, is gritty with the dust that has been scattered upon it. But see – can it be? Stretch a hand high, quick, and reach it down; the first, the sweetest, the dearest rose of June. Not yet expected, for the time is between the may and the roses, least of all here in the hot and dusty highway; but it is found – the first rose of June.

Still the pageant moves. The song-talk of the finches rises and sinks like the tinkle of a waterfall. The greenfinches have been by me all the while. A bullfinch pipes now and then further up the hedge where the brambles and thorns are thickest. Boldest of birds to look at, he is always in hiding. The shrill tone of a gold-finch came just now from the ash branches, but he has gone on. Every four or five minutes a chaffinch sings close by, and another fills the interval near the gateway. There are linnets somewhere, but I cannot from the old apple tree fix their exact place. Thrushes have sung and ceased; they will begin again in ten minutes. The blackbirds do not cease; the note uttered by a blackbird in the oak yonder before it can drop is taken up by a second near the top of the field, and ere it falls is caught by a third on the left-hand side. From one of the top-most boughs of an elm there fell the song of a willow warbler for awhile; one of the least of birds, he often seeks the highest branches of the highest tree.

A yellowhammer has just flown from a bare branch in the gateway, where he has been perched and singing a full hour. Presently he will commence again, and as the sun declines will sing him to the horizon, and then again sing till nearly dusk. The yellowhammer is almost the longest of all the singers; he sits and sits and has no inclination to move. In the spring he sings, in the summer he sings, and he continues when the last sheaves are being carried from the wheat field. The redstart yonder has given forth a few notes, the whitethroat flings himself into the air at short intervals and chatters, the shrike calls sharp and determined, faint but shrill calls descend from the swifts in the air. These descend, but the twittering notes of the swallows do not reach so far – they are too high to-day. A cuckoo has called by the brook, and now fainter from a greater distance. That the titlarks are singing I know, but not within hearing from here; a dove, though, is audible, and a chiffchaff has twice passed. Afar beyond the oaks at the top of the field dark specks ascend from time to time, and after moving in wide circles for awhile descend again to the corn. These must be larks; but their notes are not powerful enough to reach me, though they would were it not for the song in the hedges, the hum of innumerable insects, and the ceaseless 'crake, crake' of landrails. There are at least two landrails in the mowing-grass; one of them just now seemed coming straight towards the apple tree, and I expected in a minute to see the grass move, when the bird turned aside and entered the tufts and wild parsley by the hedge. Thence the call has come without a moment's pause, 'crake, crake', till the thick hedge seems filled with it. Tits have visited the apple tree over my head, a wren has sung in the willow, or rather on a dead branch projecting lower down than the leafy boughs, and a robin across under the elms in the opposite hedge. Elms are a favourite tree of robins – not the upper branches, but those that grow down the trunk, and are the first to have leaves in the spring.

The yellowhammer is the most persistent individually, but I think the blackbirds when listened to are the masters of the fields. Before one can finish another begins, like the summer ripples succeeding behind each other, so that the melodious sound merely changes its position. Now here, now in the corner, then across the field, again in the distant copse, where it seems about to sink, when it rises again almost at hand. Like a great human artist, the blackbird makes no effort, being fully conscious that his liquid tone cannot be matched. He utters a few delicious notes, and carelessly quits the green stage of the oak till it pleases him to sing again. Without the blackbird, in whose throat the sweetness of the green fields dwells, the days would be only partly summer. Without the violet all the bluebells and cowslips could not make a spring, and without the blackbird, even the nightingale would be but half welcome. It is not yet noon, these songs have been ceaseless since dawn; this evening, after the yellowhammer has sung the sun down, when the moon rises and the faint stars appear, still the cuckoo will call, and the grasshopper lark, the landrail's 'crake, crake' will echo from the mound, a warbler or a blackcap will utter his notes, and even at the darkest of the summer night the swallows will hardly sleep in their nests. As the morning sky grows blue, an hour before the sun, up will rise the larks singing and audible now, the cuckoo will recommence, and the swallows will start again on their tireless journey. So that the songs of the summer birds are as ceaseless as the sound of the waterfall which plays day and night.

Richard Jefferies, *The Life of the Fields*

HARVESTING

The sunbeams sank deeper and deeper into the wheat-ears, layer upon layer of light, and the colour deepened by these daily strokes. There was no bulletin to tell the folk of its progress, no Nileo-meter to mark the rising flood of the wheat to its hour of overflow. Yet there went through the village a sense of expectation, and men said to each other, 'We shall be there soon'. No one knew the day – the last day of doom of the golden race; everyone knew it was nigh. One evening there was a small square piece cut at one side, a little notch, and two shocks stood there in the twilight. Next day the village sent forth its army with their crooked weapons to cut and slay. It used to be an era, let me tell you, when a great farmer gave the signal to his reapers; not a man, woman, or child that did not talk of that. Well-to-do people stopped their vehicles and walked out into the new stubble. Ladies came, farmers, men of low degree, everybody – all to exchange a word or two with the workers. These were so terribly in earnest at the start they could scarcely acknowledge the presence even of the squire. They felt themselves so important, and were so full, and so intense and one-minded in their labour, that the great of the earth might come and go as sparrows for aught they cared. More men and more men were put on day by day, and women to bind the sheaves, till the vast field held the village, yet they seemed but a handful buried in the tunnels of the golden mine: they were lost in it like the hares for as the wheat fell, the shocks rose behind them, low tents of corn. Your skin or mine could not have stood the scratching of the straw, which is stiff and sharp, and the burning of the sun, which blisters like red-hot iron. No one could stand the harvest field as a reaper except he had been born and cradled in a cottage, and passed his childhood bareheaded in July heats and January snows. I was always fond of being out of doors, yet I used to wonder how these men and women could stand it, for the summer day is long, and they were there hours before I was up. The edge of the reap-hook had to be driven by force through the stout stalks like a sword, blow after blow, minute after minute, hour after hour; the back stooping, and the broad sun throwing his fiery rays from a full disc on the head and neck. I think some of them used to put handkerchiefs doubled up in their hats as pads, as in the East they wind the long roll of the turban about the head, and perhaps they would have done better if they had adopted the custom of the South and wound a long scarf about the middle of the body, for they were very liable to be struck down with such internal complaints as come from great heat. Their necks grew black, much like black oak in old houses. Their open chests were always bare, and flat, and stark, and never rising with rounded bust-like muscle as the Greek statues of athletes.

The breast-bone was burned black, and their arms, tough as ash, seemed cased in leather. They grew visibly thinner in the harvest-field, and shrunk together – all flesh disappearing, and nothing but sinew and muscle remaining. Never was such work. The wages were low in those days, and it is not long ago, either – I mean the all-year-round wages; the reaping was piece-work at so much per acre – like solid gold to men and women who had lived on dry bones, as it were, through the winter. So they worked and slaved, and tore at the wheat as if they were seized with a frenzy; the heat, the aches, the illness, the sunstroke, always impending in the air – the stomach hungry again before the meal was over, it was nothing. No song, no laugh, no stay – on from morn till night, possessed with a maddened desire to labour, for the more they could cut the larger the sum they would receive, and what is man's heart and brain to money? So hard, you see, is the pressure of human life that these miserables would have prayed on their knees for permission to tear their arms from the socket, and to scorch and shrivel themselves to charred human brands in the furnace of the sun.

Does it not seem bitter that it should be so? Here was the wheat, the beauty of which I strive in vain to tell you, in the midst of the

flowery summer, scourging them with the knout of necessity; that
which should give life pulling the life out of them, rendering their
existence below that of the cattle, so far as the pleasure of living
goes. Without doubt many a low mound in the churchyard –
once visible, now level – was the sooner raised over the nameless
dead because of that terrible strain in the few weeks of the gold
fever. This is human life, real human life – no rest, no calm enjoyment of the scene, no generous gift of food and wine lavishly
offered by the gods – the hard fist of necessity for ever battering
man to a shapeless and hopeless fall.

The whole village lived in the field; a corn-land village is always
the most populous, and every rood of land thereabouts, in a sense,
maintains its man. The reaping, and the binding up and stacking
of the sheaves, and the carting and building of the ricks, and the
gleaning, there was something to do for every one, from the
'olde, olde, very olde man', the Thomas Parr of the hamlet, down
to the very youngest child whose little eye could see, and whose
little hand could hold a stalk of wheat. The gleaners had a way of
binding up the collected wheatstalks together so that a very large
quantity was held tightly in a very small compass. The gleaner's
sheaf looked like the knot of a girl's hair woven in and bound. It
was a tradition of the wheat-field handed down from generation
to generation, a thing you could not possibly do unless you had
been shown the secret – like the knots the sailors tie, a kind of
hand art. The wheatstalk being thick at one end makes the sheaf
heavier and more solid there, and so in any manner of fastening
it or stacking it, it takes a rounded shape like a nine-pin; the round
ricks are built thick in the middle and lessen gradually toward the
top and toward the ground. The warm yellow of the straw is very
pleasant to look at on a winter's day under a grey sky; so, too, the
straw looks nice and warm and comfortable, thrown down thickly
in the yards for the roan cattle.

After the village has gone back to its home still the work of the
wheat is not over; there is the thatching with straw of last year,

which is bleached and contrasts with the yellow of the fresh-gathered crop. Next the threshing; and meantime the ploughs are at work, and very soon there is talk of seed-time.

Richard Jefferies, Field and Hedgerow

UNEMPLOYED

One morning a labouring man came to the door with a spade, and asked if he could dig the garden, or try to, at the risk of breaking the tool in the ground. He was starving; he had had no work for two months; it was just six months, he said, since the first frost started the winter. Nature and the earth and the gods did not trouble about him, you see; he might grub the rock-frost ground with his hands if he chose – the yellowish black sky did not care. Nothing for man! The only good he found was in his fellow-men; they fed him after a fashion – still they fed him. There was no good in anything else. Another aged man came once a week regularly; white as the snow through which he walked. In summer he worked; since the winter began he had had no employment, but supported himself by going round to the farms in rotation. They all gave him a trifle – bread and cheese, a penny, a slice of meat – something; and so he lived, and slept the whole of that time in outhouses wherever he could. He had no home of any kind. Why did he not go into the workhouse? 'I be afeared if I goes in there they'll put me with the rough uns, and very likely I should get some of my clothes stole.' Rather than go into the workhouse he would totter round in the face of the blasts that might cover his weak old limbs with drift. There was a sense of dignity and manhood left still; his clothes were worn, but clean and decent; he was no companion of rogues; the snow and frost, the stray of the outhouses, was better than that. He was struggling against age, against nature, against circumstance; the entire weight of society, law, and order pressed upon him to force him to lose his self-respect and liberty. He would rather risk his life in the

snowdrift. Nature, earth, and the gods did not help him; sun and
stars, where were they? He knocked at the doors of the farms and
found good in man only – not in Law or Order, but in individual
man alone.

Richard Jefferies, *Field and Hedgerow*

WORK AND PLAY

From the time he was nine Joseph would spend long, lonely days
in school vacations and on Saturdays scaring crows off the short,
green corn. He had a wooden clapper, but if he saw no one for
hours he took to shouting so as to hear a human voice. This
method had another convenience; you couldn't cry while you
shouted. Another job by which he earned pennies was throwing
swedes or turnips to the man turning the wheel of the cutter.

Joseph left school some time before his eleventh birthday in
June 1870, and work began for him in earnest that summer. By
accidents of weather, haymaking was late that year and yet the
corn harvest was full early. Elizabeth took Joseph with her to help
with both the hay and the corn on Bald Knob farm, not far from
home. For several weeks the two earned good wages. They
depended on these harvest moneys, as did many folk, to buy boots
and the like for winter. How few now know what it was ninety
years ago to get in a harvest! Though the disinherited had no great
part of the fruits, still they shared in the achievement, the deep
involvement and joy of it. In the hay-time Joseph was up sometimes at half-past-three in the morning, and out in the fields with
the men half a mile away by four. The mowers worked six or
nine in a row, each cutting a swath behind another. Their scythes
went singing through the grass, and the triumph of the scythe and
the rhythmic fall of the swath continued like a long, slow, sacred
dance. Though the men might not have expressed it that way,
they felt the drama to the full, as labourers in any village today
watch the felling of trees. After a while the men would stop at the

leader's sign, and the scythe would sing a lighter brisker tune on higher notes as the men drew their whetstones back and forth along the blades.

The heat at midday – it was half-way through July – brought thirst-quenching with beer or cold tea, and then there was the brief, deep sleep. In the afternoon, work seemed to have settled down to a routine, if the weather were good, because senses and minds were a little dulled. But under threatening clouds the work became a battle, with odds exhilarating or overwhelming!

The number of workers in the fields would seem extraordinary today – there might, in a big field, be three groups of several mowers, and when about half the field was cut as many women would come and begin to turn the first-cut swathes. In harvest, because labour was cheap in this district, much corn was still being cut by the sickle. A very neat, small instrument it was; a good worker dropped hardly a straw where the corn stood up well. A dozen, or maybe twenty, reapers, largely women, would work in one field, with men following to tie up the sheaves and another group to set them in shucks. With the weather a little less hot than in the haying time there was talk and banter and flirting and yarn-spinning during the meals under the hedge. But the great task dominated minds for all that.

Sharing these labours and emotions, Joseph had little need of myths; his courage grew and his heart ripened upon them, as other boys' did on reading the *Iliad* and the *Odyssey*. After the corn had dried in the shucks, and was being carried away to the stack-yards on the yellow and brown wagons, extended by rafts to carry the great cargoes, women and children waited at the gate to exercise, in the form of a privilege, one of the last of the old customary rights of pre-enclosure days. Each woman, with the children she had been able to bring, took a 'land' or ploughing ridge, laid out a sheet with a stone at each corner, and then the whole company began to move slowly up the ridges, all the figures bending, hands deep in the stubble, 'leasing' fallen ears. Each gleaner had a linsey-woolsey bag hanging from her waist. Tiny boys and girls had tiny bags. Long straggling straws were gathered into the left hand, while broken-off ears were dropped into the bag. As the bunches grew too large to be held, they were tied and dropped, to be picked up on the walk back to the headland. The family's total gleanings were laid on the sheet and bundled for carrying. Later on, this corn would be sent to the miller and ground, and several weeks' bread might be made from the flour.

In late September the harvest was over. Elizabeth counted her money and surveyed the family's gleanings. She tidied the house for normal life to be resumed, and paid her small debts. Shoes must be bought for the three children, pattens for herself, and some unbleached calico, stout and cheap and warm – you could make almost any garment with it, if you must. Joseph was a wage-earner now; he had left school. You could be proud of him in a field, the tall, rosy, shapely lad, talking and laughing with every-one, quick at the work. Offers of permanent 'places' for him had been made; his new status must be marked. So Elizabeth and Joseph went to Banbury to do the shopping together. Seats were bespoken on the carrier's cart for the return, but eightpence would be saved by walking the outward journey – nine miles of field-paths to follow, crossing metalled roads only at two points. It was luxurious at first to walk through stubble or grass without rake or sickle in hand, with no heavy sheaves or aching back. Other families had the same errand, and groups passed or were passed by mother and son. When they were within a mile or so of Banbury, Elizabeth made a little speech. 'Joe, I've been reckoning; I've brought thirty shillings with me. The shoes and calico will never cost all that. You've had to leave school, and we can't help it, but you shall have money to spend on books. Here be three shillings. You've read all I've got. It'll do you good to have some new. You shall choose 'em; I won't interfere, my bwoy.'

Nine miles were a long and tiring way, but the astonishing sight of Banbury rapt Joseph out of all his other sensations. Around

the Horse Fair and the markets, and Bridge Street and Sheep
Street, wherever the streets broadened out, or houses stood back
behind a little space, and in the inn yards, stood rows of carrier
carts, hundreds of them, with their hinged shafts turned skywards
to make close setting possible. 'Nijni Novgorod!', breathed Joseph
as the sight burst upon him. (His last school reading-book had
contained a rich collection of descriptions of the world's oddities.
There he had read of a giant fair in the Russian city.) His mother
went off to do her errands and left him to find his way. 'You go
by yourself,' she said, 'and if we don't see one another before,
meet me by John Gardner's cart in the Stagyard.' The three
shillings filled both minds. 'Buy what seems you good. There's
the stall in the market and Mr North's shop in Parson's Street. He
preaches for the Wesleyans; he'll not let you buy any harm. You
ought to get three books with three shillings, and good'ns too –
ones that'll last.' So she went off to the mercer's and he to turn
over the books on the stall. Choosing in public embarrassed the
boy. That this was a momentous affair the bookseller saw by
Joseph's solemn look. 'What sort o' thing d'you want? Not sermons, eh? Not Walter Scott? Borrow them anywhere! Want to
larn something?' At the last phrase Joseph brightened. The stall-
holder's hand fell on a book with paper covers of heavenly blue
and a brilliant yellow label on the back. As he rustled the leaves
over, triangles and polygons fell into a procession. 'Top class does
those at school, beginning geometry', Joseph stammered. 'Well,
that's mensuration', said the salesman, turning to the title. 'Teach
you to find out how high the Church tower is; measure everything under the sun.' The books bought at Mr North's shop were
perhaps not a successful purchase, but they were cherished. I turn
their pages now. There were, in fact, three volumes; the *History
of Rasselas, Prince of Abyssinia* consisted of two small dark leather
volumes, printed in 1759, just a hundred years before Joseph was
born.[26] For his mother Joseph bought a little book, also in dark
leather, containing recipes for every kind of thing – for curing

diseases, curing children's faults, aiding the memory, making wine, removing stains – John Wesley's book. One is not a sceptic at eleven, and John Wesley was a great name.[27]

Elizabeth never expressed surprise at these additions to the bookshelf. She and Joseph shared, at any rate, the *Rasselas*. Both of them would quote it later, without pointing out their borrowings. 'There are many conclusions in which nothing is concluded', was one of their words. And many years later Joseph would quote with a little pompous fun, 'My curiosity does not very strongly lead me to survey piles of stones or mounds of earth; my business is with man'.

It was the book on mensuration the boy lost himself in on the way home. He mastered quite a few pages, for halfway to Tysoe a man left the carrier's cart to take a parcel to a farmhouse across the field, asking Master Gardner to wait for him. Wait he did, till at last the passengers murmured and the truant was left behind. Do all the days in a life have as much significance at this one of Joseph's? Twenty years later, Joseph saw Carrier Gardner balancing a sixpence on his finger-tip. 'I met John Watson just now,' he said, 'and he paid me this. D'you remember a day you and your mother rid wi' me back from Banbury? You were raidin' a book, like the chap you be. Watson got out afoor he paid. Bin tryin' to pay me this tanner for twenty year. Never could find the right minute. He says as I've allus bin busy, or talkin' to somebody.' What a world of slow pace and scruple some folk lived in then.

After the Harvest Home supper at Bald Knob, Joseph became a farm boy on another farm, a regular wage-earner. He was to work mainly with the shepherd in the winter and lambing time, and then with the carter and ploughman for the spring ploughing. He had little contact with the farmer, Master Ainge, a sickly, elderly man who left the day-to-day work of the farm largely to the men.

John Makepeace, the shepherd, was nearing sixty-five and looked older. He was shrivelled and bent and dirty, for he lived alone in an old, low-roofed cottage on the edge of one of Mr Ainge's two farmyards. Here he used only one room, cooked his meals on a fire of sticks in a little three-legged cauldron; his smocks he washed once a year, so it was said, in the nearest brook. He had no right to his name, someone told Joseph. An ancestor of his had been born in a ditch, of a wayfaring woman, who had died before the babe was heard crying and taken to the nearest farm. There he grew up in kitchen and stables and became Makepeaces' John, and now his descendant was John Makepeace. Living between Whatcote and Tysoe, he seldom visited either. He had never taken a near view of Compton Wynyates though it was just over the hill. It was half a century since he had entered a church – and this in 1870, when Sabbath keeping was universal. A pagan was Makepeace. Absorbed in the fields, in the animal life and in the murky jobs in his cottage, there was no room in his life for ideal or abstraction. Yet he had his comment on such matters. Periodically the Vicar hunted him down and told him he had a soul to save. 'If I never gus to church I never gus to chapel', was his ritual reply, as if that at least should please the parson.

Something of a struggle went on between shepherd and carter over Joseph. Jasper seemed suspicious of Makepeace, the boy noticed. He himself was fascinated and pleased by the strange old fellow, who showed him hares' forms and taught him how to watch badgers and foxes. There was something very remarkable about Makepeace's knowledge of plants. He knew every one. Of course, he never spoke of their beauty; the plants were 'yarbs', good for this and that, liked by this animal and that bird; and he had Adam's joy in naming. 'Never 'eard nobody call it,' he would say, 'but I calls it "old yellow spiky", or "jumping Jack", "smoky Jinny" or "little yeavy yed".'

John's flocks were scraggy and harsh in wool, but they were a healthy lot, and he knew the ways of each. He could manage any captive animal, tame or wild. He would catch and hold quiet the savage cats and tempestuous kittens born in the cattleyard. His dogs and ferrets were well trained. On the whole John was a silent fellow, but at first Joseph did not notice this. In his constant activity through the long days Makepeace would be, as it were, half-turned towards the youngster, correcting by example some mistaken way of handling a hurdle, drawing his attention without words to a movement in a pool; or he would stop a moment when some bird-song was heard in isolation and tap out its rhythm with wood on wood and simply name the bird. All this was a form of conversation, but John could also use words. Occasionally he would tell Joseph some long, circumstantial tale, as we shall see.

Jasper, Joseph's co-master, was beginning to look elderly. He was tall and a little stooping, with a long face, long hands to match, mild blue eyes and a slow smile. Sometimes in a busy season he would join the shepherd in folding the sheep, or tending the in-lamb ewes, and then Joseph would consider that Jasper and not John was the good shepherd of metaphor. He looked the part and acted it too: he would handle tenderly the 'poor-doing' lambs, whereas John would sometimes surreptitiously finish their little lives.

Jasper was a pious churchgoer, and never missed a meeting of his Friendly Society, the Foresters' Club. Though he could neither read nor write, he loved to be read to; especially he wished to have the Gospels read to him, and on Saturday evenings, after a fairly early knocking-off, Joseph would go to his cottage near the Old Tree and read three or four chapters to him. But Jasper wanted more worldly news also, and they would turn to the *Banbury Guardian* and read the farmers' letters in the correspondence column, and (but this was a year or two later) the reports of [Joseph] Arch's meetings. The best of these times occurred in the summer. Jasper was never so much at ease inside his cottage as out in the garden, for his wife nagged and was a slattern. Inside the cottage a spoiled life was patiently endured, but outside Jasper had precious friends and experiences.

Gradually and still rather vaguely, Joseph understood Jasper's

suspicion of Makepeace. The latter would watch – and hold
Joseph's arm so that he must watch too – a fight of cats and rats
in the barn, or a hawk after little birds, a weasel circling a fascinated rabbit, and never show an impulse to save the weaker creature.
When the little drama reached its deadly end, his grasp on Joe's
arm would tighten oddly and he would give a little cluck-cluck
of satisfaction.

Then there were Makepeace's stories. Once Joseph saw Jasper
follow Makepeace into a cowstall, in a grimly purposeful way.
'Your taales', he said to Makepeace's back, 'beant fit for a bwoy's
ears. If you tells that bwoy . . .', and then soon silence and presumably some dumb show. But Makepeace had already told a good
deal.

During Joseph's second winter on Ainge's farm there was a buzz
of talk for miles round. The skeleton of a man had been found in
a barn a few miles away. There was a great mystery as to how the
skeleton came to be there. The skull had been broken; foul play,
but by whom? When?

It was not a mystery to Makepeace. When he was young he had
worked for a while in yon parish. (The name of it eludes me,
perhaps happily: we will call it Radford.) The parson there had
been murdered and the murderer was never found. 'Good reason
for why not', Makepeace said. 'Nobody daren't tell o' nobody
else. They were all in it, you might say . . . there beant no naame
in Radford the same as forty yurr agoo, bar a laabourer or two.
They be all gone, good raison for why.' One after another, it
seemed, as they could find another farm or shop or 'public', the
families had gone. Did they all know, asked Joseph, about the
skeleton? 'Not they; they daredn't know thaat', said Makepeace,
'but there were summat as they knowed.' It took a good part of
the day and half the night (they were sitting up with a calving
cow) for the whole story to be told. The parson at Radford was
newish, a family man and poor. He insisted on his tithes – the
tenth egg and fruit and piglet and chicken. 'They were little men

down theer, ne'er a big farmer. They couldn't affoord the tithes.'
But the man who was always talking about tithes was the publican, better off than any of them. The village grew to be full of
hate and agitation. 'There weredn't no Methodists, nor no
Quaakers neither, to stop 'em 'aatin' and tell 'em to look to the
sky.'

There was a barmy, that is a yeasty, fellow in the village, excited
sometimes, often sulky. 'It weredn't saafe to cross 'im in 'is fits –
quoiet enough for the mooast.' One day when the parson was
walking up the lane from one of his glebe fields to the parsonage,
at his usual time, he had been 'knocked down wi' a spaade and
killed'. And then the barmy fellow had been missing. That was
what everybody had known, but they knew no more, and now
the story was forgotten. Joseph asked a question or two and got
short answers. Then there was a fit of silence and irritability and,
finally, in the dark, the whole story. The skeleton was accounted
for. 'If you ever tells', Makepeace said, 'I'll say as you gets silly
taales out o' them books as you brings along wi' your fodder.'
Talk in the public-house had begun the affair. Two or three men
had talked to the barmy fellow, inciting him to the deed, promis-
ing him twenty sovereigns. The publican had shown him the
money, putting it into a linen bag with its neck in a ring (just like
Makepeace's own purse) before his eyes. The deed done, Barmy
vanished and the men grew frightened. Barmy couldn't be far
away, he hadn't the money; he would tell about the bribe. They
had hunted for him and found him skulking in some outhouse.
(From this point, Joseph became sure, Makepeace had seen what
happened.) The money and more was proffered to Barmy, but on
condition that he made off once for all and emigrated. If he didn't
go . . . But Barmy sulked. He wouldn't answer, he wouldn't
move. The men went to him again and described the horrors of
the court, of hanging, so that he dared no longer stay in one place.
But he would not be off. He had slept one night in a dry ditch, and
the next night, when the Sheriff's men were known to be coming,

he stole into a barn. But he had been watched and his enemies followed. Again they cajoled and threatened. The barn was half full of corn and beans. There was a heap of sand at one end, and ploughs, and hanging on wooden pegs in the walls were flails and other tools. Barmy raved at the men, showing his teeth like a dog, and then suddenly turned his back on them all and threw himself down on the sand. Then the publican took the lead. 'Leave 'im to me', he shouted. 'Goo away all on y'.' And they all went – except one, a young 'un who slipped back and clung to a chink in the barn doors. He could not see the whole extent inside, but heard everything – a thud and a dreadful groan.

There had been other stories, taking a boy – after all, a tenderly reared child – back into a hellish world. One other remained clear in the mind, but was never told in full. It concerned a shepherd and his betrayal, or supposed betrayal, of other labourers for poaching, or maybe worse, and the revenge they had taken after following him one night to his lonely place with the sheep. They had – can I write it? – skinned him alive.

It was well, perhaps, that Joseph should know to what villages had descended, from what they had had to climb up. Though his own village had known nothing so terrible as the worst deeds Makepeace could tell of, it was not for nothing that Tysoe Quakers and Methodists had their rigid exclusions – their objections to song and tale and joke.

The time came for Joseph to be with Jasper. Ploughing was far harder work than waiting on the shepherds. On drizzling days, walking beside Jasper's team of three horses, on the low clayland under Windmill Hill, what 'rainy marching in the painful field!' It was an effort to pull each foot from the clinging, sticky earth, and one had a hundred feet! But on the red, light soil of the upper fields work went well, even with a team of only two. Elderly man and boy would look out together over the great green vale, telling each other that it was always changing. Always the light was throwing up some field, or a distant little spinney never seen from here before. More travelled eyes might have found the green expanse a little lifeless, lacking visible water, but for these it was perfect. Its stillness and greenness was its character. But there were days when its staidness vanished, swept away by wind, together with the clouds that seemed almost to bowl along the sky.

When they stopped for bread and lard at half-past nine, Jasper would ask Joseph whether he had any poetry for him, and Joseph would recite his scraps of Shakespeare, always the lines about 'warriors for the working day'. 'The best things be in books, Joe', Jasper said, and gave his little proof. 'Look at the letters you rades me out o' the *Banbury Guardian*. Who'd think there was any sense in Jeff Southerton to hear him talk? But when he writes a letter to the *Guardian* about the waages or the schoolin' he has somewh't to say. He's wrong, but there's a pinch o' sense in it. And they lines you says to me, nobody couldn't *talk* like that. It's the pen, you see . . . To think, bwoy, as you can rade the hull Bible. Yoor mother has read it time and again, I'll be bound. But,' he hastened to say lest he should seem envious, 'I knows my pieces. "The Lord is my Shepherd; I shall not want; He leadeth me beside the still waters . . ." '

The two shared some outstanding experiences. There was the late February day of dreadful windstorm. They had taken a cart up to the windmill with sacks of corn. On their way back they had to pass a little farmyard, derelict since the enclosures. The smaller buildings were already roofless, but there was still one high, ancient, thatched barn. It looked majestic to eyes which had seen so few buildings of height. That day as they came down towards it, they saw pale patches on the near side of its roof – the top straw had been blown off and left unweathered straw beneath. The edges of the patches were fringes blowing in the wind, inviting it to take them. Then it was dreadful to see the wind lift great gobs and gouts of thatch and fling them sodden and heavy far across the yard. The skeleton of the roof began to show. For an old reason the two were compelled to watch. The scene stood for age and uncomprehending youth, for the fragility of the created thing before primeval force. They tried to express the symbol. 'A sick 'ooman', said Jasper, 'losing 'er locks.' 'An old man grieving.' Neither could murmur 'Lear', for they had not read of him, but when Joseph did he would see the old barn in its trouble.

Jasper remembered Joe's lack of a father. He was the first person to speak to him about his own powers. 'Dooan't you stop a laabourer, bwoy, twun't do for a lad like you. What be schools for? Ever thought about them chapel folk? They rades and they says their thoughts. I dooan't want to be a chapel man, but, bwoy, you goo and see what they doos. Parson Francis be middling good, but he dooan't know what goes on in yoor yed, and dooan't want to, and he wun't help you.'

In the conflict between the two ways of life, Makepeace's and Jasper's, the latter gained Joseph's mind. He presently completely forgot Makepeace's ugly stories; they only returned to him long after when his mind was preoccupied by the past.

There were some social occasions on the farm, even in the winter. Sometimes the midday meal would be taken down at the farm-yard in Jasper's little harness room beside the stables, with horses' collars and harness hanging round. Here Jasper and Joe would meet the other labourers on the farm – the yardmen, the second ploughman, and Makepeace might be there too. A little brick chimney had been run up through the shed, and each man would carry in a piece of dry, rotten wood, and they would frizzle small pieces of raw bacon. The shelter and warmth were heaven. Talk often fell on old times, old sports and farming ways, and especially on food.

The old amusements were the topic on happier days. Those which had totally disappeared were the favourites – cock-fighting and bull-baiting. Some of the men had seen cock-fighting and told how the cocks were fed and trained. The cock-pit had been on an island of village green near the home of one of them. He

and Joseph went and looked for traces of it and found them very
clear. Pitch-and-toss gambling was only lost to view, being illegal
but easily hidden. The men said Methodism had killed the sports
because the best sportsmen had been converted. But Jasper said it
was due to a change in the Church too; the clergy and the gentle-
men-farmers had ceased to be spectators. Altogether, the matches
had lost interest.

One old sport survived still – wrestling, generally between two
wrestlers, but still occasionally pick-a-back wrestling in two lines.
Joseph himself had seen this. It was an accident that he saw the
very last match of another kind, for his mother would have
objected had she known. Two men who had a quarrel fought it
out in a crude duel, with bare fists, but in a regular way, with a
few rough rules – times fixed and seconds present to see fair play.
Unfortunately, there was trouble. One of the men died of exhaus-
tion on the field, and presently his opponent was tried for man-
slaughter. After serving his sentence he went off to New Zealand,
and thus came to an end the old rough sports.

The meagre diet of some years back was mentioned often. Men
used to start the day on a breakfast of bread soaked in hot water,
salted and peppered. Bread and onions had been eaten in the fields
at dinner-time. A man's wage would not buy bread for a family,
let alone any meat. 'No, nor it wun't now', said Jasper, 'if there be
any childer.' Someone told of an occasion when a family of parents
and nine children had shared a single bloater at Sunday dinner.
Cabbage had been a great standby. The young children, they said,
had lived on cabbage and lard. 'My old 'ooman', said one of them,
'says cabbage killed many a babby, but kept the next biggest alive.'
Now in the seventies the men brought a bit of cheese as well as
an onion. When they ate at home they might have suet pudding
with scraps of bacon rolled in it and mushrooms, too, once or
twice a year, and then it was the richest of dishes. Usually this talk
was cheerful; times were not so bad as they had been, but sometimes a darker spirit ruled. Life was hard laabour abroad, squalling

babbies at whum, and the workus at last. The workus was hell, but a cold un. And all, mark you, in a land of plenty. There was nothing to live for.

Ainge's farm itself was talked of. Fifteen years before it had had a plough-team of oxen – old Gloucester long-horns, with horns a yard long. Blacksmith made cow-knobs to stop their stabbing one another in the sheds. It had been the last farm to make the shallow, pale Banbury cheese, the last good-sized farm to thresh with the flail, and now Makepeace's sheep were the last of the old sort. As to the value of the new ways, there was no proof of more profit.

One day an adder was killed in the woods beyond Sunrising Hill, and there was some excitement. 'What a to-do,' said one of the men, 'adders used to be as common as 'ares on th' 'eeaths. Badgers be gooin' too. And what ought to goo, that be Raynard, but 'e dooant.'

The heaths? Where were they, Joseph asked. 'You better goo and talk to old Tom Lynes; 'e sin the first 'edge planted.' Jasper took Joe to old Tom. Tom was ninety, but strong still. He did not look like a labourer, for he had a massive frame and well-formed features, not wrecked even now. He had been born before the worst of the famine years. On his forehead were tiny white hollows; when he was six, Tysoe's last great epidemic of smallpox had occurred. All his family had been ill; his mother had been carried on a stretcher to the pockhouse at Westcote, two miles from Church Town. Tom had been sixteen when the first hedge had been planted along the top above the Red Way. He could still walk through the three fields on to the lower slopes of Old Lodge, and from there he named all the fields within sight. It was as if the hedges shrivelled, and the natural country revealed itself. Along the hills to the east of the parish were 'moors' and 'heaths' – Westcote Heath and Mere Hill. Over Old Lodge in Shenington parish were the First, Second and Far Barnacombe Fields. Barna, then, must be the name of the tiny stream that flowed through them, thought Joe, though no one ever named it now. 'Barna' –

like Hook-a-Norton – barn, bourn! Burns; burn! Why, it must mean brook! Lynes as he talked named every path and spinney. Small things and great were alike to him each with its name or its past. Did Joe ever see that loop in yon hedge? A grett tree had stood theer and the hedge was planted round it. He could explain, if you waited long enough, some very strange names – Duffus, on the Manor farm, was where the dove-house used to be; Tithekers had to do with tithes, he didn't remember quite what. On the flat clay land, all newly enclosed in Lynes's time, the names were taken simply from the shapes cut out of the common – the Picked (or pointed) Ground, the Three-corner Field.

Jasper and old Lynes discussed the days before the hedges. The lower slopes of the old heaths were very tolerable grassland now, where they had grown only furze; thyme and harebell could only be seen now on Bald Knob and the hill walks. Enclosures would have done good if there had been justice in 'em. 'They give folks allotments now instid o' ther rights – on a slope so steep a two-legged animal can't stand, let alone dig!' In the old days you could walk all through the parish and all round it by the balks and head-lands and cut wood on the waste, if there was any. 'And what can you do now, Jasper?' asked Lynes. 'Make a farmer mad and you be done.' Fall on evil days then, and your own parish looked after you. 'This bwoy 'ere now, wi'out a dad, 'e'd a bin prenticed to any traade 'e'd a wanted, a bright un such as 'e be. Now they 'as that noisy grett school and pitches 'im out on it afore 'e 'as begun to learn. A good bwoy should be under teachin' till 'e's nineteen, at a good traade, saame as I could 'a bin only I wanted to be out on the land. But dooan't you taake no notice of us old fellows, bwoy, we be only meahnderin'.'

All that arose out of Joseph's work. All the children then spent more time with the men and women than they would later, for no one thought of school as carrying the real burden of their training. Besides, when the men and the youngsters came home from work they had not earned the wherewithal to live, only part of it. Wood had to be collected and dragged home from the lanes, water drawn from the well, gardens dug and planted. When the diphtheria epidemic at Brailes had horrified the district, purer water must be carried from standpipes, two or three only in each town. The children shared these jobs and chopped sticks, picked fruit, ran errands and went mushrooming. The better the home, the greater their responsibilities were.

When the men had big works going on at home, building or thatching a shed, maybe, or cleaning out the well, or emptying the privy pit, boys must be there to fetch and carry, flying like the wind for the tools or wedges or nails the men had need of. Looking on, a boy would get absorbed in the men's skill, yet not beyond a certain degree, for it was a boy's deepest disgrace to fail, when a crisis came, to see where his weight was needed to supplement the men's, or when his smaller hand must be thrust in.

Some of the labours were communal. As a biggish lad, Joseph carried his mother's corn to the Upper Town tithe barn near the Old Tree, where several men were already threshing with their 'stick-na-halfs', as they called flails. The boys would be allowed to take short turns while the men shook themselves free of the horrid, pricking dust and slaked the thirst it gave them. The call to share work was so frequent that where a job was concerned men and boys came to take all the world for neighbours. They would put shoulder to a clogged wheel if it belonged to Old Nick himself. In accident there was no doctor, in calamity no fire brigade at call; squeamishness and fastidiousness were lower than crime. If a labourer's boy had not the courage or will to throw himself into the breach, the word went forth that he was of no account. In such labours and crises it was perhaps not the more imaginative lads, such as Joseph and his young brother, but some boy more silent and slow who got the accolade, 'You be near a man, you be'.

One part of the neighbourly training in these out-of-school and after-work hours was done by the women. Elizabeth would send her boys to carry some old woman's water, or to chop her wood, or dig her potato plot – not usually very welcome work, but wise old women had always some small treat for the boys when the job was done – some bite or sup within doors, a hot roast potato or a glass of metheglin, though sometimes they would be taxed to find anything. It was not labour that hurt even the very young; it was the insufficiency of the harvest when gathered – the low feeding, the lack of clothes, the draughty houses. It was always one of the most moving experiences to young Joseph to see inside another house, like peeping into another world. He was too young to 'observe', but a fresh eye registered on its periphery what would come to its clear notice later. He knew exactly how and what the cottage women cooked in the one big oval pot, with also perhaps a little old bronze, three-legged cauldron to seethe the potatoes in their skins. Into the boiler went everything else – the bacon, the greens in a net, the dumplings of flour and fat which were taken out as the first course, blunting the appetite so that the meat could be decently shared. As for his own meals, they were not quite so limited. His mother had one of the small stoves, with a little oven. He was aware that only the raven gave his mother the where-withal for the better meals – the gift of pieces of chine after pig-killing, the rabbit left inside the kitchen door. There were a few sad sights in the houses – the two idiots, a child and a man, and a poor invalid 'in a decline'. Out in the street, he saw old Mrs Wells's heavy ancient pewter dishes carried along home, after their grisly use, to restrain the bloating of some corpse; and his mother, making broth over her fire, exclaimed about the horrible messes offered to the dying.

Of course, there were homes different in kind. Joseph went on errands to his Aunt Hannah Rouvray. Her cottage, a fine large one, was furnished with rosewood and mahogany. There were many small pieces of china, with hand-painted flowers and moulded fruits. The path from her garden gate to her door was bordered deep with flowers, from snowdrop-time to the last tiny yellow chrysanthemum. If you visited her, she offered you a glass of

French wine on a painted tray. The only work Joseph ever saw
her do was her fantastic patchwork, and such gardening as could
go with wearing of a full, black silk dress. Just inside Hannah's
door hung a tiny, deep rosewood frame containing a print – the
certificate of Adolphe Rouvray's admission to the Chairmakers'
Guild. Could chairmaking have provided her with the mysterious
sources of her living? The village thought not. But it had no
grounds at all for its thoughts. On her little fortune in the Funds
the widow lived very completely to herself. She was not very
neighbourly, but she was good-natured, kindly-mannered. Altogether she was good for something in the education of young boys
– for a little vision of comfort and leisure and propriety and for a
streak of colour.

But, of course, there was sheer play at times. There were 'ducks
and drakes' on the green – a good, slow play for fine evenings
when there were the air and the scene to enjoy. Cricket itself was
coming; the fame of Surrey and Wiltshire county cricket had
reached Tysoe, and the boys were making home-made bats and
bowling along the smoother bits of road. Every year, in the
lengthening evenings of late spring, the echoing cries of a race of
giants filled the village. The eleven- and twelve-year-olds had
need to be giants – they were getting so strong and yet not growing into men. Joseph and his brother, George, liked this play well
and made stilts every springtime. Their posse of playmates would
act the beginning of half a dozen stories on their stilts. One boy
would suggest some stronghold to be attacked, and they would
start on their way towards it, and then someone would shout,
'No, no, tisn't fun; I know what we'll do'. Half a dozen starts
would be made, two or three evenings spent in elevation, and
then the boys would feel the need for speedy movement and
reality. The stilts were thrown down, all magic gone from the
clumsy sticks, and soon they were broken for the fire. We have
one clear, momentary glimpse of Joseph himself at play. It is a
verbal photograph, often handed around long after the event. The

scene was the village green at the south end where it widens into a rough square, on which in the seventies the speeches and out-of-door sermons took place. As late as the fifties the old games used to be held here, and in the sixties the boys played their version of them. Two long lines of boys, each with another on his back, stand ready for a pick-a-back battle. The riders will wrestle together till one line is riderless and the other has won. There they stand ready for the fray. Round the corner from the Back Lane comes Joseph running, a rider on his shoulders – a donkey foal's skin stuffed with straw. He joins his line and makes for his opponent; the little grey head wags and wags, and the little form moves so comically that onlookers and wrestlers are all undone by helpless laughter, and the battle is off. That was Joseph always – a serious fellow and yet merrier than the merry.

But it was not always spring and summer. Amusement and information came in the winter, as also to a lesser extent in other seasons, from the lighter side of religious life. The Church especially, and Joseph was a Churchman, hatched out and gathered under its wings many minor groups – an Insurance Society, a Band of Hope, a penny bank, penny readings, the list changing with need and fashion. It was from the missionary meetings and leaflets that Joseph gained his early introduction, all in exotic mode, to the world beyond the seas. Melanesia, India, Africa would always have a more homely, familiar feeling for him than France or Germany. There was, for example, the visit of Mr Florin, the missionary from Norfolk Island. He drew back curtains from a wonderful scene. Passion fruits, pineapples, grapes made the mouth water. In the big, cold barn-school, the warmth of the Island was felt and the cliff-bound coast vividly seen.

Tysoe had adopted a Melanesian boy, Buha, but he was no longer in the mission school. At twelve years of age he had been sent home for a time, but he returned with a girl to be his wife. Then her relations had come in boats to rescue her and presently Buha had gone away too. The natives, though tractable and lovable, had their customs. Give offence to a chief and you must expiate it by an offering of human heads. Thus had perished some young officers of a British naval vessel; there had been no hatred in the slaughter, only necessity from the Melanesian point of view.

What impressed Joseph equally with the foreign warmth and wealth was the missionary's justice of mind. His first picture of India was less happy. The Vicar allowed his mother to read a letter from a lady-missionary who had been governess to the Vicar's daughters. She was so tired, she wrote, of Ahmed Jugger – 'Those unmelodious voices dinning incessantly' in her ears were more than she could endure any longer. She would go to Calcutta, the Bengalis were well educated and understood English. She had been at the Cathedral at Bombay; the organ sounded heavenly in contrast to the yelling natives she always heard at the Marathi services. She was trying to buy land for a school, but it was difficult to get a safe title; the natives were such rogues – they cheated at every turn!

Then there were the 'treats'. The Vicar was at his best on festive occasions such as the Church Sunday School treat. It was a very fine affair. First, the afternoon service in the Church, with the Vicar and curate officiating and four clergymen from the neighbouring villages in the procession. Recitations in the school followed and then tea on the Vicarage lawn. There was cake at this tea – a wonderful change from bread and lard. Games on the slope of Old Lodge, the beloved familiar hill rising behind the Vicarage, finished the day for the young children. But on one occasion Joseph lingered to see what the grown-ups did during the later hours. At six the Vicar's own friends, four or five other clergymen and their families, came spanking up in gigs and dog-carts. Mrs Francis led off with one of them in a country dance and the big village children looked on till, after cake and lemonade, they were despatched home. But Joseph sat among the branches of a tree and saw Chinese lanterns lit and hung among the green-black leaves of the laurels round the lawn, making great blobs of colour, glowing yet pale.

Many of these experiences of my father's early days come back to me in his own voice, but of murky stories and the uglier hardships I heard nothing directly from him. He kept them in his mind to correct what might have become a rose-coloured vision, and though not to be recounted in his home they could be charmed from him in outline by my brothers working with him out in a field.

M. K. Ashby, *Joseph Ashby of Tysoe*

COTTAGERS AND THEIR HOMES

The hamlet stood on a gentle rise in the flat, wheat-growing north-east corner of Oxfordshire. We will call it Lark Rise because of the great number of skylarks which made the surrounding fields their springboard and nested on the bare earth between the rows of green corn . . .

A few of the houses had thatched roofs, whitewashed outer walls and diamond-paned windows, but the majority were just stone or brick boxes with blue-slated roofs. The older houses were relics of pre-enclosure days and were still occupied by descendants of the original squatters, themselves at that time elderly people. One old couple owned a donkey and cart, which they used to carry their vegetables, eggs, and honey to the market town and sometimes hired out at sixpence a day to their neighbours. One house was occupied by a retired farm bailiff, who was reported to have 'well feathered his own nest' during his years of stewardship. Another aged man owned and worked upon about an acre of land. These, the innkeeper, and one other man, a stonemason who walked the three miles to and from his work in the town every day, were the only ones not employed as agricultural labourers . . .

The first charge on the labourers' ten shillings was house rent. Most of the cottages belonged to small tradesmen in the market town and the weekly rents ranged from one shilling to half a crown. Some labourers in other villages worked on farms or estates where they had their cottages rent free; but the hamlet people did not envy them, for 'Stands to reason,' they said, 'they've allus got to do just what they be told, or out they goes, neck and crop, bag and baggage.' A shilling, or even two shillings a week, they felt, was not too much to pay for the freedom to live and vote as they liked and to go to church or chapel or neither as they preferred.

Every house had a good vegetable garden and there were allotments for all; but only three of the thirty cottages had their own water supply. The less fortunate tenants obtained their water from a well on a vacant plot on the outskirts of the hamlet, from which the cottage had disappeared. There was no public well or pump. They just had to get their water where and how they could; the landlords did not undertake to supply water . . .

At the back or side of each cottage was a lean-to pigsty and the house refuse was thrown on a nearby pile called 'the muck'll'. This was so situated that the oozings from the sty could drain into it; the manure was also thrown there when the sty was cleared, and the whole formed a nasty, smelly eyesore to have within a few feet of the windows. 'The wind's in the so-and-so,' some woman indoors would say, 'I can smell th' muck'll', and she would often be reminded of the saying, 'Pigs for health', or told that the smell was a healthy one.

It was in a sense a healthy smell for them; for a good pig fattening in the sty promised a good winter. During its lifetime the pig was an important member of the family, and its health and condition were regularly reported in letters to children away from home, together with news of their brothers and sisters. Men callers on Sunday afternoons came, not to see the family, but the pig, and would lounge with its owner against the pigsty door for an hour, scratching piggy's back and praising his points or turning up their own noses in criticism. Ten to fifteen shillings was the price paid for a pigling when weaned, and they all delighted in getting a bargain. Some men swore by the 'dilling', as the smallest of a litter was called, saying it was little and good, and would soon catch up; others preferred to give a few shillings more for a larger young pig.

The family pig was everybody's pride and everybody's business. Mother spent hours boiling up the 'little taturs' to mash and mix with the pot-liquor, in which food had been cooked, to feed to the pig for its evening meal and help out the expensive barley meal. The children, on their way home from school, would fill their arms with sow thistle, dandelion, and choice long grass, or roam along the hedgerows on wet evenings collecting snails in a pail for the pig's supper. These piggy crunched up with great relish. 'Feyther', over and above farming out the sty, bedding down, doctoring, and so on, would even go without his nightly half-pint when, towards the end, the barley-meal bill mounted until 'it fair frightened anybody'. . .

When the pig was fattened – and the fatter the better – the date of execution had to be decided upon. It had to take place some time during the first two quarters of the moon; for, if the pig was killed when the moon was waning the bacon would shrink in cooking, and they wanted it to 'plimp up'. The next thing was to engage the travelling pork butcher, or pig-sticker, and, as he was a thatcher by day, he always had to kill after dark, the scene being lighted with lanterns and the fire of burning straw which at a later stage of the proceedings was to singe the bristles off the victim . . .

On the following Sunday came the official 'pig feast', when fathers and mothers, sisters and brothers, married children and grandchildren who lived within walking distance arrived to dinner.

If the house had no oven, permission was obtained from an old couple in one of the thatched cottages to heat up the big bread-baking oven in their wash-house. This was like a large cupboard with an iron door, lined with brick and going far back into the wall. Faggots of wood were lighted inside and the door was closed upon them until the oven was well heated. Then the ashes were swept out and baking-tins with joints of pork, potatoes, batter puddings, pork pies, and sometimes a cake or two, were popped inside and left to bake without further attention.

Meanwhile, at home, three or four different kinds of vegetables would be cooked, and always a meat pudding, made in a basin. No feast and few Sunday dinners were considered complete without that item, which was eaten alone, without vegetables, when a joint was to follow. On ordinary days the pudding would be a roly-poly containing fruit, currants, or jam; but it still appeared as a first course, the idea being that it took the edge off the appetite. At the pig feast there would be no sweet pudding, for that could be had any day, and who wanted sweet things when there was plenty of meat to be had!

But this glorious plenty only came once or twice a year, and there were all the other days to provide for. How was it done on ten shillings a week? Well, for one thing, food was much cheaper than it is to-day. Then, in addition to the bacon, all vegetables, including potatoes, were home-grown and grown in abundance. The men took great pride in their gardens and allotments and there was always competition amongst them as to who should have the earliest and choicest of each kind. Fat green peas, broad beans as big as a halfpenny, cauliflowers a child could make an armchair of, runner beans and cabbage and kale, all in their seasons went into the pot with the roly-poly and slip of bacon.

Then they ate plenty of green food, all home-grown and freshly pulled; lettuce and radishes and young onions with pearly heads and leaves like fine grass. A few slices of bread and home-made lard, flavoured with rosemary, and plenty of green food 'went down good' as they used to say.

Bread had to be bought, and that was a heavy item, with so many growing children to be fed; but flour for the daily pudding and an occasional plain cake could be laid in for the winter without any cash outlay. After the harvest had been carried from the fields, the women and children swarmed over the stubble picking up the ears of wheat the horse-rake had missed. Gleaning, or 'leazing', as it was called locally . . .

At the end of the fortnight or three weeks that the leazing lasted, the corn would be thrashed out at home and sent to the miller, who paid himself for grinding by taking toll of the flour. Great was the excitement in a good year when the flour came home – one bushel, two bushels, or even more in large, industrious families. The mealy-white sack with its contents was often kept for a time on show on a chair in the living-room and it was a common thing for a passer-by to be invited to 'step inside an' see our little bit o' leazings'. They liked to have the product of their labour before their own eyes and to let others admire it, just as the artist likes to show his picture and the composer to hear his opus played. 'Them's better'n any o' yer oil-paintin's,' a man would say, pointing to the flitches on his wall, and the women felt the same about the leazings.

Here, then, were the three chief ingredients of the one hot meal a day, bacon from the flitch, vegetables from the garden, and flour for the roly-poly. This meal, called 'tea', was taken in the evening, when the men were home from the fields and the children from school, for neither could get home at midday.

About four o'clock, smoke would go up from the chimneys, as the fire was made up and the big iron boiler, or the three-legged pot, was slung on the hook of the chimney-chain. Everything was cooked in the one utensil; the square of bacon, amounting to little more than a taste each; cabbage, or other green vegetables in one net, potatoes in another, and the roly-poly swathed in a cloth. It sounds a haphazard method in these days of gas and electric cookers; but it answered its purpose, for, by carefully timing the putting in of each item and keeping the simmering of the pot well regulated, each item was kept intact and an appetising meal was produced. The water in which the food had been cooked, the

G

potato parings, and other vegetable trimmings were the pig's share . . .

For other meals they depended largely on bread and butter, or, more often, bread and lard, eaten with any relish that happened to be at hand. Fresh butter was too costly for general use, but a pound was sometimes purchased in the summer, when it cost ten-pence. Margarine, then called 'butterine', was already on the market, but was little used there, as most people preferred lard, especially when it was their own home-made lard flavoured with rosemary leaves. In summer there was always plenty of green food from the garden and home-made jam as long as it lasted, and sometimes an egg or two, where fowls were kept, or when eggs were plentiful and sold at twenty a shilling . . .

'Poverty's no disgrace, but 'tis a great inconvenience' was a common saying among the Lark Rise people; but that put the case too mildly, for their poverty was no less than a hampering drag upon them. Everybody had enough to eat and a shelter which, though it fell far short of modern requirements, satisfied them. Coal at a shilling a hundredweight and a pint of paraffin for lighting *had* to be squeezed out of the weekly wage; but for boots, clothes, illness, holidays, amusements, and household re-newals there was no provision whatever. How did they manage?

Boots were often bought with the extra money the men earned in the harvest field. When that was paid, those lucky families which were not in arrears with their rent would have a new pair all round, from the father's hobnailed dreadnoughts to little pink kid slippers for the baby. Then some careful housewives paid a few pence every week into the boot club run by a shopkeeper in the market town. This helped; but it was not sufficient, and how to get a pair of new boots for 'our young Ern or Alf' was a prob-lem which kept many a mother awake at night.

Girls needed boots, too, and good, stout, nailed ones for those rough and muddy roads; but they were not particular, any boots would do. At a confirmation class which Laura attended, the clergyman's daughter, after weeks of careful preparation, asked her catechumens: 'Now, are you sure you are all of you thoroughly prepared for to-morrow. Is there anything you would like to ask me?'

'Yes, miss,' piped up a voice in a corner, 'me mother says have you got a pair of your old boots you could give me, for I haven't got any fit to go in.'

Alice got her boots on that occasion; but there was not a confirmation every day. Still, boots were obtained somehow; nobody went barefoot, even though some of the toes might sometimes stick out beyond the toe of the boot . . .

But, in spite of their poverty and the worry and anxiety attending it, they were not unhappy, and, though poor, there was nothing sordid about their lives. 'The nearer the bone the sweeter the meat', they used to say, and they were getting very near the bone from which their country ancestors had fed. Their children and children's children would have to depend wholly upon whatever was carved for them from the communal joint, and for their pleasure upon the mass enjoyments of a new era. But for that generation there was still a small picking left to supplement the weekly wage. They had their home-cured bacon, their 'bit o' leazings', their small wheat or barley patch on the allotment; their knowledge of herbs for their homely simples, and the wild fruits and berries of the countryside for jam, jellies, and wine, and round about them as part of their lives were the last relics of country customs and the last echoes of country songs, ballads, and game rhymes. This last picking, though meagre, was sweet.

Flora Thompson, *Lark Rise to Candleford*

MEN AFIELD

Very early in the morning, before daybreak for the greater part of the year, the hamlet men would throw on their clothes, breakfast on bread and lard, snatch the dinner-baskets which had been packed for them overnight, and hurry off across fields and over stiles to the farm. Getting the boys off was a more difficult matter. Mothers would have to call and shake and sometimes pull boys of eleven or twelve out of their warm beds on a winter morning. Then boots which had been drying inside the fender all night and had become shrunk and hard as boards in the process would have to be coaxed on over chilblains. Sometimes a very small boy would cry over this and his mother to cheer him would remind him that they were only boots, not breeches. 'Good thing you didn't live when breeches wer' made o' leather,' she would say, and tell him about the boy of a previous generation whose leather breeches were so baked up in drying that it took him an hour to get into them. 'Patience! Have patience, my son', his mother had exhorted. 'Remember Job.' 'Job!' scoffed the boy. 'What did he know about patience? He didn't have to wear no leather breeches.

Leather breeches had disappeared in the 'eighties and were only remembered in telling that story. The carter, shepherd, and a few of the older labourers still wore the traditional smock-frock topped by a round black felt hat, like those formerly worn by clergymen. But this old country style of dress was already out of date; most of the men wore suits of stiff, dark brown corduroy, or, in summer, corduroy trousers and an unbleached drill jacket known as a 'sloppy'.

Most of the young and those in the prime of life were thick-set, red-faced men of good medium height and enormous strength who prided themselves on the weights they could carry and boasted of never having had 'an e-ache nor a pa-in' in their lives. The elders stooped, had gnarled and swollen hands and walked badly, for they felt the effects of a life spent out of doors in all weathers and of the rheumatism which tried most of them. These elders wore a fringe of grey whisker beneath the jaw, extending from ear to ear. The younger men sported drooping walrus moustaches. One or two, in advance of the fashion of their day, were clean-shaven; but as Sunday was the only shaving day, the effect of either style became blurred by the end of the week.

They still spoke the dialect, in which the vowels were not only broadened, but in many words doubled. 'Boy' was 'boo-oy', 'coal', 'coo-al', 'pail', 'pay-ull', and so on. In other words, syllables were slurred, and words were run together, as 'brenbu'er' for bread and butter. They had hundreds of proverbs and sayings and their talk was stiff with simile. Nothing was simply hot, cold, or coloured; it was 'as hot as hell', 'as cold as ice', 'as green as grass', or 'as yellow as a guinea'. A botched-up job done with insufficient materials was 'like Dick's hatband that went half-way round and tucked'; to try to persuade or encourage one who did not respond was 'putting a poultice on a wooden leg'. To be nervy was to be 'like a cat on hot bricks'; to be angry, 'mad as a bull'; or any one might be 'poor as a rat', 'sick as a dog', 'hoarse as a crow', 'as ugly as sin', 'full of the milk of human kindness', or 'stinking with pride'. A temperamental person was said to be 'one o' them as is either up on the roof or down the well'. The dialect was heard at its best on the lips of a few middle-aged men, who had good natural voices, plenty of sense, and a grave, dignified delivery. Mr. Frederick Grisewood of the B.B.C. gave a perfect rendering of the old Oxfordshire dialect in some broadcast sketches a few years ago. Usually, such imitations are maddening to the native born, but he made the past live again for one listener.

The men's incomes were the same to a penny; their circumstances, pleasures, and their daily field work were shared in common; but in themselves they differed, as other men of their day differed, in country and town. Some were intelligent, others slow at the uptake; some were kind and helpful, others selfish; some vivacious; others taciturn. If a stranger had gone there looking for the conventional Hodge, he would not have found him.

Nor would he have found the dry humour of the Scottish peasant, or the racy wit and wisdom of Thomas Hardy's Wessex. These men's minds were cast in a heavier mould and moved more slowly. Yet there were occasional gleams of quiet fun. One man

who had found Edmund crying because his magpie, let out for her
daily exercise, had not returned to her wicker cage, said, 'Doo'nt
'ee take on like that, my man. You goo an' tell Mrs. Andrews
about it [naming the village gossip] and you'll hear where your
Maggie's been seen, if 'tis as far away as Stratton.'

Their favourite virtue was endurance. Not to flinch from pain
or hardship was their ideal. A man would say, 'He says, says he,
that field o' oo-ats's got to come in afore night, for there's a rain
a'comin'. But we didn't flinch, not we! Got the last loo-ad under
cover by midnight. A'moost too fagged-out to walk home; but
we didn't flinch. We done it!' Or, 'Ole bull he comes for me, wi's
head down. But I didn't flinch. I ripped off a bit o' loose rail an'
went for he. 'Twas him as did th' flinchin'. He! he!' Or a woman
would say, 'I set up wi' my poor old mother six nights runnin';
never had me clothes off. But I didn't flinch, an' I pulled her
through, for she didn't flinch neither.' Or a young wife would say
to the midwife after her first confinement, 'I didn't flinch, did I?
Oh, I do hope I didn't flinch' . . .

Around the farmhouse were grouped the farm buildings; stables
for the great stamping shaggy-fetlocked carthorses; barns with
doors so wide and high that a load of hay could be driven through;
sheds for the yellow-and-blue painted farm wagons, granaries
with outdoor staircases; and sheds for storing oilcake, artificial
manures, and agricultural implements. In the rickyard, tall, pointed, elaborately thatched ricks stood on stone straddles; the dairy
indoors, though small, was a model one; there was a profusion of
all that was necessary or desirable for good farming.

Labour, too, was lavishly used. Boys leaving school were taken
on at the farm as a matter of course, and no time-expired soldier
or settler on marriage was ever refused a job. As the farmer said,
he could always do with an extra hand, for labour was cheap and
the land was well tilled up to the last inch.

When the men and boys from the hamlet reached the farmyard
in the morning, the carter and his assistant had been at work for

an hour, feeding and getting ready the horses. After giving any
help required, the men and boys would harness and lead out their
teams and file off to the field where their day's work was to be
done.

If it rained, they donned sacks, split up one side to form a hood
and cloak combined. If it was frosty, they blew upon their nails
and thumped their arms across their chest to warm them. If they
felt hungry after their bread-and-lard breakfast, they would pare
a turnip and munch it, or try a bite or two of the rich, dark brown
oilcake provided for the cattle. Some of the boys would sample
the tallow candles belonging to the stable lanterns; but that was
done more out of devilry than from hunger, for, whoever went
short, the mothers took care that their Tom or Dicky should have
'a bit o' summat to peck at between meals' – half a cold pancake
or the end of yesterday's roly-poly.

With 'Gee!' and 'Wert up!' and 'Who-a-a, now!' the teams
would draw out. The boys were hoisted to the backs of the tall
carthorses, and the men, walking alongside, filled their clay pipes
with shag and drew the first precious puffs of the day, as, with
cracking of whips, clopping of hooves and jingling of harness, the
teams went tramping along the muddy byways.

The field names gave the clue to the fields' history. Near the
farmhouse, 'Moat Piece', 'Fishponds', 'Duffus [i.e. dovehouse]
Piece', 'Kennels', and 'Warren Piece' spoke of a time before the
Tudor house took the place of another and older establishment.
Farther on, 'Lark Hill', 'Cuckoos' Clump', 'The Osiers', and
'Pond Piece' were named after natural features, while 'Gibbard's
Piece' and 'Blackwell's' probably commemorated otherwise long-
forgotten former occupants. The large new fields round the ham-
let had been cut too late to be named and were known as 'The
Hundred Acres', 'The Sixty Acres', and so on according to their
acreage. One or two of the ancients persisted in calling one of these
'The Heath' and another 'The Racecourse'.

One name was as good as another to most of the men; to them

it was just a name and meant nothing. What mattered to them about the field in which they happened to be working was whether the road was good or bad which led from the farm to it; or if it was comparatively sheltered or one of those bleak open places which the wind hurtled through, driving the rain through the clothes to the very pores; and was the soil easily workable or of back-breaking heaviness or so bound together with that 'hemmed' twitch that a ploughshare could scarcely get through it.

There were usually three or four ploughs to a field, each of them drawn by a team of three horses, with a boy at the head of the leader and the ploughman behind at the shafts. All day, up and down they would go, ribbing the pale stubble with stripes of dark furrows, which, as the day advanced, would get wider and nearer together, until, at length, the whole field lay a rich velvety plum-colour.

Each plough had its following of rooks, searching the clods with side-long glances for worms and grubs. Little hedgerow birds flitted hither and thither, intent upon getting their tiny share of whatever was going. Sheep, penned in a neighbouring field, bleated complainingly; and above the ma-aing and cawing and twittering rose the immemorial cries of the land-worker: 'Wert up!' 'Who-o-o-a!' 'Go it, Poppet!' 'Go it, Lightfoot!' 'Boo-oy, be you deaf, or be you hard of hearin', dang ye!'

After the plough had done its part, the horse-drawn roller was used to break down the clods; then the harrow to comb out and leave in neat piles the weeds and the twitch grass which infested those fields, to be fired later and fill the air with the light blue haze and the scent that can haunt for a lifetime. Then seed was sown, crops were thinned out and hoed and, in time, mown, and the whole process began again . . .

The labourers worked hard and well when they considered the occasion demanded it and kept up a good steady pace at all times. Some were better workmen than others, of course; but the major-ity took a pride in their craft and were fond of explaining to an outsider that field work was not the fool's job that some townsmen considered it. Things must be done just so and at the exact moment, they said; there were ins and outs in good land work which took a man's lifetime to learn. A few of less admirable build would boast: 'We gets ten bob a week, a' we yarns every penny of it; but we doesn't yarn no more; we takes hemmed good care o' that!' But at team work, at least, such 'slack-twisted 'uns' had to keep in step, and the pace, if slow, was steady.

While the ploughmen were in charge of the teams, other men went singly, or in twos or threes, to hoe, harrow, or spread manure in other fields; others cleared ditches and saw to drains, or sawed wood or cut chaff or did other odd jobs about the farmstead. Two or three highly skilled middle-aged men were sometimes put upon piecework, hedging and ditching, sheep-shearing, thatching, or mowing, according to the season. The carter, shepherd, stockman, and blacksmith had each his own specialized job. Important men, these, with two shillings a week extra on their wages and a cottage rent free near the farmstead . . .

At twelve by the sun, or by signal from the possessor of one of the old turnip-faced watches which descended from father to son, the teams would knock off for the dinner-hour. Horses were unyoked, led to the shelter of a hedge or a rick and given their nosebags and men and boys threw themselves down on sacks spread out beside them and tin bottles of cold tea were uncorked and red handkerchiefs of food unwrapped. The lucky ones had bread and cold bacon, perhaps the top or the bottom of a cottage loaf, on which the small cube of bacon was placed, with a finger of bread on top, called the thumbpiece, to keep the meat untouched by hand and in position for manipulation with a clasp-knife. The consumption of this food was managed neatly and decently, a small sliver of bacon and a chunk of bread being cut and conveyed to the mouth in one movement. The less fortunate ones munched their bread and lard or morsel of cheese; and the boys with their ends of cold pudding were jokingly bidden not to get 'that 'ere treacle' in their ears.

The food soon vanished, the crumbs from the red handkerchiefs were shaken out for the birds, the men lighted their pipes and the boys wandered off with their catapults down the hedgerows. Often the elders would sit out their hour of leisure discussing politics, the latest murder story, or local affairs; but at other times, especially when one man noted for that kind of thing was present, they would while away the time in repeating what the women spoke of with shamed voices as 'men's tales'.

These stories, which were kept strictly to the fields and never repeated elsewhere, formed a kind of rustic *Decameron*,[28] which seemed to have been in existence for centuries and increased like a snowball as it rolled down the generations. The tales were supposed to be extremely indecent, and elderly men would say after such a sitting, 'I got up an' went over to th' osses, for I couldn't stand no more on't. The brimstone fair come out o' their mouths as they put their rascally heads together.' What they were really like only the men knew; but probably they were coarse rather than filthy. Judging by a few stray specimens which leaked through the channel of eavesdropping juniors, they consisted chiefly of 'he said' and 'she said', together with a lavish enumeration of those parts of the human body then known as 'the unmentionables'.

Songs and snatches on the same lines were bawled at the ploughtail and under hedges and never heard elsewhere. Some of these ribald rhymes were so neatly turned that those who have studied the subject have attributed their authorship to some graceless son of the Rectory or Hall. It may be that some of these young scamps had a hand in them, but it is just as likely that they sprung direct from the soil, for, in those days of general churchgoing, the men's minds were well stored with hymns and psalms and some of them were very good at parodying them.

There was 'The Parish Clerk's Daughter', for instance. This

damsel was sent one Christmas morning to the church to inform
her father that the Christmas present of beef had arrived after he
left home. When she reached the church the service had begun
and the congregation, led by her father, was half-way through the
psalms. Nothing daunted, she sidled up to her father and intoned:

'Feyther, the me-a-at's come, an' what's me mother to d-o-o-o
w'it?'

And the answer came pat: 'Tell her to roast the thick an' boil
th' thin, an' me-ak a pudden o' th' su-u-u-u-et.'

But such simple entertainment did not suit the man already
mentioned. He would drag out the filthiest of the stock rhymes,
then go on to improvise, dragging in the names of honest lovers
and making a mock of fathers of first children. Though nine out
of ten of his listeners disapproved and felt thoroughly uncomfort-
able, they did nothing to check him beyond a mild 'Look out, or
them boo-oys'll hear 'ee!' or 'Careful! some 'ooman may be
comin' along th' roo-ad.'

But the lewd scandalizer did not always have everything his
own way. There came a day when a young ex-soldier, home from
his five years' service in India, sat next to him. He sat through one
or two such extemporized songs, then, eyeing the singer, said
shortly, 'You'd better go and wash out your dirty mouth.'

The answer was a bawled stanza in which the objector's name
figured. At that the ex-soldier sprung to his feet, seized the singer
by the scruff of his neck, dragged him to the ground and, after a
scuffle, forced earth and small stones between his teeth. 'There,
that's a lot cleaner!' he said, administering a final kick on the
buttocks as the fellow slunk, coughing and spitting, behind the
hedge.

A few women still did field work, not with the men, or even in
the same field as a rule, but at their own special tasks, weeding and
hoeing, picking up stones, and topping and tailing turnips and
mangel; or, in wet weather, mending sacks in a barn. Formerly,
it was said, there had been a large gang of field women, lawless,

slatternly creatures, some of whom had thought nothing of having four or five children out of wedlock. Their day was over; but
the reputation they had left behind them had given most country-
women a distaste for 'goin' afield'. In the 'eighties about half a
dozen of the hamlet women did field work, most of them being
respectable middle-aged women who, having got their families
off hand, had spare time, a liking for an open-air life, and a longing
for a few shillings a week they could call their own . . .

On Friday evening, when work was done, the men trooped up
to the farmhouse for their wages. These were handed out of a
window to them by the farmer himself and acknowledged by a
rustic scraping of feet and pulling of forelocks. The farmer had
grown too old and too stout to ride horseback, and, although he
still made the circuit of his land in his high dogcart every day, he
had to keep to the roads, and pay-day was the only time he saw
many of his men. Then, if there was cause for complaint, was the
time they heard of it. 'You, there! What were you up to in Causey
Spinney last Monday, when you were supposed to be clearing the
runnels?' was a type of complaint that could always be countered
by pleading. 'Call o' Nature, please, sir.' Less frequent and harder
to answer was: 'I hear you've not been too smart about your work
lately, Stimson. 'Twon't do, you know, 'twon't do! You've got to
earn your money if you're going to stay here.' But, just as often,
it would be: 'There, Boamer, there you are, my lad, a bright and
shining golden half-sovereign for you. Take care you don't go
spending it all at once!' or an inquiry about some wife in childbed
or one of the ancients' rheumatism. He could afford to be jolly and
affable: he paid poor old Monday Morning to do his dirty work
for him.

Apart from that, he was not a bad-hearted man and had no idea
he was sweating his labourers. Did they not get the full standard
wage, with no deduction for standing by in bad weather? How
they managed to live and keep their families on such a sum was
their own affair. After all, they did not need much, they were not

used to luxuries. He liked a cut off a juicy sirloin and a glass of good port himself; but bacon and beans were better to work on. 'Hard liver, hard worker' was a sound old country maxim, and the labouring man did well to follow it. Besides, was there not at least one good blow-out for everybody once a year at his harvest-home dinner, and the joint of beef at Christmas, when he killed a beast and distributed the meat, and soup and milk-puddings for anybody who was ill; they had only to ask for and fetch them.

He never interfered with his men as long as they did their work well. Not he! He was a staunch Conservative himself, a true blue, and they knew his colour when they went to vote; but he never tried to influence them at election times and never inquired after-wards which way they had voted. Some masters did it, he knew, but it was a dirty, low-down trick, in his opinion. As to getting them to go to church – that was the parson's job.

Although they hoodwinked him whenever possible and referred to him behind his back as 'God a'mighty', the farmer was liked by his men. 'Not a bad sort,' they said; 'an' does his bit by the land.' All their rancour was reserved for the bailiff.

There is something exhilarating about pay-day, even when the pay is poor and already mortgaged for necessities. With that morsel of gold in their pockets, the men stepped out more briskly and their voices were cheerier than ordinary. When they reached home they handed the half-sovereign straight over to their wives, who gave them back a shilling for the next week's pocket-money. That was the custom of the countryside. The men worked for the money and the women had the spending of it. The men had the best of the bargain. They earned their half-sovereign by hard toil it is true, but in the open air, at work they liked and took an inter-est in, and in congenial company. The women, kept close at home with cooking, cleaning, washing, and mending to do, plus their constant pregnancies and a tribe of children to look after, had also the worry of ways and means on an insufficient income.

Many husbands boasted that they never asked their wives what they did with the money. As long as there was food enough, clothes to cover everybody, and a roof over their heads, they were satisfied, they said, and they seemed to make a virtue of this and think what generous, trusting, fine-hearted fellows they were. If a wife got in debt or complained, she was told: 'You must larn to cut your coat accordin' to your cloth, my gal.' The coats not only needed expert cutting, but should have been made of elastic.

On light evenings, after their tea-supper, the men worked for an hour or two in their gardens or on the allotments. They were first-class gardeners and it was their pride to have the earliest and best of the different kinds of vegetables. They were helped in this by good soil and plenty of manure from their pigsties; but good tilling also played its part. They considered keeping the soil constantly stirred about the roots of growing things the secret of success and used the Dutch hoe a good deal for this purpose. The process was called 'tickling'. 'Tickle up old Mother Earth and make her bear!' they would shout to each other across the plots, or salute a busy neighbour in passing with: 'Just tickling her up a bit, Jack?'

The energy they brought to their gardening after a hard day's work in the fields was marvellous. They grudged no effort and seemed never to tire. Often, on moonlight nights in spring, the solitary fork of some one who had not been able to tear himself away would be heard and the scent of his twitch fire smoke would float in at the windows. It was pleasant, too, in summer twilight, perhaps in hot weather when water was scarce, to hear the *swish* of water on parched earth in a garden – water which had been fetched from the brook a quarter of a mile distant. 'It's no good stintin' th' land,' they would say. 'If you wants anything out you've got to put summat in, if 'tis only elbow-grease.' . . .

For a few days or a week or a fortnight, the fields stood 'ripe unto harvest'. It was the one perfect period in the hamlet year. The human eye loves to rest upon wide expanses of pure colour:

the moors in the purple heyday of the heather, miles of green down-land, and the sea when it lies calm and blue and boundless, all delight it; but to some none of these, lovely though they all are, can give the same satisfaction of spirit as acres upon acres of golden corn. *There* is both beauty and bread and the seeds of bread for future generations . . .

In the fields where the harvest had begun all was bustle and activity. At that time the mechanical reaper with long, red, revolving arms like windmill sails had already appeared in the locality; but it was looked upon by the men as an auxiliary, a farmers' toy; the scythe still did most of the work and they did not dream it would ever be superseded. So while the red sails revolved in one field and the youth on the driver's seat of the machine called cheerily to his horses and women followed behind to bind the corn into sheaves, in the next field a band of men would be whet-ting their scythes and mowing by hand as their fathers had done before them.

With no idea that they were at the end of a long tradition, they still kept up the old country custom of choosing as their leader the tallest and most highly skilled man amongst them, who was then called 'King of the Mowers'. For several harvests in the 'eighties they were led by the man known as Boamer. He had served in the Army and was still a fine, well-set-up young fellow with flashing white teeth and a skin darkened by fiercer than English suns.

With a wreath of poppies and green bindweed trails around his wide, rush-plaited hat, he led the band down the swathes as they mowed and decreed when and for how long they should halt for 'a breather' and what drinks should be had from the yellow stone jar they kept under the hedge in a shady corner of the field. They did not rest often or long; for every morning they set themselves to accomplish an amount of work in the day that they knew would tax all their powers till long after sunset. 'Set yourself more than you can do and you'll do it' was one of their maxims, and some of their feats in the harvest field astonished themselves as well as the onlooker.

Old Monday, the bailiff, went riding from field to field on his long-tailed, grey pony. Not at that season to criticize, but rather to encourage, and to carry strung to his saddle the hooped and handled miniature barrel of beer provided by the farmer.

One of the smaller fields was always reserved for any of the women who cared to go reaping. Formerly all the able-bodied women not otherwise occupied had gone as a matter of course; but, by the 'eighties, there were only three or four, beside the regular field women, who could handle the sickle. Often the Irish harvesters had to be called in to finish the field . . .

After the mowing and reaping and binding came the carrying, the busiest time of all. Every man and boy put his best foot forward then, for, when the corn was cut and dried it was imperative to get it stacked and thatched before the weather broke. All day and far into the twilight the yellow-and-blue painted farm wagons passed and repassed along the roads between the field and the stack-yard. Big cart-horses returning with an empty wagon were made to gallop like two-year-olds. Straws hung on the roadside hedges and many a gatepost was knocked down through hasty driving. In the fields men pitchforked the sheaves to the one who was building the load on the wagon, and the air resounded with *Hold tights* and *Wert ups* and *Who-o-oas*. The *Hold tight!* was no empty cry; sometimes, in the past, the man on top of the load had not held tight or not tight enough. There were tales of fathers and grandfathers whose necks or backs had been broken by a fall from a load, and of other fatal accidents afield, bad cuts from scythes, pitchforks passing through feet, to be followed by lockjaw, and of sunstroke; but, happily, nothing of this kind happened on that particular farm in the 'eighties.

At last, in the cool dusk of an August evening, the last load was brought in, with a nest of merry boys' faces among the sheaves on the top, and the men walking alongside with pitchforks on shoulders. As they passed along the roads they shouted:

Harvest home! Harvest home!
Merry, merry, merry harvest home!

and women came to their cottage gates and waved, and the few passers-by looked up and smiled their congratulations. The joy and pleasure of the labourers in their task well done was pathetic, considering their very small share in the gain. But it was genuine enough; for they still loved the soil and rejoiced in their own work and skill in bringing forth the fruits of the soil, and harvest home put the crown on their year's work.

As they approached the farm-house their song changed to:

Harvest home! Harvest home!
Merry, merry, merry harvest home!
Our bottles are empty, our barrels won't run,
And we think it's a very dry harvest home.

and the farmer came out, followed by his daughters and maids with jugs and bottles and mugs, and drinks were handed round amidst general congratulations. Then the farmer invited the men to his harvest home dinner, to be held in a few days' time, and the adult workers dispersed to add up their harvest money and to rest their weary bones. The boys and youths, who could never have too much of a good thing, spent the rest of the evening circling the hamlet and shouting 'Merry, merry, merry harvest home!' until the stars came out and at last silence fell upon the fat rickyard and the stripped fields.

On the morning of the harvest home dinner everybody prepared themselves for a tremendous feast, some to the extent of going without breakfast, that the appetite might not be impaired. And what a feast it was! Such a bustling in the farm-house kitchen for days beforehand; such boiling of hams and roasting of sirloins; such a stacking of plum puddings, made by the Christmas recipe;

such a tapping of eighteen-gallon casks and baking of plum loaves would astonish those accustomed to the appetites of to-day. By noon the whole parish had assembled, the workers and their wives and children to feast and the sprinkling of the better-to-do to help with the serving. The only ones absent were the aged bedridden and their attendants, and to them, the next day, portions, carefully graded in daintiness according to their social standing, were carried by the children from the remnants of the feast. A plum pudding was considered a delicate compliment to an equal of the farmer; slices of beef or ham went to the 'bettermost poor'; and a ham-bone with plenty of meat left upon it or part of a pudding or a can of soup to the commonalty.

Long tables were laid out of doors in the shade of a barn, and soon after twelve o'clock the cottagers sat down to the good cheer, with the farmer carving at the principal table, his wife with her tea urn at another, the daughters of the house and their friends circling the tables with vegetable dishes and beer jugs, and the grandchildren, in their stiff, white, embroidered frocks, dashing hither and thither to see that everybody had what they required. As a background there was the rickyard with its new yellow stacks and, over all, the mellow sunshine of late summer.

Passers-by on the road stopped their gigs and high dog-carts to wave greetings and shout congratulations on the weather. If a tramp looked wistfully in, he was beckoned to a seat on the straw beneath a rick and a full plate was placed on his knees. It was a picture of plenty and goodwill.

It did not do to look beneath the surface. Laura's father, who did not come into the picture, being a 'tradesman' and so not invited, used to say that the farmer paid his men starvation wages all the year and thought he made it up to them by giving that one good meal. The farmer did not think so, because he did not think at all, and the men did not think either on that day; they were too busy enjoying the food and the fun.

After the dinner there were sports and games, then dancing in the home paddock until twilight, and when, at the end of the day, the farmer, carving indoors for the family supper, paused with his knife poised to listen to the last distant 'Hooray!' and exclaimed, 'A lot of good chaps! A lot of good chaps, God bless 'em!' both he and the cheering men were sincere, however mistaken.

Flora Thompson, Lark Rise to Candleford

THE VALE OF THE WYLYE[29]

It is a green valley – the greenness strikes one sharply on account of the pale colour of the smooth, high downs on either side – half a mile to a mile in width, its crystal current showing like a bright serpent for a brief space in the green, flat meadows, then vanishing again among the trees. So many are the great shade trees, beeches and ashes and elms, that from some points the valley has the appearance of a continuous wood – a contiguity of shade. And the wood hides the villages, at some points so effectually that looking down from the hills you may not catch a glimpse of one and imagine it to be a valley where no man dwells. As a rule you do see something of human occupancy – the red or yellow roofs of two or three cottages, a half-hidden grey church tower, or column of blue smoke, but to see the villages you must go down and look closely, and even so you will find it difficult to count them all. I have tried, going up and down the valley several times, walking or cycling, and have never succeeded in getting the same number on two occasions. There are certainly more than twenty, without counting the hamlets, and the right number is probably something between twenty-five and thirty, but I do not want to find out by studying books and maps. I prefer to let the matter remain unsettled so as to have the pleasure of counting or trying to count them again at some future time. But I doubt that I shall ever succeed. On one occasion I caught sight of a quaint, pretty little church standing by itself in the middle of a green meadow, where it looked very solitary with no houses in sight and not even a cow grazing near it. The river was between me and the church, so I went up-stream, a mile and a half, to cross by the bridge, then doubled back to look for the church, and couldn't find it! Yet it was no illusory church; I have seen it again on two occasions, but again from the other side of the river, and I must certainly go back some day in search of that lost church, where there may be effigies, brasses, sad, eloquent inscriptions, and other memorials of ancient tragedies and great families now extinct in the land.

This is perhaps one of the principal charms of the Wylye – the sense of beautiful human things hidden from sight among the masses of foliage. Yet another lies in the character of the villages. Twenty-five or twenty-eight of them in a space of twenty miles; yet the impression left on the mind is that these small centres of population are really few and far between. For not only are they small, but of the old, quiet, now almost obsolete type of village, so unobtrusive as to affect the mind soothingly, like the sight of trees and flowery banks and grazing cattle. The churches, too, as is fit, are mostly small and ancient and beautiful, half-hidden in their tree-shaded churchyards, rich in associations which go back to a time when history fades into myth and legend.

But let us look at the true cottages. There are, I imagine, few places in England where the humble homes of the people have so great a charm. Undoubtedly they are darker inside, and not so convenient to live in as the modern box-shaped, red-brick, slate-roofed cottages, which have spread a wave of ugliness over the country; but they do not offend – they please the eye. They are smaller than the modern-built habitations; they are weathered and coloured by sun and wind and rain and many lowly vegetable forms to a harmony with nature. They appear related to the trees amid which they stand, to the river and meadows, to the sloping downs at the side, and to the sky and clouds over all. And, most delightful feature, they stand among, and are wrapped in, flowers as in a garment – rose and vine and creeper and clematis. They are mostly thatched, but some have tiled roofs, their deep, dark red clouded and stained with lichen and moss; and these roofs, too, have their flowers in summer. They are grown over with yellow stonecrop, that bright cheerful flower that smiles down at you from the lowly roof above the door, with such an inviting expression, so delighted to see you no matter how poor and worthless a person you may be or what mischief you may have been at, that you begin to understand the significance of a strange vernacular name of this plant – Welcome-home-husband-though-never-so-drunk.

But its garden flowers, clustering and nestling round it, amid which its feet are set – they are to me the best of all flowers. These are the flowers we know and remember for ever. The old, homely, cottage-garden blooms, so old that they have entered the soul. The big house garden, or gardener's garden, with everything growing in it I hate, but these I love – fragrant gilly-flower and pink and clove-smelling carnation; wallflower, abundant periwinkle, sweet-william, larkspur, love-in-a-mist, and love-lies-bleeding, old-woman's-nightcap, and kiss-me-John-at-the garden-gate, sometimes called pansy. And best of all and in greatest profusion, that flower of flowers, the marigold.

How the townsman, town born and bred, regards this flower, I do knot know. He is, in spite of all the time I have spent in his company, a comparative stranger to me – the one living creature on the earth who does not greatly interest me. Some over-populated planet in our system discovered a way to relieve itself by discharging its superfluous millions on our globe – a pale people with hurrying feet and eager, restless minds, who live apart in monstrous, crowded camps, like wood ants that go not out to forage for themselves – six millions of them crowded together in one camp alone! I have lived in these colonies, years and years, never losing the sense of captivity, of exile, ever conscious of my burden, taking no interest in the doings of that innumerable multitude, its manifold interests, its ideals and philosophy, its arts and pleasures. What, then, does it matter how they regard this common orange-coloured flower with a strong smell? For me it has an atmosphere, a sense or suggestion of something immeasurably remote and very beautiful – an event, a place, a dream perhaps, which has left no distinct image, but only this feeling unlike all others, imperishable, and not to be described except by the one word Marigold.

But when my sight wanders away from the flower to others blooming with it – to all those which I have named and to the taller ones, so tall that they reach half-way up, and some even quite up, to the eaves of the lowly houses they stand against – hollyhocks and peonies and crystalline white lilies with powdery gold inside, and the common sunflower – I begin to perceive that they all possess something of that same magical quality.

These taller blooms remind me that the evening primrose, long naturalized in our hearts, is another common and very delightful cottage-garden flower; also that here, on the Wylye, there is yet another stranger from the same western world which is fast winning our affections. This is the golden-rod, grandly beautiful in its great, yellow, plume-like tufts. But it is not quite right to call the tufts yellow: they are green, thickly powdered with the minute golden florets. There is no flower in England like it, and it is a happiness to know that it promises to establish itself with us as a wild flower.

Where the village lies low in the valley and the cottage is near the water, there are wild blooms, too, which almost rival those of the garden in beauty – water agrimony and comfrey with ivory-white and dim purple blossoms, purple and yellow loosestrife and gem-like, water forget-me-not; all these mixed with reeds and sedges and water-grasses, forming a fringe or border to the potato or cabbage patch, dividing it from the stream.

W. H. Hudson, *A Shepherd's Life*

THE UNCONSCIOUS ART

The infallible and unconscious art of adjusting buildings to the ground on which they stood has been utterly lost. To see a modern building in the country (unless it has been built by the squire) which so fits into the landscape as to be part of it is as rare as to see a bee-eater, waxwing or golden oriole. The reason goes deep; it is because we no longer live in organic relation with our native land. This contrast is best seen in the winter months when there is no leafage to veil the modern house in its crude heresy against the natural law of fitness to environment. The earth revenges itself for its urban conquest by an unsparing exposure of the gracelessness and irrelevance of houses built of imported materials and unsited. No satirist could reveal the sham and shame of these houses as does the nakedness of the earth on which they have been so blindly set. The conquest of the country by the town is achieved by them, but how barbarous a one the earth shows it to be! Contrast them with the traditional ones that do express an organic relation with their surroundings. The earth is in repose and all colouring is subdued, all tones are modulated to the moods of the wintry skies. The cottages, barns and farmsteads seem to sink into this patient relaxed earth, as though her cloak were thrown over them. They are subdued to earth as earth is to sky. Subdued too in the sense of accepting their limitations by the building of them in the local materials. But from this acceptance springs their variety and individuality.

H. J. Massingham, *Where Men Belong*

THE LABOURER

He seemed the embodiment of the constant fatalistic living thread of our history; that power of quietness in him went back from generation to generation, born of the earliest arts of life, of the inherited intuitive knowledge of the best way to live within the framework of natural law. And it struck me that that something, to which it is difficult to give any name, but which is inherent in the older country labourer's manner – that difference between him and the rest of England to-day – ought to be my theme. This is a thing quite apart from 'morality', inability to spell correctly, or whatever is termed narrow-mindedness. Whatever we are gaining in bath-rooms and panel dentistry, we are without doubt losing something much less easily classified. One may call it individual authority, personal sanction for living; at any rate, it is a thing of humble beginnings, of a knowledge of process and of natural law. It is something about a countryman that is like the weather, something that, in a word with him on the commonest subject, gives you a vista of generations. The spark of true culture is there, which has fed the language, the music and all the arts of English life. It is a mistake to think that these gifts fall like manna out of heaven – they flow up to us from what is considered (since we became divided into 'classes') the lowest stratum in our social system. It may be a matter of paradox, but there is no need to stress the illiterate man's power of expression. His life has been a hard one, materially a grotesque anomaly with industrial 'prosperity' – yet in conditions of poverty and degradation we find the same steady power.

His life in the open air, the domestic arts that his cottage sheltered, have been the making of the English countryside as we know it . . . Merrie England is not a matter of surmise; there is first-hand evidence of that genius which enclosures maimed and industrialism killed. Before the tension of competitive money-making, of the need to support a certain social standard of amenity, paralysed the individual life; before water and heat became commodities and the machine departmentalised and insulated vocations one from another; before the grooves of specialisation became so deep that the mind was blinkered and ran in one track, the knowledge of a craft gave a man intuitively a power of judgment over all other branches of life. Because the basic arts of life were homogeneous. Broadcasting, swift communications, give an illusory appearance of unification; they mask the real dispersion of mind that is taking place, the insulation of man from man.

Adrian Bell, Introduction to *The Open Air*

3

LIVING AT WORK: CRAFTS AND SKILLS

INTRODUCTION

The farm labourer enjoyed his work; there is abundant testimony
for that. Even though he was not working for himself, he was
part of a self-explanatory and acceptable order when he was in
employment. The range of jobs on a farm and the round of the
seasons ensured variety; the most wearisome of tasks did not go
on indefinitely. Labelled 'unskilled', he had in fact to exercise a
good number of skills to survive. Incompetence in broadcast
sowing, scything, loading, rick-making, knotting straw and
making straw ropes, thatching, wood-cutting and sometimes
building drystone walls, quickly showed its wasteful results.
Skill and the wit to profit by traditional knowledge enabled the
village carpenter to drill a tree trunk along its length, for a well;
to make the slightly curved rafters needed for roofs; to build
staircases; and to make for the mills large spur wheels, each with
120 mortices for cogs. Other crafts similarly involved an intimate
knowledge of the neighbourhood – the materials it yielded and
the requirements it imposed – the ability to apply ancient tech-
niques, and dexterity with tools, as extensions of the worker's
self. Sturt has much to say about tools. Expatiating on the wealth
of associations evoked by a hundred-year-old device for digging
potatoes, he concludes, 'Those who use such tools do not stop to
admire the summer, they co-operate with it.' He learned himself
to use one 'with a kind of gratitude for its uses', and watching a
man at work he writes: 'I began to recognise once more the

health-giving influence of working with tools. As the workman gets deeper and deeper into the fibre of materials, strength comes back to him from them: it is a re-assertion of his "animal" life, even as the touch of one's knuckles on the boarding, or in the wayside grass' (*Journals*, p. 765). Wordsworth agreed; he extols them not only for their products, but also because they cut out 'the impertinent and ceaseless strife of proofs and reasons' (*Excursion* v, 601-21).

Walter Rose the carpenter often insists on the harmony of tool and use; and as frequently he stresses the beauty of work in tune with the countryside and a part of the latter's own comeliness. Beauty stemmed first from utility: the chamfering of a waggon's timbers to secure lightness added grace; the tapering of the top of a gate for strength where most needed pleased the eye (cf. Edward Thomas in *The Heart of England*: 'the beautiful five-barred gates, with their noble top bars, tapered and shaped like a gunstock and barrel'); the functional shape of a pot that is now something prized by collectors, and so on. The conditions of necessity, in the words of Sturt's *Journals* 'the frictions and strains and stresses which are the inexorable lawgivers to all crafts, in all time', produced what Rose in *The Village Carpenter* called 'the hallmark of the craftsman, the little touch of beauty engraved on the article of utility'. Next came the addition of some feature just for the pleasure it gave, such as the ornamentation of the top of a wooden pump: 'No pump', he wrote, 'was every made in our yard without this slight touch of beauty carved on its side – the edict of sentiment handed down over the centuries from ancient woodworkers to be faithfully preserved and reproduced.' Ornaments on ricks, the scroll on a gate, combing on a pot, are finishing touches that grew out of function, completing the basic design – examples of the traditional unconscious arts, the folk song and the folk music 'that are indigenous in most peoples and wither away before culture and civilisation' (Sturt, *Journals*, p. 247).

The example of folk song reminds one that in England and

Scotland at least song was rooted in the getting of a living, an integral part of life. 'Every event and occasion was celebrated [Alfred Williams wrote] . . . they left nothing untouched, and no part of life unreflected or unrepresented' (*Folk-Songs of the Upper Thames*). Flora Thompson is another witness:

Most of the men sang or whistled as they dug or hoed. There was a good deal of outdoor singing in those days. Workmen sang at their jobs; men with horses and carts sang on the road; the baker, the miller's men, and the fish-hawker sang as they went from door to door; even the doctor and parson on their rounds hummed a tune between their teeth. People were poorer and had not the comforts, amusements, or knowledge we have today; but they were happier.

Lark Rise to Candleford

Thomas Hennell, writing fifty years ago, says that 'some sheep-shearing songs, such as "Old Job", still exist in the memories of the older farmers and labourers here and there, but with the decline of the old ritual at sheepshearing festivals they are remembered only in a casual fragmentary way'. The ox-man, he adds, 'had three or four songs which he sang continually over and over again; and when he stopped singing, the oxen stood still in their tracks '(*Change in the Farm*). In Scotland it was the business of the 'gaudsman' to encourage the team of oxen by whistling. Hennell again tells us that the 'bagster' used to keep up a song as he stamped or danced the hops into a sack. Williams lists a number of such occupational songs, and describes at length the singing matches that took place in wet weather, when outdoor work was at a standstill.

Williams and others have also remarked the common error of 'imagining that the inhabitants of a locality are incapable of appreciating their ballads and songs', and later assures us that the taste for good things still remains; 'the wonderful taste of the rustic population' was evident in the kind of flowers they grew, their furniture, and their songs. Sturt however noted that by his time the 'peasant taste for beautiful things' was dying out (*Journals*,

p. 569); and a generation later, as H. J. Massingham records, it had disappeared: 'What suffered most visibly was the inborn aesthetic faculty, once a common possession of all countrymen. Almanacs for samplers, the "Present from Brighton" for willow pattern, novelettes for the Bible, Richardson and travel books, coarse, machined embroidery for point-lace, cheap shoddy for oak and mahogany' (Introduction to *Lark Rise* ...). When Sturt wrote in the *Journals* that 'From production for *use*, there would arise delight, instead of indifference, and instead of ugliness, art', he was, up to a point, echoing William Morris, who saw that the split between art and labour was at the core of the degradation inflicted by industry; art (and readers of Sturt will add 'and a good deal else in the way of cultural value') was now divorced from the ordinary world of men. Conversely, 'The more I think of art (in its modern sense, i.e. divorced from necessary labour) the more puzzled I get to know what it is, and why people do it, or buy it.' He did not commit himself to the view, apparently held by Morris, that given machine-made leisure and other advantages, men would take to producing and enjoying art. A generation later Eric Gill restated the position:

These necessary works (food, clothing, shelter and entertainment) have hitherto been man's chief means to the very thing which he is now expected to gain without doing them, namely culture – the knowledge and love of HIGHER THINGS. Hitherto the vast majority of men have gained such culture as they have gained (and it has often been both great and high) by cultivating the arts of agriculture and gardening; cooking and making drinks; weaving and spinning and dressmaking; pottery, metal working, and wood working; building in all its multitude of branches (from chicken coops to cathedrals); and every kind of dance and song and music and poetry. Henceforth these things are not to be man's means to culture. He is to gain culture in his spare time, not by the practice of these multifarious and necessary arts, because being necessary they will all be done or supplied by machines.

Unemployment (a pamphlet) (1933)

The passages that follow show that, when not unemployed or brutally driven, both those who worked on the farm and those who supplied its wants enjoyed their work, because it brought into play many of the qualities that make up a human being. They lived as they worked. All exercised skill, learned a craft or two, and used their muscles to some purpose; all found their creative impulses satisfied. As Sturt and others have recorded, much more accrued to the worker than a livelihood. What they needed, their work provided; they did not want leisure, because they did not know the meaning of the word. After a long hard day's work, they could come home and ardently cultivate their gardens. The only art they knew was that which formed part of their lives, and they needed no other. In the words of Sturt's *Journals*, 'people who know what the crops mean have small use for the interpretations of art'.

H

THE WHEELWRIGHTS' WAY OF LIFE

Buying

One aspect of the death of Old England and of the replacement of the more primitive nation by an 'organised' modern state was brought out forcibly and very disagreeably by the War against Germany. It was not only that one saw the beautiful fir-woods going down, though that was bad. The trees, cut into lengths, stripped of their bark and stacked in piles, gave to many an erst secluded hill-side a staring publicity. This or that quiet place, the home of peace, was turned into a ghastly battle-field, with the naked and maimed corpses of trees lying about. Bad enough, all this was. Still, trees might grow again; the hollows might recover their woodland privacy and peace for other generations to enjoy. But what would never be recovered, because in fact War had found it already all but dead, was the earlier English understanding of timber, the local knowledge of it, the patriarchal traditions of handling it. Of old there had been a close relationship between the tree-clad country-side and the English who dwelt there. But now, the affection and the reverence bred of this – for it had been with something near to reverence that a true provincial beheld his native trees – was all but gone. A sort of greedy prostitution desecrated the ancient woods. All round me I saw and heard of things being done with a light heart that had always seemed to me wicked – things as painful to my sympathies as harnessing a carriage-horse to a heavy dray, or as pulling down a cathedral to get building-stone. I resented it; resented seeing the fair timber callously felled at the wrong time of year, cut up too soon, not 'seasoned' at all. Perhaps the German sin had made all this imperative; yet it was none the less hateful. Not as waste only was it hateful: it was an outrage on the wisdom of our forefathers – a wanton insult put upon Old England, in her woods and forests.

The new needs were so different from the old. What had been prized once was prized no more. The newer vehicles, motor-drawn, were not expected to last longer than eight or ten years at the most; five years, oftener, found them obsolete, and therefore durability was hardly considered in the timber used for their construction. But it was otherwise in the earlier time, in the old-fashioned wheelwright's shop. Any piece of work had to last for years. Fashion, or invention, didn't affect it. So it was held a shame to have to do work twice over because the original material had been faulty; and I have known old-fashioned workmen refuse to use likely-looking timber because they held it to be unfit for the job.

And they knew. The skilled workman was the final judge. Under the plane (it is little used now) or under the axe (it is all but obsolete) timber disclosed qualities hardly to be found otherwise. My own eyes know because my own hands have felt, but I cannot teach an outsider, the difference between ash that is 'tough as whipcord,' and ash that is 'frow as a carrot,' or 'doaty,' or 'biscuity.' In oak, in beech, these differences are equally plain, yet only to those who have been initiated by practical work. These know how 'green timber' (that is, timber with some sap left in it, imperfectly 'seasoned') does not look like properly dried timber, after planing. With axe or chisel or draw-shave they learn to distinguish between the heart of a plank and the 'sap.' And again, after years of attention, but nohow else, timber-users can tell what 'shakes' are good and what bad. For not all shakes, all natural splits, in seasoned timber are injurious. On the contrary it was an axiom in my shop that good timber in drying was bound to 'open' (care had to be taken to prevent it from opening too far) and that timber must be bad, must have lost all its youthful tough-ness, if the process of drying developed no shakes in it.

A wheelwright had to be quite familiar with little truths like these in buying his timber, and then not forget other considera-tions. In my shop we bought trees 'in the round' – as they lay in the wood or the hedgerow where they had been felled or 'thrown'. And, immediately, the season of throwing came into question. Some oak, cut down in the dead of the winter, was called 'winter-cut.' It dried into excellent material, the sap almost as hard, though nothing like so durable, as the heart. Winter-cut oak always had the bark on it. And for this reason it was scarce, and 'spring-cut' was commoner, the bark having a high market-value for tanning. Most oak therefore was thrown early in spring, when the running of the sap allowed the bark to be stripped off easily. A further advantage was that this spring-cut oak lent itself so well to the craft of 'cleaving' spokes and laths.

It followed that the expeditions to buy oak were always in the late spring or the summer. The bark had been stripped then – it stood in big brown stacks beside the shining butter-coloured 'sticks' or butts of timber, where they lay in the brambles and newly springing fern. The 'lop and top' – the branches and twigs – had also been stacked, the bigger branches into cordwood, good for fires, the smaller – the twiggy boughs – into 'bavins' or 'sprays' such as bakers want for their ovens or potters for their kilns. So, the ground was clear enough for the wheelwright to examine his trees, and to measure them if he bought. And a delightful outing he had of it.

For his quest took him into sunny woodland solitudes, amongst unusual things and with country men of a shy type good to meet. It was while looking at some oak (near the Hog's Back) that I first heard the word 'puckeridge,' when a startled bird flitted away into a shady thicket. 'Nasty p'isonous birds,' said the man with me. Another time, as I pushed through some brambles in 'Alice Holt'[30] and came to a patch of spurge (or it may have been a mist of blue-bells), the tall young forester who was showing me the oak-trees suddenly dropped forward his full length without bending; and when he stood up he had got a rabbit in his hands.

Other timber than oak (always, of whatever sort, felled in winter) invited the timber-buyer into the winter woods or along leafless hedgerows. It was in stodging from hedge to hedge across wet water-meadows in February to look at some ash that my father took the chill which started his last illness. Elm was rather a haphazard crop with us: it would keep so long in the round that the season of throwing was not much if at all regarded – though I have seen it 'perished' by its own sap imprisoned in the unopened log. With beech it is just the reverse. During the war vast quantities of beech were spoiled, in the prevailing ignorance when to throw it and open the timber. Spoiled, I mean, for old-fashioned wheelwright work, chiefly in axle-trees. For this purpose beech should be hard as bone, and should therefore be cut down in November (they used to say in my shop) and opened into quarters by Christmas.

Another matter the wheelwright buyer had to know about was the soil the timber grew on. Age-long tradition helped him here. I, for instance, knew from my father's telling, and he perhaps from his father's, that the best beech in the district came from such and such a quarter: that the very limbs from the elm in one park would yield good 'stocks' (hubs for wheels); and that in a certain luxuriant valley the beautiful-looking oaks had grown too fast and when opened were too shaky to be used. Yet I didn't know (and paid for not knowing) that on the clay, in one hollow of Alice Holt, the oak had a nasty trick of going 'foxy-hearted.' I bought a small 'parcel' of trees there. They looked well enough too in the yard until the winter, when the sawyers began to saw them open. But then – tree after tree, sound at the butt, began about two feet up to disclose the 'foxy' middle, the rusty-looking pith like rotten string or rope running far up. I don't think my father or grandfather would have bought timber from that hollow. They knew 'England' in a more intimate way.

One point further concerned the timber-buyer. The best of trees, thrown at the right time, was after all useless if it could not for any reason be hauled up on to timber-carriage, or swung under 'nib' or 'timber-bob' (the same thing), for bringing home to the

saw-pit. So it behoved the wheelwright buyer to refuse if, as sometimes happened, a tree had fallen in an inaccessible place. In steep
hanger, or over shelving stream-banks, it might be impossible to
place the skids from ground to wheel-top for rolling the tree up
on to the 'carriage.' Running-chains and horse-power availed nothing then. The tree must rot where it lay. A slighter difficulty
was a very miry road. The broadest wheels were not always broad
enough to save the heavily-laden timber-carriage from sinking
inextricably into a very soft surface. If the buyer of the tree could
wait for dry weather, well and good. But what if the sawyers
should have finished for him and gone away while his trees were
stuck in the mud? These things had to be considered.

When the bargain was settled it remained to measure the timber
– a pleasant and interesting job. To get the string between tree
and ground (I never found a 'tape' measure of any use) I had a
'needle' or 'sword' – a slender and curved rod of iron – to push
under the tree. At its end the needle was forged into a small hook
like a button hook, and the looped string was then easily drawn
back and so the circumference of the tree was taken. From that,
to the 'girt', allowing for the thickness of the bark, and then (with
slide-rule) calculating how many cubic feet of timber the tree
held, was child's play. I liked it well, clambering over the prone
tree-stems, amongst foxgloves and ferns perhaps. To guess the
'misure' of a tree, before actually taking its 'misure' – that in itself
was a game. And, afterwards, the timber-carter liked to be told
what the 'meetins' were – what was the average size of the trees
he was sending his horses out to bring home.

Kindly feeling

I should soon have been bankrupt in business in 1884 if the public
temper then had been like it is now – grasping, hustling, competitive. But then no competitor seems to have tried to hurt me. To
the best of my remembrance people took a sort of benevolent
interest in my doings, put no difficulties in my way, were slow to

take advantage of my ignorance. Nobody asked for an estimate – indeed there was a fixed price for all the new work that was done. The only chance for me to make more profit would have been by lowering the quality of the output; and this the temper of the men made out of the question. But of profits I understood nothing. My great difficulty was to find out the customary price. The men didn't know. I worked out long lists of prices from the old ledgers, as far as I could understand their technical terms.

Commercial travellers treated me well – Sanders from Auster & Co., Bryant from Simpson's, Dyball from Nobles & Hoare. The last-named, I remember, fearing that I was in danger of over-stocking, could hardly be persuaded to book an order for four gallons of varnish, when he was expecting it to be for only two gallons. It was not until customers had learnt to be shy of my book-learned ignorance, my simplicity, my Ruskinian absurdi-ties, that they began to ask for estimates, or to send their work elsewhere.

The steadiness of the men was doubtless what saved me from ruin. Through them I felt the weight of the traditional public attitude towards industry. They possibly (and properly) exagger-ated the respect for good workmanship and material; and I cannot blame them if they slowed down in pace. Workmen even to-day do not understand what a difference this may make to an employer. The main thing after all (and the men in my shop were faithful to it) was to keep the business up to a high level, preserving the reputation my father and grandfather had won for it. To make it pay – that was not their affair. Certainly they taught me how to be economical, in 'lining-out' the timber and so on; but the time came when I found it needful to curb their own extravagance, scheming all sorts of ways, for instance, to get three shafts out of a plank, where a too fastidious workman would have cut only two. It rarely happened the other way about, rarely happened that the condemnation of a piece of timber came from me; but it did happen, not infrequently, that a disgusted workman would refuse to use what I had supplied to him.

In this temper the shop, I feel sure, turned out good work. Especially the wheels which George Cook used to make were, I am bound to think, as good as any that had been built under the eyes of two experts like my father and his father. Cook, it is pretty sure, took his own time; but what a workman he was! There was another wheelwright in the shop whose wife used to take out garden produce in a little van: and when the van wanted new wheels, this man would not make them himself but asked that George Cook might make them. Truly, it was a liberal education to work under Cook's guidance. I never could get axe or plane or chisel sharp enough to satisfy him; but I never doubted, then or since, that his tiresome fastidiousness over tools and handiwork sprang from a knowledge as valid as any artist's. He knew, not by theory, but more delicately, in his eyes and fingers. Yet there were others almost his match – men who could make the wheels, and saw out on the saw-pit the other timbers for a dung-cart, and build the cart and paint it – preparing the paint first; or, if need be, help the blacksmith tyring the wheels. And two things are notable about these men. Of the first, indeed, I have already given some hint: it is, that in them was stored all the local lore of what good wheelwright's work should be like. The century-old tradition was still vigorous in them. They knew each customer and his needs; understood his carters and his horses and the nature of his land; and finally took a pride in providing exactly what was wanted in every case. So, unawares, they lived as integral parts in the rural community of the English. Overworked and underpaid, they none the less enjoyed life, I am sure. They were friends, as only a craftsman can be, with timber and iron. The grain of the wood told secrets to them.

The other point is, that these men had a special bond of comfort in the regard they felt for my own family. This was of old standing. Consideration had been shown to them – a sort of human thought-

THE WHEELWRIGHTS' WAY OF LIFE 221

fulness – for very long. My grandfather, I heard more than once, wanting to arrange his wayzgoose[31] for Christmas, had been careful not to fix it for the same day as the wayzgoose at Mason's, the carpenter's, but to have it so that the sawyers, who worked for both firms, could attend both feasts. My father had been habitually considerate. 'The men' sought his advice as if they were his trusting children. He and his brothers had all mastered the trade: they were looked up to as able workmen; they always chose the hardest work for themselves. It was my father who was furnaceman at 'shoeing' (putting the iron tyres on the wheels); who sharpened the pit-saws, acted as 'striker' to the smiths for special jobs, stacked the timber – never spared himself. Thanks largely to him a sort of devotion to the whole family had grown up in the shop, and in time was of incalculable help to me, all inexperienced. For some years I was called familiarly by my Christian name; and when at last it was more usual to hear myself called 'the guv'ner,' still something like affection followed me; not because I was an able workman (I had had no apprenticeship for that), but because I was heir to a tradition of friendly behaviour to 'the men.' Older than myself though most of them were, while all were abler, they seemed to me often like a lot of children – tiresome children sometimes. And still they came to me for help and advice, in their own small business difficulties.

Waggons

Long after the peaceful period these chapters deal with, I was really pained at the sight of an old farm-waggon being trundled along with a load of bricks towards what had been a quiet country place on the Surrey and Hampshire border. It was bad enough for bricks to be going there at all – to desecrate some ancient heath or woodland or field. Too plainly Old England was passing away; villas were coming, the day of farm-waggons was done. Here was this stately implement forced, like the victim of an implacable conqueror, to carry the materials for its own undoing. No circumstance of tyranny was omitted. Ignominy was piled upon ignominy. I felt as if I were watching a slave subjected to insult and humiliation. It was not so much that bricks were out of place. True, the delicate lines of the waggon-timbers had been shaped for other uses – for hay or for corn-sheaves, or flour-sacks or roots – but waggons have been used for 'brick-cart' often enough, and no wrong done. But here the shame seemed emphasised by the tractor. Instead of quiet beautiful cart-horses, a little puffing steam-engine was hurrying this captive along, faster than ever farm-waggon was designed to go. The shafts had been removed – as when Samson was mutilated to serve the ends of his masters – and although I couldn't see it, I knew only too well how the timbers would be trembling and the axles fretting at the speed of this unwonted toil. I felt as if pain was being inflicted; as if some quiet old cottager had been captured by savages and was being driven to work on the public road.

Very likely it was silly to feel so keenly as I felt then for a dead thing, and yet – the truth is, farm-waggons had been adapted, through ages, so very closely to their own environment that, to understanding eyes, they really looked almost like living organisms. They were so exact. Just as a biologist may see, in any limpet, signs of the rocky shore, the smashing breakers, so the provincial wheelwright could hardly help reading, from the waggon-lines, tales of haymaking and upland fields, of hilly roads and lonely woods and noble horses, and so on. The age-long effort of Englishmen to fit themselves close and ever closer into England was betokened in my old farm-waggon; and this the little puffing steam-tractor seemed to flout.

But where begin to describe so efficient an organism, in which all the parts interacted until it is hard to say which was modified first, to meet which other? Was it to suit the horses or the ruts, the loading or the turning, that the front wheels had to have a diameter of about four feet? Or was there something in the average height of a carter, or in the skill of wheel-makers, that fixed these dimensions? One only knew that, by a wonderful compromise, all these points had been provided for in the country tradition of fore-wheels for a waggon. And so all through. Was it to suit these same wheels that the front of a waggon was slightly curved up, or was that done in consideration of the loads, and the circumstance merely taken advantage of for the wheels? I could not tell. I cannot tell. I only know that in these and a hundred details every well-built farm-waggon (of whatever variety) was like an organism, reflecting in every curve and dimension some special need of its own country-side, or, perhaps, some special difficulty attending wheelwrights with the local timber.

Already, indeed, when I entered the business, the heyday of waggon-building was over and that decline had set in from which the old craft is now wellnigh dead. In details to be discussed in another chapter, the new wheels of 1884 were made more cheaply than of old: for the countryman was growing so commercial that he would not – perhaps could not – afford to have work done with a single eye to its effectiveness. So with the waggon-bottoms. Just before my time a change for the worse had been introduced. The floors were now cross-boarded, although . . . the costlier long-boarding had been a more useful if not a stronger device. This, as I say, was giving way to something cheaper. The earlier adjustments, which in fact had given the beauty as of an organism, were being neglected. Yet this neglect did not, could not, spread far. For years the old country traditions of waggon-building continued to be faithfully followed. Details which might not be cheapened still achieved the superb adjustments, and waggons grew into beauty, not to please artists who gushed about them, but to satisfy carters and to suit the exigencies of field and crop and road.

'Jobbing'

Those who had been duly apprenticed were wont to say, in my shop, that a man learnt more as an 'Improver,' in the first twelve months after his apprenticeship was over, than in all the six or seven years of 'serving his time.' Although there may have been some swank about this, I think there was some truth too. It was not only that an improver was liable to be discharged, and had to try at last to work well, if he had never tried before. This was what the skilled men chiefly meant, and it was true. A youth, turning from apprentice to improver, must now prove his worth or 'get the sack.' But more than this: experienced judgment was called for in many jobs that an apprentice could hardly be trusted to do, and this the elder men understood. The case was probably the same in other trades. A watch-maker assured me that, while it was comparatively easy for a youth at a technical school to learn how to make a new watch, the test of a true workman was at the repairing bench. Certainly this applied to wheelwrights. A machine could turn out a wheel – of sorts – but to mend one required, in many cases, long experience. Because this was so, I learnt to dislike employing either an old pensioner from the army or a young boy from a technical class. The soldier (besides being usually out of the habit of steady work) could not bring any experience of his own to bear and was afraid to move without orders. The army had killed his initiative. The boy, on the other hand, with no experience at all, was wont to think he already knew enough. He would not be told, and he was too vain to learn the lessons constantly coming from repairs.

From repairs, in fact, came the teaching which kept the wheelwrights' art strongly alive. A lad might learn from older workmen all about the tradition – all that antiquity had to teach – but at repairs he found out what was needful for the current day; what this road required, and that hill; what would satisfy Farmer So-and-So's temper, or suit his pocket; what the farmer's carter favoured or his team wanted. While 'new-work' was largely controlled by proven theories and by well-tried fashions, on the other hand repairs called for ingenuity, adaptiveness, readiness to make shift. It wasn't quite enough to know how to do this or that; you needed also to know something about why, and to be ready to think of alternative dodges for improvising a temporary effect, if for any reason the time-honoured methods known to an apprentice could not be adopted.

You had to be prepared to cope with queer and inconvenient accidents – if a horse ran away and snapped a shaft, or turned a cart over, or if a tyre came off a wheel. Sometimes a message would come that a waggon-axle had broken asunder out at Where-is-it, a mile away, or Farmer What's-his-Name would send asking for a man because a dung-cart wheel was jammed and would not go round. In such cases, and their variety was legion, an apprentice would have been helpless. Nor would it do to send an army pensioner too timid to do the smallest detail without instructions. What was wanted was an experienced man, sure of himself and well versed in the use of odd apparatus and handy tackle for emergencies.

Such a man going to 'pick-up' a break-down – a waggon on the road, say, with a wheel run off – would know what to take with him – a screw-jack, a 'chopping-block' or two, several levers, an old wheel, perhaps a handful of oak wedges, one or two sledge-hammers – for it might well be that all these things would be wanted. And, reaching the break-down, he would know how to lever it to the road-side out of the way of other traffic, and how to scotch-up one side of it safely while he worked on the other side. With none of the conveniences of the shop at hand, he could improvise a bench, a vice. The road was his 'wheel-block.' A stone might serve a useful turn.

Perhaps the trouble was a cart brought to the shop with a wheel that wanted greasing, that squeaked hideously and seemed likely to catch fire with friction, yet refused to be taken off the arm. 'Coomed-up' the wheelwright would say, possibly instead of gummed-up, but certainly meaning that the old grease, which should have been periodically cleaned away (any old sack would have served), had hardened into solid obstruction round the lynch-pin, or the collar, or the washers. Then the skilled man knew perfectly well how to turn the cart over, how to get his sledge-hammer to work without smashing the wheel, and, when he had got the wheel off, how to burn the old grease away from the axle-arm without spoiling the 'temper' of the case-hardened iron.

Sometimes, in an ignorant attempt to correct 'too much fore-way, a carter had got the stock of a wheel so saturated with grease that the oak wedges no longer held and the cast-iron box, grown loose, had worn away too large a hole through the centre of the wheel. It fell to the wheelwright, then, first to fill up the superflu-ous space round the box; next, so to drive in new wedges that they would hold in spite of the grease; and, lastly, to find out what had been the origin of the mischief and to put it right. The employer had many other things to see to and could not always give personal attention to every one of these details. An experienced and self-reliant man was wanted.

While problems like these just instanced were common enough, other repairs, arising out of normal wear and tear, were part of the daily routine of the shop. This or that piece of iron-work, or of wood-work, had fairly worn out, or had been damaged and needed replacing. This it was especially that kept the ancient traditions still young and vigorous. For here the workman – whose apprenticeship had but brought him into contact with a skilled senior – came into contact with the forces of weather, of sun and rain and frost, of road-grit and horse-strength – the frictions and strains and stresses which are the inexorable law-givers to all crafts, in all time.

Day after day the work from this source – 'jobbing-work' – came to the shop. Often the yard was crowded with carts and waggons brought in for some slight attention; though, to be sure, in bad winter weather whole days would go by when nothing – not so much as a wheelbarrow – came, and I began to wonder what to set the men at. In the first year or two this didn't matter so much. There were spokes to be dressed, felloes 'turned out' by the sawyers to be shaped; the woodmen had enough to do. In after years the purchase of ready-shaped timber made winter a difficult season to get through, as no 'short time' had ever been worked in my shop. The farmers never helped me out, in those circumstances. Truly exasperating it was. Sometimes I knew of a certain cart wanting a new wheel, a certain waggon with the boards worn out, a pair of shafts that would need a new 'bolt' (cross-bar) before they could be used next spring. I knew where these things stood in their sheds, getting covered with dust, and I would suggest to their owners to let me have them now, in a slack time. Yet I don't remember ever getting any work that way.

But, by and by, when spring brought a change of weather and the shop was busy and the yard full, when the farmer wanted his wheel, or his waggon, or his decrepit shafts urgently by next day, then would come peremptory messages, unreasonable demands, to get the job done forthwith or it would be taken away to some other shop. Yet not seldom it happened that, after a job had actually been taken out of its proper turn and the owner notified, it would be left in the yard in the way for a week or two. In summer weather, though, there was not much time for grieving about such things. Every hour brought its fresh job, or saw some old one fetched away. Now and then some member of the staff, acting for me while I was myself busy, would make an inconvenient promise. Then he became unduly urgent about the job he had taken in, wanting to attend to it first. Or he had some favourite customer, or another had tipped him, or he had a fancy for doing this tailboard, that splinter-bar, rather than the wheel I wanted him to repair next. These, however, were but problems of management. They did not affect the problems of wear and tear, which taught more than the apprentice could be shown.

These were so various – each illustrating some detail in the craft – it is hard to choose amongst them. Much might be told about repairs to shafts. Hardly a day passed without some of this. For instance, when a horse was being 'shut-in' (backwards, of course) it was only too liable to set a heavy hind hoof on the fore end of a shaft and cause it to 'spring.' The only thing to do then was to splice the shaft. As this involved taking out the iron-work the opportunity was seized of mending it in the blacksmith's fire before it was put back. Did the hooks want lining? Would the ridge-tie serve another turn, or were its links getting so thin as to make a new ridge-tie necessary? Nothing but experience could instruct one on these matters. It was useful experience again – it taught a lot about shafts – to watch Will Hammond with his tongs, winding and nailing a red-hot 'wroppin-cleat' as he called it – a narrow band of hooping – round each end of a splice. He knew, if you didn't, just where the strength was wanted.

Shafts had to be spliced, sometimes, not because of any break but because, lasting too long, they had actually worn sharp at the points from being dropped down on to the ground so often. It was enough to make you shudder to see a horse shut-in to shafts like that. He had but to stumble sideways and the ash would pierce his shoulder like a sharpened stake. But, though humanity counselled splicing, there were several details to consider. Perhaps it would suffice just to saw off the dangerous end and round-up the stump a little? In no case must the shaft be made so long or so short as to wear into the horse-collar; a consideration that showed why new shafts and shaft-planks were sawed out to a certain length. At the same time it became clear why just that curve was chosen for them. The shafts, having approached the horse's shoulders and collar conveniently close, were better turned away again slightly, just at the very end.

Prices

It has been already explained how, having no other guidance, I priced the work to my customers by my father's and my grand-father's charges, making schedules of figures from an old ledger. This plan was only not quite disastrous because, as also has been explained, there was in fact a local traditional price for new work and new parts, which nobody dared to exceed. This much was painfully proved to me long afterwards. A certain standard cart, I ascertained, was being sold throughout the neighbourhood at less than cost price. Accordingly I tried to get sundry rivals to join me in raising the price. One of these however made the project known to a good customer of mine and succeeded in getting that customer's work away from me. This was one of the many occasions when I should have welcomed pressure from a strong Trade Union, to compel other employers to make the changes I could not introduce alone.

My father had probably known for years how unprofitable some of the trade was. New work, he used to say, did not pay. Even in his time, and under his able management, it was only worth doing at all for the sake of keeping the staff together and getting the 'jobbing' – the repairs; for, as there could be no standard in them, it was still possible to make a profit at jobbing. On the subject of profits other tradesmen in the district were as ignorant and simple as myself. Although Farnham fancied itself a little town, its business was being conducted in the spirit of the village – almost indeed of the mediaeval manor. Men worked to oblige one another. Aldershot was almost as bad; Alton was if possible worse; and the most conservative village in the whole neighbourhood set the rate to which my own trade lived down. I doubt if there was a tradesman in the district – I am sure there was no wheelwright – who really knew what his output cost, or what his profits were, or if he was making money or losing it on any particular job. In later years, after the habit of giving estimates had become common (as it was unknown in 1884), I several times lost work to rivals who, I found out, were working for less than the mere iron and timber were to cost them. They never knew. Nor did they know if on to-morrow's estimate they were to make a fabulous profit. Well on into the present century these matters, in my trade, were settled by guess-work, not by calculation. We knew nothing, thought nothing, of how much we ought to have.

But it was very needful to know how much our customer would pay.

This strange way of conducting business had possibly worked out well enough, say in Queen Anne's time when the shop was founded. In the course of generations errors would get corrected and a reasonable charge standardised. Neighbours, with little or no competition, would find out the fair prices of things and not dream of departing from them. Even in my grandfather's day the traditional prices would often hold good. Then, there were no 'overhead' expenses – rates, fire-insurance, railway carriage, office charges, and so on – to compare with those of the present century. The wages left the employer a good margin. Thus, my grandfather paid but 17s. a week where my father paid 24s. Material cost less.

But by the time I dropped into the business many changes had begun. Some of the old work was growing obsolete, unexampled work was coming into vogue all round. Not only was it that 'The Iron Age' (as already pointed out) was on the move again, after years of quiescence. Better roads, and imported foodstuffs too, broke up the old farm-life on which my shop had waited. Instead of waggons, vans to run twice as fast were wanted, and their springs and brakes and lighter wheels revolutionised the industry my men had taught me. At the same time the break-down of village industries was introducing changes which were reflected in my shop in the shape of butchers' carts and bread-carts – unknown of old – and in brewers' drays and in millers' vans, not to mention vehicles for bricks and other building materials.

While novelties were pouring in upon the trade from one side, on the other side an unexampled competition began to be felt, keeping the prices still low. Things were not as in the pre-railway days. Now, discontented customers would buy 'steam wheels' from London. Lighter wheels than any that could be made in my shop – wheels imported ready-made from America – had to be kept in stock along with the ancient sort of naves and felloes. But

the prices were effectually kept down also by competition of another sort, or rather of a very ancient sort. Dorset villages, Wiltshire villages, entered into the rivalry. Thanks to their lower wages
and rents, and their far less costly timber, places one had never
heard of were able to supply local farmers at so cheap a rate that
it was worth the farmers' while to ignore, or to sacrifice, the advantage of vehicles made locally with a view to local conditions.
The circle of my competitors widened out by hundreds of miles.

In all these circumstances it is not wonderful that the price of
wheelwright's work by no means kept pace with the cost of it.
To tell the truth, the figures in my shop in 1884 (as extracted by
myself from the old books) were not much in excess of those
which Arthur Young found current in the southern counties in
1767.[32] For a waggon the price had risen from about £21 then,
to £29 or £30 in my father's time; but carts, which at the later
date were but £12 or less, had averaged as much as £10 even a
century earlier.

Conceivably a man in so small a way of business as to do much
of his work himself – and this must have been the case with many
a village wheelwright – could make both ends meet even at these
prices, even in 1884; and this the more if he got 'jobbing' work to
keep him going and to confuse his calculations. I knew one man
who threw up a situation he had held for years in a rival's shop –
probably under the impression that it was a profitable thing to be
an employer even without capital; and began building new carts
for a pound or so less than the local price. I am fairly certain that
he kept no accounts to show him how much less his profits amounted to now than his weekly wages had been of old. Perhaps he
never would have known this had there been plenty of repairs for
him to do; but as it was, he had to close-down within twelve
months, being too honest a man to profit by bankruptcy.

In these circumstances it is not surprising that I began at last to
feel a need of some change or other. It is true, I knew nothing
about 'Costing.' Methods for that were not devised until years

later; but, in the simpler things, I did after four or five years – say in 1889 – know well enough that some of the work was not paying its way – was even being done at a loss. Yet too often I saw work going elsewhere which I felt ought to have come to me. And one thing, if not certain, was probable: under my ignorant management the men had grown not so much lazy as leisurely. I knew this but too well; but I did not know how to mend the matter. Too early, indeed, I had realised how impossible it would be to carry out any of the Ruskinian notions, any of the fantastic dreams of profit-sharing, with which I had started. The men in the shop, eaten up with petty jealousies, would not have made any ideals work at all. But to discharge them was not to be thought of. How could I even find fault with those who had taught me what little I knew of the trade and who could but be only too well aware how little that was? Moreover, they were my friends. Business was troublesome enough even on the best of terms, but I could not have found the heart to go on with it all at the cost of the friction which must have come if I had begun trying to 'speed-up' my friends and instructors. Meanwhile, none the less, the trade these friends of mine depended on for a living was slipping away, partly by their own fault.

What was to be done? How long I thought it over is more than I can at all tell now; but eventually – probably in 1889 – I set up machinery: a gas-engine, with saws, lathe, drill and grindstone. And this device, if it saved the situation, was (as was long afterwards plain) the beginning of the end of the old style of business, though it did just bridge over the transition to the motor-trade of the present time.

I suppose it did save the situation. At any rate there was no need for dismissals, and after a year or two there was trade enough – of the more modern kind – to justify my engaging a foreman, whom I ultimately took into partnership. It proved a wise move from every point of view save the point of sentiment. The new head had experience and enterprise enough, without offending the men too, to develop the new commercial side – the manufacture of trade-vans and carts – when the old agricultural side of the business was dying out. Wood-work and iron-work were still on equal terms. Neither my partner nor myself realised at all that a new world (newer than ever America was to the Pilgrim Fathers) had begun even then to form all around us; we neither of us dreamt that the very iron age itself was passing away or that a time was actually near at hand when (as now) it would not be worth any young man's while to learn the ancient craft of the wheelwright or the mysteries of timber-drying. It might be that improved roads and plentiful building were changing the type of vehicles wheelwrights would have to build; but while horses remained horses and hill and valley were hill and valley, would not the old English provincial lore retain its value? We had no provocation to think otherwise, and yet: –

And yet, there in my old-fashioned shop the new machinery had almost forced its way in – the thin end of the wedge of scientific engineering. And from the first day the machines began running, the use of axes and adzes disappeared from the well-known place, the saws and saw-pit became obsolete. We forgot what chips were like. There, in that one little spot, the ancient provincial life of England was put into a back seat. It made a difference to me personally, little as I dreamt of such a thing. 'The Men,' though still my friends, as I fancied, became machine 'hands.' Unintentionally, I had made them servants waiting upon gas combustion. No longer was the power of horses the only force they had to consider. Rather, they were under the power of molecular forces. But to this day the few survivors of them do not know it. They think 'Unrest' most wicked.

Yet it must be owned that the older conditions of 'rest' have in fact all but dropped out of modern industry. Of course wages are higher – many a workman to-day receives a larger income than I was ever able to get as 'profit' when I was an employer. But no higher wage, no income, will buy for men that satisfaction which of old – until machinery made drudges of them – streamed into their muscles all day long from close contact with iron, timber, clay, wind and wave, horse-strength. It tingled up in the niceties of touch, sight, scent. The very ears unawares received it, as when the plane went singing over the wood, or the exact chisel went tapping in (under the mallet) to the hard ash with gentle sound. But these intimacies are over. Although they have so much more leisure men can now taste little solace in life, of the sort that skilled hand-work used to yield to them. Just as the seaman to-day has to face the stoke-hole rather than the gale, and knows more of heat-waves than of sea-waves, so throughout. In what was once the wheelwright's shop, where Englishmen grew friendly with the grain of timber and with sharp tool, nowadays untrained youths wait upon machines, hardly knowing oak from ash or caring for the qualities of either. And this is but one tiny item in the immensity of changes which have overtaken labour through-out the civilised world. The products of work are, to be sure, as important as ever – what is to become of us all if the dockers will not sweat for us or the miners risk their lives? That civilisation may flourish a less-civilised working-class must work. Yet others wonder at working-class 'unrest.' But it remains true that in modern conditions work is nothing like so tolerable as it was say thirty years ago; partly because there is more hurry in it, but largely because machinery has separated employers from employed and has robbed the latter of the sustaining delights which materials used to afford to them. Work is less and less pleasant to do – unless, perhaps, for the engineer or the electrician.

But, leaving these large matters, I would speak of a smaller one. Is there – it is worth asking – such laughter about labour, such fun, such gamesome good temper, as cheered the long hours in my shop in 1884? Are we not taking industry too seriously to be sensible about it? Reading of 'Scientific Management' I recall something quite different from that – something friendly, jolly, by no means scientific – which reached down to my time from an

older England. A mischievous spirit itself freshened one up sometimes. One day there came, knocking at my office-door, an inno-
cent apprentice-boy with a message from the wheelwright who
was teaching him his trade. 'Please sir,' the boy said, 'Mr — sent
me to get a straight hook.' Of course I ought to have been angry
with the man for wasting time in sending the boy off on a fool's
errand, and with the boy for coming to me when he must assuredly
have been sent to the blacksmiths. But in fact I could not be angry.
I sent the boy back. 'Go and tell Mr — if he wants a straight hook
to come and ask me for it himself.'

And though there cannot have been any profit in that trans-
action I have always valued the good temper it betokened all round,
as a product of industry too much overlooked in modern times.
There ought really to be a little fun in work, for the workman's
sake. And I think he will insist on it, even at the cost of a little less
Civilisation for the Employing Classes.

George Sturt, *The Wheelwright's Shop*

RESPONSE TO NEED:
THE CARPENTER'S WORK

The shop

My father's workshop – which still exists – was formerly the stable
of a manorial farmstead. Large banners and festoons of cobweb,
hoary with age and the accumulated dust of years, hung from its
English timber roof. A date, 'Dec. 12th, 1569', was chalked on a
transverse beam; this represented the date when the property was
first acquired by my family, on each anniversary of which my
father treated the men to beer and the lads to minerals. The method
of celebrating the event was much appreciated and it was never
allowed to pass forgotten. Since then the discovery of the actual
purchase deeds has proved that the year is correct, but that the
date was 18 August.

The original stone cobble floor was lined with oak slabs, uneven and slippery with use and always needing repair; these were laid concave side downward and the cavity beneath became filled with sawdust that filtered through the rude joints. Large heavy benches lined the walls, their tops dented and crevassed with age and the wear of many tools, on to which the light, none too good for a workshop, streamed through lead diamond and quarried windows. Each bench was furnished with a screw vice and each man had his regular bench. On the walls were fitted racks for the smaller tools – chisels, gouges and bradawls, etc. – and each saw hung on its special nail.

In the middle of the workshop were double benches made and arranged for two men to work at, one on each side. Rude four-legged stools, always made without nails, their tops scored with hundreds of saw cuts, also formed part of the shop equipment. A strong odour of wood pervaded the place, a mingled scent of newly cut pine, oak and elm; occasionally, but not often, the rather sickly smell of ash was added: this was properly the wheel-wright's wood – our use of it was mostly confined to handles for tools for our own use and for the farms for which we catered.

Very few of our regular men had ever worked for any other master. They had begun, years before my time, as handy men to help in the timber yard, chopping and sawing and doing the more laborious work. As helpers to experienced carpenters they had acquired a knowledge of the craft, finally becoming proficient joiners able to undertake anything that was required and with a permanent bench in the workshop. Each possessed his complete set of tools, jealously prized, cared for, and guarded. Each man to us was part of the firm, his individuality a feature of its sentiment.

From these simple-minded men, I began at fourteen to learn the countryside craft. They taught me how to saw upright and square, with the time-honoured threat of 'hanging a plumb-bob from my nose' when I erred. They taught me the peculiar art of sharpening a saw, the irregular teeth of which were once described as 'sow and pigs'. With infinite patience they showed me how to plane wood straight, square and 'out of wind'; how to drive a nail home without splitting or leaving the indent of the hammer on the face of the wood; the purpose and use of the various tools, the art of sharpening the rounds, hollows, and moulding planes, and the importance of keeping the left hand out of the danger zone when using a chisel, away from any slip that might occur. My neglect of this precaution resulted in a bad cut and a stiff finger joint, which remains stiff as a valuable reminder to this very day.

One of those men – a good joiner – could read but had never learned to write. I often wrote his time for the week, the hours at the different jobs, on a tenon lap. My father never aspired to printed time sheets, and the side-cuttings from tenons were used for that purpose. A little stack of them lay each Saturday on the office table waiting for his pen to strike out the items as he entered them into the books.

But the man who could not write could sharpen a saw from heel to point in graduated perfection as no other man I have ever met. Our men excelled at saw-sharpening, probably from the experience gained at the saw-pit. I have watched them sawing splays – the crucial test of correct sharpening – without the saw once leaving the line. I have seen them saw the pyramidical tops to gate posts absolutely true each side without any finish with the plane being required. The wood they used was not easy to work; much of it was tough English oak and elm, hard with long seasoning; and all the work done to it after it had left the saw-pit was done in the workshop, by labour with the hands.

The work that we executed was closely related to the life of the village, and of the district for a few miles round. There was continual going and coming from the shop to the places for which the work was intended; a few days' work in the shop, making doors, windows, or other fitments for a house or farm, then a period at the place fixing the work, and doing what else was required there.

Thus we were ever in contact with the life of the village, and a necessary part of its communal existence.

No field for miles around but had its gate that sooner or later would need repair: no farmer who did not need his new cow-cribs, sheep-troughs, or ladders. No house, from the vicarage to the labourer's cottage, but had at some time or other a defect in its woodwork for which the services of our men would be required.

Thus the lore of the village became interwoven with the lore of our workshop, which, in fact, was part of the village life, a definite feature inseparable from its conduct; as also were the workshops of the wheelwright, the blacksmith, the saddler, the bootmaker, and the village tailor. But, whereas the wheelwright worked solely at his shop and yard and sent his product away on wheels when finished, our work needed to be carried or carted to its destination, and usually one, or two, or three of us would have to accompany it to fix it in its place. This took us on to the farms and into the homes of the village. Not a house but we knew the run of it, the condition of its structure and the peculiar mentality of the folk that inhabited it. Not a farm but we knew the disposition of the farmer, and many of them – little lords on their small domains – needed some suiting!

Most of our clients had their favourite workman, one who had worked there before and found favour. It was a feature of our business diplomacy to see that favourite men should go again to the same places. The experiences whilst away were brought back and told again over the bench, many of them humorous. 'Tell your master that I think he must be very short of wood', said a woman who was dissatisfied with the amount of repairs to an old bedroom floor. 'I could do the work myself if I had the tools', was the caustic remark of another in her vain endeavour to persuade the workman to do the work in a contrary fashion. 'Here are the tools, Madam', politely answered the man, offering her his kit.

The work we undertook was very varied and included some

regular items that are rarely made by joiners to-day. Who does not remember the joiner-made washing tray of wide yellow pine with splayed sides and ends? Every thrifty wife in our village possessed one, and almost all of them were made in our shop. We kept a small pot of white lead especially for the sealing of their joints; but it was well known that no tray, howsoever well grooved, jointed and sealed, would hold water until it had been soaked for a time. I believe the same is true of tubs and barrels made of wood.

Another item often made was the travelling clothes box. No maid leaving the village for domestic service was properly equipped without her box made by the village carpenter. It was strongly made: it was expected to last a lifetime, and no one dreamed that the time was near when it would be discarded in favour of the tin trunk. The making of such a clothes box was reckoned a day's work; it involved planing all the wood and dovetailing each angle. The finished box was fitted with lock and key and iron handles at each end.

At that period wide yellow pine could be easily obtained of any timber merchant, but afterwards it became increasingly difficult to get and is now rarely used for joinery. It still turns up occasion-ally in old counter tops. Its softness and freedom from tendency to warp makes it a desirable wood for a drawing-board.

As much of our work was done for farms in the district a good proportion of English wood was used in our workshop: oak for gates and posts, elm for mangers and partitions of stables and so on. At the same time imported deal was the wood everywhere used for general joinery work. From far-off countries this timber was brought to our bench for us to transform into articles for the use of mankind. Could those long straight deals have spoken, what stories they might have told of the vast dense forests of Russia, Norway and Sweden, countries of mystery to us that we had never seen, nor hoped to see. It was different with the English wood that oft-times we had helped to fell. We remembered the trees; the places where they had grown from saplings to maturity usually had some association with our lives, and when the plank or board was at length before us its quality would be critically appraised. To us it was a question of responding to the tools. To the woodworker the varied dispositions of woods are almost human: even in the same species they differ, some yielding to his wishes as though glad to co-operate, others stubborn and intractable. The quality of a tree was remembered to the last fragment after the bulk of the log had been used. In any carpenter's yard there are piles of oddments – small pieces left over from many trees – but though they are all mixed up, it is usually remembered from which tree each piece was cut.

English oak, ash, walnut, and elm have qualities of strength, durability and appearance unsurpassed by the same species grown in other parts of the world, but the English fir, our representative of the tree that provides the foreign deal, is of a decidedly inferior quality and is quite unsuitable for joinery, although it serves very useful purposes for rustic work and fences out-of-doors. Foreign deal is therefore a necessity of our national life until such time – if ever it should be – that we learn how to grow the same quality on the hills and dales of England.

For centuries the difficulty of transport hampered the use of foreign deal in our inland towns and villages. Small quantities would doubtless be brought by carrier from the London docks; and this may still be found in the excellent Georgian houses and in works of the Adam order, in wainscot work with large wide panels, and corner cupboards with arched tops and domed interiors, and in the substantial windows of that period with wooden sashes specially made for the newly discovered 'crown', or 'wheel-spun' glass.

But with the construction of canals the imported deal found its way into the heart of England. My father said that at first it was always supplied in large chopped baulks, and that when purchasing them he has walked from one to the other as they lay floating in the canal water. The baulks were sawn at our pit: the outside into joists and rafters, and the inside into floor and other boards. An examination of many houses built at this period will reveal that the rafters have one chopped side.

But when I started work the timber merchants had taken over the preparation of floor-boards and matched boards, which they supplied machine-planed and thicknessed. Thus I escaped their preparation by hand, a monotonous hard job formerly held to be a punishment task for refractory apprentices.

Every joiner will readily grant to the machine-saw the credit of cutting boards straight and of equal thickness, a job not easy for two men to do so well at a pit. The boards that came from the pit to the bench to be prepared for a floor often varied in thickness, and to obtain the equality necessary for a level floor the sash fillister was used as a gauge on each edge, and the boards were levelled across with the chisel only where they would have to rest on the joists; a system that retained the full thickness of wood between the joists, where the strain was greatest.

With the exception of floor-boards and grooved and tongued boards all the joinery for a new house was prepared by hand at the workshop, where not even a hand-morticer existed. The making of 4½ × 3 in. solid outer door frames with oak sills; the preparation of inside door linings and stop fillets; the panel and ledged doors; the solid casement or hollow sliding sash windows, all in rotation were prepared ready for fixing as the house advanced.

The making of a simple four-panel inside door was considered a good day's work. As this involved ripping the 9 × 1½ in. planks down the centre for the styles and the planing and thicknessing of all the wood, it left no time for ease and relaxation. The outside doors to the ordinary house were made to the still well-known orders of 'bead and butt' or 'bead and flush'; in each case the panels are of one-inch board inserted with the face level with the framework. The distinction between 'butt' and 'flush' is that the ornamental bead worked on the panel edges is either butted to the frame or continued all round the panel. Of the two systems the 'butt' is the most weatherproof.

The making of the usual Victorian windows, with hollow frames and sashes to slide up and down with cords and weights, was then a job cherished by the joiner. Each workman aspired to possess his complete set of sash ovolo moulding planes; his sash fillister for taking out the rebates to receive the glass; his brass-ended mitres for fitting the ends of the sash bars; his double-tooth gauge and mortice chisels. In addition, many would keep specially prepared steel scribing blades with points ranged at the exact distance apart for setting out the sashes.

A venerable item of the equipment of our workshop was the 'sticking board', a length of wood, prepared to lie flat on the bench, made with special rebates and grooves to hold the sash bars in each successive stage of preparation. It is still with me, bearing the marks of ancient usage – the scores left by countless bench knives – a relic of old-time craft, to old-time joiners familiar, to the present generation a curiosity.

Work on the farm

Some of my father's men never claimed to be joiners, and rarely worked in the workshop. Theirs was a ruder kind of craft, wood-craft of the open fields, the hillside and the valleys. I have heard such work contemptuously called 'hedge-carpentry'; but the slightest knowledge would convince anyone of its value, and a little reflection would also reveal that it constituted art, in its natural, simple state.

It always appealed to me. I did not pause to reason why, but now I recognise that the work these men did was in perfect harmony with the spirit of earth, closely allied to nature and quite free from hard and fast convention. The beauty of it was that these men had never learned what is termed the higher order of the carpenter's craft. They continued to work on primitive lines, with the axe and saw, and a few other elementary tools.

Thus they had never become enslaved to line and level; their minds had not been trained to revolt if their work deviated from the square, or if it was slightly on the twist and the faces of their joints not absolutely flush. They themselves made no claim to art – I doubt if they knew the meaning of the word. But the work they did was part of the beauty of the countryside; the cleft fence-rails and posts split from oak saplings, with the bark left on in places, and the rough knots trimmed with axe or drawing knife.

From a distance I have seen them at work repairing the gates and fences of the broad open field, a herd of cows looking on. Old Johnnie up to his hips in a deep post-hole from which he was heaving large spits of earth; Old Enoch spiking a big stoop on to the prostrate post. Both of them were of the old order of men, an order even then fast dying out. Their memories went back to pre-enclosure days and to the open-field system with its separate acre strips, each an individual holding; to the days of the common herd that grazed on the fallow field and on the long meads that flanked the streams on each side of the parish.

Of all this I have heard them speak – of the dividing of the mowing grass at hay-time; and the 'foreign' shepherds who brought large flocks of sheep from a distance, buying up strips of keep for them, and selling or adding to their flock as they travelled.

These old workmen had never been separated from the land, and so they understood the ways of the farms and the needs of the farmers as no town carpenter could possibly have done. They knew from long experience all there was to know about the erection of new farm buildings and repairs to the old, the making and repairing of gates and fences in the fields, of cattle cribs and sheep troughs and all that pertained to the farm. They had always been used to this work and they asked nothing higher from life.

The tools they possessed were primitive – a good axe and saw, a clawed hammer, shell augers of different sizes with a mallet and gouge for cutting a disk in the wood where the hole was required to be bored, a few 'parsors' (sometimes called gimlets), and a bradawl. Add to these a smoothing plane and a few strong chisels, an iron square, a rule, and a chalk-line wound on a wooden reel. All these were arranged in a large flag carpenter's basket lined with canvas, in the inner pocket of which would be found a nail punch, a pot containing grease for the saw and a file for sharpening it. They would carry this basket many miles to the outlying farms with an axe helve passed through the handles, its blade just behind the nape of the bearer's neck where the webbing-bound handles formed a comfortable pad to the shoulders.

So in my early youth I went with one or another of them on many a summer morning, the dew still on the lush grass, over field after field to some buried farm, often by ways that I had never been before, but well known to the old workman whose unflagging steps I followed; his pace never faster, never slower; his broad back half obscured by the large tool basket, out of which the end of the saw projected.

These glimpses of farm life always interested me. There was the long cool whitewashed dairy in which were ranged, side by side, large shallow lead flats full of rich milk off which the dairy-maids carefully skimmed the cream, the large copper for the brewing of small ale for the labourers, the salted flitches and hams suspended from the ceiling of the kitchen.

Even in comparison with my native old-fashioned village it was a step further back in time, for these farmsteads were remote and self-contained, and still deeply rooted in the soil where they had been planted long ago when the land was first reclaimed from the forest.

The carpentry of the open countryside ought not to savour too much of the joiner's bench. In fact, it is a separate craft and should be kept so. Each district has its own variations of method and design to suit the particular needs of the place.

Formerly the country carpenters looked to the trees growing near by to see how each could be used for the work that was to be done. This developed a folk-craft peculiar to each district. In some localities larch fir in the round, or sawn down the centre, or quartered, is the material for fences, gates and porches to cottages; in others, cleft oak, or willow, or chestnut, according to the timber that thrives in the district. This specialisation in particular kinds of wood, having gone on for centuries, has developed special local skill and given definite character to a place.

I did not realise it at the time, but now I see that precisely in this way our men understood and served the particular need of our district and no other.

Old Enoch's age was more than seventy, but he was hale and strong. His mind harked back to the days of hand-made nails, and when he would praise his claw-hammer – of which he was very fond – he would base his argument on the number of fourpenny, sixpenny, or eightpenny nails that it would save in a day. He remembered the number of each to a pound (though I have forgotten) and he would reason it out quite well – the number of nails saved, and their value, and the consequent greater value per day of a man using such a hammer.

My father told me that when nails were made by hand the different sizes and lengths were known by their price per pound from 4d. to 1s.: the longer ones, involving less labour, cost the least.

Old Enoch also chopped his wood pins square with his axe, whereas all other of our men rounded them with chisel or plane, He said that formerly they were always left square, which I myself have noticed in very old roofs, where the rafters are fastened to the plates with wood pins instead of nails. Enoch said that square pins held better.

He was an amiable old man, tending throughout life to take the line of least resistance. If he did his work wrong – as he often did – and my father called his attention to the mistake, Enoch would always be ready with the same answer: 'Blam-me, master, I was just thinking the same thing.'

Such was the harmless quality of what the workshop called 'his

I

lies'. But he once said seriously what was often quoted to his credit: that throughout life he had never wilfully told a lie. His yarns were, at times, decidedly tall, but I incline to the belief that many had been added to since they first left his lips. The best remembered and most often quoted yarn was his claim that in the days of his prime he had made a forty-round ladder in one day and raised it with one hand when finished.

His stock expression, never used by anyone else save when repeating his yarns, was 'Blam-me'. No one knew what it meant. It was emphatic, but it was not considered a swear word; in fact, my father never allowed bad language, and old Enoch was always clean of speech, allowing himself no more than this one departure from orthodox English.

'Slatter,' said grandfather irascibly, 'that post is six inches out of upright.'

Enoch sighted it, his axe helve between his fingers instead of a plumb-bob. The answer came amiably, 'Blam-me, master, so 'tis; exactly six inches.'

'You old liar,' raged grandfather, 'you wouldn't have known whether it was or not if I hadn't told you.'

I should like to meet Enoch again, and hear his tales.

Old Johnnie – we all called him 'Johnnie, the big man with a small voice' – asked nothing more of life than regular work not exceeding the grasp of his mentality. The pathway of his life in my father's employ was from farm to farm. The farmers knew him well and he knew the run of their farms as well as any of their labourers. They called him 'John'. 'I'll get you to send John over for a few days' work' a farmer would say to my father at market. And John would arrive at the farm with tool-basket at his back to receive from the farmer instructions about the work to be done.

The 'few days' would pass and no John return. Nor did my father expect him; he understood the ways of farm life too well. As he anticipated, he would learn from the farmer at market that a score of unexpected jobs had turned up. All the men on the farm had hailed John's advent with joy. The carter reported holes in the manger, and the cowman said that 'the browsings wanted seeing to', also that 'one of the clopses was broke'. And all the gates in the meadows were more or less out of order. 'John may as well see to the lot now that he's with us', the farmer would say. So the few days' work would extend to weeks, Johnnie walking to and fro each day, regular to the minute and coming to the yard each Saturday for his wage. There he would pick up nails, screws, hinges, etc. and give my father notice of any timber that he wanted sent over. Father, if in the neighbourhood, would call, often only to learn that Johnnie was working in some remote part of the farm, repairing a gate, a stile, or a fence, to reach which would involve a tramp of half a mile and full knowledge of the locality. Johnnie was usually booked in advance: and another farm would expect him when the end of the work in hand was definitely reached.

Johnnie never felt the cold. 'Cold! what's the use of feeling the cold?' he would say, on being asked his opinion of bitter weather. Once, at a job of roofing, when the weather, by reason of wind and snow, was so inclement that the men decided to abandon the work and return home, Johnnie merely said, 'It will be worse to-morrow', whereupon they all agreed to stick it out.

His stature was that of a giant, but he had a weak, squeaky, husky voice. I doubt if he could have shouted to save his life. 'You have sent me a big man with a small voice', said a new employer to my father at market, and this description stuck to Johnnie for the rest of his life.

I have heard him laugh – the rippling laugh of a child. Something had tickled his obscure mentality, which no one ever thoroughly probed. Yet I never knew him out of temper, or impatient, or in a hurry. As for working for anyone else, I doubt if the thought ever entered his mind; and I am certain that it was equally unthinkable to all of us.

No one disagreed with Johnnie; in fact there was no cause to do so. He was always happy to take the rough, toilsome work that no one else wanted to do. He was always requisitioned for the job of lifting heavy beams and for any other work demanding brute strength.

On my first experience of tree felling, the wedges driven in at the base of the tree failed to cause it to fall. Johnnie pushed it: the tree fell at once. He was never short of money, although his weekly wage never exceeded 17s. His cottage, owned by himself, was always neat, and his wife happy. Folk even whispered that they had a well-filled stocking indoors. He was surely nature's child, one who had never unlearned the art of filling to perfection the little niche which had been provided for him by destiny.

Walter Rose, *The Village Carpenter*

A SHEPHERD OF THE DOWNS

Caleb cherished an admiration and reverence for his father's memory which were almost a worship, and he loved to describe him as he appeared in his old age, when upwards of eighty. He was erect and tall, standing six feet two in height, well proportioned, with a clean-shaved, florid face, clear, dark eyes, and silver-white hair; and at this later period of his life he always wore the dress of an old order of pensioners to which he had been admitted – a soft, broad, white felt hat, thick boots and brown leather leggings, and a long, grey cloth overcoat with red collar and brass buttons.

According to Caleb, he must have been an exceedingly fine specimen of a man, both physically and morally. Born in 1800, he began following a flock as a boy, and continued as shepherd on the same farm until he was sixty, never rising to more than seven shillings a week and nothing found, since he lived in the cottage where he was born and which he inherited from his father. That a man of his fine powers, a head-shepherd on a large hill-farm, should have had no better pay than that down to the year 1860, after nearly half a century of work in one place, seems almost incredible. Even his sons, as they grew up to man's estate, advised him to ask for an increase, but he would not. Seven shillings a week he had always had; and that small sum, with something his wife earned by making highly finished smock-frocks, had been sufficient to keep them all in a decent way; and his sons were now all earning their own living. But Caleb got married, and resolved to leave the old farm at Bishop to take a better place at a distance from home, at Warminster, which had been offered him. He would there have a cottage to live in, nine shillings a week, and a sack of barley for his dog. At that time the shepherd had to keep his own dog – no small expense to him when his wages were no more than six to eight shillings a week. But Caleb was his father's favourite son, and the old man could not endure the thought of losing sight of him; and at last, finding that he could not persuade him not to leave the old home, he became angry, and told him that if he went away to Warminster for the sake of the higher wages and barley for the dog he would disown him! This was a serious matter to Caleb, in spite of the fact that a shepherd has no money to leave to his children when he passes away. He went nevertheless, for, though he loved and reverenced his father, he had a young wife who pulled the other way; and he was absent for years, and when he returned the old man's heart had softened, so that he was glad to welcome him back to the old home.

Meanwhile at that humble cottage at Winterbourne Bishop great things had happened; old Isaac was no longer shepherding on the downs, but living very comfortably in his own cottage in the village. The change came about in this way.

The downland shepherds, Caleb said, were as a rule clever poachers; and it is really not surprising, when one considers the temptation to a man with a wife and several hungry children, besides himself and a dog, to feed out of about seven shillings a week. But old Bawcombe was an exception: he would take no game, furred or feathered, nor, if he could prevent it, allow another to take anything from the land fed by his flock. Caleb and his brothers, when as boys and youths they began their shepherding, sometimes caught a rabbit, or their dog caught and killed one without their encouragement; but, however the thing came into their hands, they could not take it home on account of their father. Now it happened that an elderly gentleman who had the shooting was a keen sportsman, and that in several successive years he found a wonderful difference in the amount of game at one spot among the hills and in all the rest of his hill property. The only explanation the keeper could give was that Isaac Bawcombe tended his flock on that down where rabbits, hares, and partridges were so plentiful. One autumn day the gentleman was shooting over that down, and seeing a big man in a smock-frock standing motionless, crook in hand, regarding him, he called out to his keeper, who was with him, 'Who is that big man?' and was told that it was Shepherd Bawcombe. The old gentleman pulled some money out of his pocket and said, 'Give him this half-crown, and thank him for the good sport I've had to-day.' But after the coin had been given the giver still remained standing there, thinking, perhaps, that he had not yet sufficiently rewarded the man; and at last, before turning away, he shouted, 'Bawcombe, that's not all. You'll get something more by and by.'

Isaac had not long to wait for the something more, and it turned out not to be the hare or brace of birds he had half expected. It happened that the sportsman was one of the trustees of an ancient charity which provided for six of the most deserving old men of the parish of Bishop; now, one of the six had recently died, and on this gentleman's recommendation Bawcombe had been elected to fill the vacant place. The letter from Salisbury informing him of his election and commanding his presence in that city filled him with astonishment; for, though he was sixty years old and the father of three sons now out in the world, he could not yet regard himself as an old man, for he had never known a day's illness, nor an ache, and was famed in all that neighbourhood for his great physical strength and endurance. And now, with his own cottage to live in, eight shillings a week, and his pensioners' garments, with certain other benefits, and a shilling a day besides which his old master paid him for some services at the farm-house in the village, Isaac found himself very well off indeed, and he enjoyed his prosperous state for twenty-six years. Then, in 1886, his old wife fell ill and died, and no sooner was she in her grave than he, too, began to droop; and soon, before the year was out, he followed her, because, as the neighbours said, they had always been a loving pair and one could not 'bide without the other.

This chapter has already had its proper ending and there was no intention of adding to it, but now for a special reason, which I trust the reader will pardon when he hears it, I must go on to say something about that strange phenomenon of death succeeding death in old married couples, one dying for no other reason than that the other has died. For it is our instinct to hold fast to life, and the older a man gets if he be sane the more he becomes like a newborn child in the impulse to grip tightly. A strange and a rare thing among people generally (the people we know), it is nevertheless quite common among persons of the labouring class in the rural districts. I have sometimes marvelled at the number of such cases to be met with in the villages; but when one comes to think about it one ceases to wonder that it should be so. For the labourer on the land goes on from boyhood to the end of life in the same everlasting round, the changes from task to task, according to the seasons, being no greater than in the case of the animals that alter their actions and habits to suit the varying conditions of the year. March and August and December, and every month, will bring about the changes in the atmosphere and earth and vegetation and in the animals, which have been from of old, which he knows how to meet, and the old, familiar task, lambing-time, shearing-time, root and seed crops, hoeing, haymaking, harvesting. It is a life of the extremest simplicity, without all those interests outside the home and the daily task, the innumerable distractions, common to all persons in other classes and to the workmen in towns as well. Incidentally it may be said that it is also the healthiest, that, speaking generally, the agricultural labourer is the healthiest and sanest man in the land, if not also the happiest, as some believe.

It is this life of simple, unchanging actions and of habits that are like instincts, of hard labour in sun and wind and rain from day to day, with its weekly break and rest, and of but few comforts and no luxuries, which serves to bind man and wife so closely. And the longer their life goes on together the closer and more unbreakable the union grows. They are growing old: old friends and companions have died or left them; their children have married and gone away and have their own families and affairs, so that the old folks at home are little remembered, and to all others they have become of little consequence in the world. But they do not know it, for they are together, cherishing the same memories, speaking of the same old, familiar things, and their lost friends and companions, their absent, perhaps estranged, children, are with them still in mind as in the old days. The past is with them more than the present, to give an undying interest to life; for they share it, and it is only when one goes, when the old wife gets the tea ready and goes mechanically to the door to gaze out, knowing that her tired man will come in no more to take his customary place and listen to all the things she has stored up in her mind during the day to tell him; and when the tired labourer comes in at dusk to find no old wife waiting to give him his tea and talk to him while he refreshes himself, he all at once realizes his position; he finds himself cut off from the entire world, from all of his kind. Where are they all? The enduring sympathy of that one soul that was with him till now had kept him in touch with life, had made it seem unchanged and unchangeable, and with that soul has vanished the old, sweet illusion as well as all ties, all common, human affection.

He is desolate, indeed, alone in a desert world, and it is not strange that in many and many a case, even in that of a man still strong, untouched by disease and good for another decade or two, the loss, the awful solitude, has proved too much for him.

Such cases, I have said, are common, but they are not recorded, though it is possible with labour to pick them out in the church registers; but in the churchyards you do not find them, since the farm-labourer has only a green mound to mark the spot where he lies.

W. H. Hudson, A Shepherd's Life

THREE CHARACTERS

One of the stories of the old Wiltshire days I picked up was from an old woman, aged eighty-seven, in the Wilton workhouse. She has a vivid recollection of a labourer named Reed, in Odstock, a village on the Ebble near Salisbury, a stern, silent man, who was a marvel of strength and endurance. The work in which he most delighted was precisely that which most labourers hated, before threshing machines came in despite the action of the 'mobs' – threshing out corn with the flail. From earliest dawn till after dark he would sit or stand in a dim, dusty barn, monotonously pounding away, without an interval to rest, and without dinner, and with no food but a piece of bread and a pinch of salt. Without the salt he would not eat the bread. An hour after all others had ceased from work he would put on his coat and trudge home to his wife and family.

The woman in the workhouse remembers that once, when Reed was a very old man past work, he came to their cottage for something, and while he stood waiting at the entrance, a little boy ran in and asked his mother for a piece of bread and butter with sugar on it. Old Reed glared at him, and shaking his big stick, exclaimed, 'I'd give you sugar with this if you were my boy!' and so terrible

did he look in his anger at the luxury of the times, that the little
boy burst out crying and ran away!

What chiefly interested me about this old man was that he was
a deer-stealer of the days when that offence was common in the
country. It was not so great a crime as sheep-stealing, for which
men were hanged; taking a deer was punished with nothing
worse than hard labour, as a rule. But Reed was never caught; he
would labour his full time and steal away after dark over the
downs, to return in the small hours with a deer on his back. It was
not for his own consumption; he wanted the money for which he
sold it in Salisbury; and it is probable that he was in league with
other poachers, as it is hard to believe that he could capture the
animals single-handed.

After his death it was found that old Reed had left a hundred
pounds to each of his two surviving daughters, and it was a wonder to everybody how he had managed not only to bring up a
family and keep himself out of the workhouse to the end of his
long life, but to leave so large a sum of money. One can only suppose that he was a rigid economist and never had a week's illness,
and that by abstaining from beer and tobacco he was able to save
a couple of shillings each week out of his wages of seven or eight
shillings; this, in forty years, would make the two hundred
pounds with something over.

It is not a very rare thing to find a farm-labourer like old Reed
of Odstock, with not only a strong preference for a particular
kind of work, but a love of it as compelling as that of an artist for
his art. Some friends of mine whom I went to visit over the border
in Dorset told me of an enthusiast of this description who had
recently died in the village. 'What a pity you did not come
sooner,' they said. Alas! it is nearly always so; on first coming
to stay at a village one is told that it has but just lost its
oldest and most interesting inhabitant – a relic of the olden
time.

This man had taken to the scythe as Reed had to the flail, and was never happy unless he had a field to mow. He was a very tall old man, so lean that he looked like a skeleton, the bones covered with a skin as brown as old leather, and he wore his thin grey hair and snow-white beard very long. He rode on a white donkey, and was usually seen mounted galloping down the village street, hatless, his old brown, bare feet and legs drawn up to keep them from the ground, his scythe over his shoulder. 'Here comes old Father Time,' they would cry, as they called him, and run to the door to gaze with ever fresh delight at the wonderful old man as he rushed by, kicking and shouting at his donkey to make him go faster. He was always in a hurry, hunting for work with furious zeal, and when he got a field to mow so eager was he that he would not sleep at home, even if it was close by, but would lie down on the grass at the side of the field and start working at dawn, between two and three o'clock, quite three hours before the world woke up to its daily toil.

The name of Reed, the zealous thresher with the flail, serves to remind me of yet another Reed, a woman who died a few years ago aged ninety-four, and whose name should be cherished in one of the downland villages. She was a native of Barford St. Martin on the Nadder, one of two villages, the other being Wishford, on the Wylye river, the inhabitants of which have the right to go into Groveley Wood, an immense forest on the Wilton estate, to obtain wood for burning, each person being entitled to take home as much wood as he or she can carry. The people of Wishford take green wood, but those of Barford only dead, they having bartered their right at a remote period to cut growing trees for a yearly sum of five pounds, which the lord of the manor still pays to the village, and, in addition, the right to take dead wood.

It will be readily understood that this right possessed by the people of two villages, both situated within a mile of the forest, has been a perpetual source of annoyance to the noble owners in modern times, since the strict preservation of game, especially of pheasants, has grown to be almost a religion to the landowners. Now it came to pass that about half a century or longer ago, the Pembroke of that time made the happy discovery, as he imagined, that there was nothing to show that the Barford people had any right to the dead wood. They had been graciously allowed to take it, as was the case all over the country at that time, and that was all. At once he issued an edict prohibiting the taking of dead wood from the forest by the villagers, and great as the loss was to them they acquiesced; not a man of Barford St. Martin dared to disobey the prohibition or raise his voice against it. Grace Reed then determined to oppose the mighty earl, and accompanied by four other women of the village boldly went to the wood and gathered their sticks and brought them home. They were summoned before the magistrates and fined, and on their refusal to pay were sent to prison; but the very next day they were liberated and told that a mistake had been made, that the matter had been inquired into, and it had been found that the people of Barford did really have the right they had exercised so long to take dead wood from the forest.

As a result of the action of these women the right has not been challenged since, and on my last visit to Barford, a few days before writing this chapter, I saw three women coming down from the forest with as much dead wood as they could carry on their heads and backs. But how near they came to losing their right! It was a bold, an unheard-of thing which they did, and if there had not been a poor cottage woman with the spirit to do it at the proper moment the right could never have been revived.

Grace Reed's children's children are living at Barford now; they say that to the very end of her long life she preserved a very clear memory of the people and events of the village in the old days early in the last century. They say, too, that in recalling the far past, the old people and scenes would present themselves so vividly to her mind that she would speak of them as of recent things, and would say to some one fifty years younger than herself, 'Can't

you remember it? Surely you haven't forgotten it when 'twas the
talk of the village!'

W. H. Hudson, *A Shepherd's Life*

JOHN BROWN

'John Brown is dead,' said an aged friend and visitor in answer to
my inquiry for the strong labourer.

'Is he really dead?' I asked, for it seemed impossible.

'He is. He came home from his work in the evening as usual,
and seemed to catch his foot in the threshold and fell forward on
the floor. When they picked him up he was dead.'

I remember the doorway; a raised piece of wood ran across it,
as is commonly the case in country cottages, such as one might
easily catch one's foot against if one did not notice it; but he knew
that bit of wood well. The floor was of brick, hard to fall on and
die. He must have come down over the crown of the hill, with his
long slouching stride, as if his legs had been half pulled away from
his body by his heavy boots in the furrows when a ploughboy.
He must have turned up the steps in the bank to his cottage, and so,
touching the threshold, ended. He is gone through the great doorway, and one pencil-mark is rubbed out. There used to be a large
hearth in that room, a larger room than in most cottages; and
when the fire was lit, and the light shone on the yellowish red
brick beneath and the large rafters overhead, it was homely and
pleasant. In summer the door was always wide open. Close by on
the high bank there was a spot where the first wild violets came.
You might look along miles of hedgerow, but there were never
any until they had shown by John Brown's.

If a man's work that he has done all the days of his life could be
collected and piled up around him in visible shape, what a vast
mound there would be beside some! If each act or stroke was
represented, say by a brick, John Brown would have stood the
day before his ending by the side of a monument as high as a

pyramid. Then if in front of him could be placed the sum and product of his labour, the profit to himself, he could have held it in his clenched hand like a nut, and no one would have seen it. Our modern people think they train their sons to strength by football and rowing and jumping, and what are called athletic exercises; all of which it is the fashion now to preach as very noble, and likely to lead to the goodness of the race. Certainly feats are accomplished and records are beaten, but there is no real strength gained, no hardihood built up. Without hardihood it is of little avail to be able to jump an inch farther than somebody else. Hardihood is the true test, hardihood is the ideal, and not these caperings or ten minutes' spurts.

Now, the way they made the boy John Brown hardy was to let him roll about on the ground with naked legs and bare head from morn till night, from June till December, from January to June. The rain fell on his head, and he played in wet grass to his knees. Dry bread and a little lard was his chief food. He went to work while he was still a child. At half-past three in the morning he was on his way to the farm stables, there to help feed the cart-horses, which used to be done with great care very early in the morning. The carter's whip used to sting his legs, and sometimes he felt the butt. At fifteen he was no taller than the sons of well-to-do people at eleven; he scarcely seemed to grow at all till he was eighteen or twenty, and even then very slowly, but at last he became a tall big man. That slouching walk, with knees always bent, diminished his height to appearance; he really was the full size, and every inch of his frame had been slowly welded together by this ceaseless work, continual life in the open air, and coarse hard food. This is what makes a man hardy. This is what makes a man able to stand almost anything, and gives a power of endurance that can never be obtained by any amount of gymnastic training.

I used to watch him mowing with amazement. Sometimes he would begin at half-past two in the morning, and continue till night. About eleven o'clock, which used to be the mowers' noon, he took a rest on a couch of half-dried grass in the shade of the hedge. For the rest, it was mow, mow, mow for the long summer day.

John Brown was dead: died in an instant at his cottage door. I could hardly credit it, so vivid was the memory of his strength. The gap of time since I had seen him last had made no impression on me; to me he was still in my mind the John Brown of the hay-field; there was nothing between then and his death.

He used to catch us boys the bats in the stable, and tell us fearful tales of the ghosts he had seen; and bring the bread from the town in an old-fashioned wallet, half in front and half behind, long before the bakers' carts began to come round in country places. One evening he came into the dairy carrying a yoke of milk, staggering, with tipsy gravity; he was quite sure he did not want any assistance, he could pour the milk into the pans. He tried, and fell at full length and bathed himself from head to foot. Of later days they say he worked in the town a good deal, and did not look so well or so happy as on the farm. In this cottage opposite the violet bank they had small-pox once, the only case I recollect in the hamlet – the old men used to say everybody had it when they were young; this was the only case in my time, and they recovered quickly without any loss, nor did the disease spread. A roomy well-built cottage like that, on dry ground, isolated, is the only hospital worthy of the name. People have a chance to get well in such places; they have very great difficulty in the huge buildings that are put up expressly for them. I have a Convalescent Home in my mind at the moment, a vast building. In these great blocks what they call ventilation is a steady draught, and there is no 'home' about it. It is all walls and regulations and draughts, and altogether miserable. I would infinitely rather see any friend of mine in John Brown's cottage. That terrible disease, however, seemed to quite spoil the violet bank opposite, and I never picked one there afterwards. There is something in disease so destructive, as it were, to flowers.

The hundreds of times I saw the tall chimney of that cottage rise out of the hill-side as I came home at all hours of the day and night! the first chimney after a long journey, always comfortable to see, especially so in earlier days, when we had a kind of halting belief in John Brown's ghosts, several of which were dotted along that road according to him. The ghosts die as we grow older, they die and their places are taken by real ghosts. I wish I had sent John Brown a pound or two when I was in good health; but one is selfish then, and puts off things till it is too late – a lame excuse verily. I can scarcely believe now that he is really dead, gone as you might casually pluck a hawthorn leaf from the hedge.

Richard Jefferies, *Field and Hedgerow*

4

THE FUTURE

LEISURE

Leisure, and the problem of using it, are new things . . . I do not mean that the older inhabitants of the valley never had any spare time. There were, doubtless, many hours when they 'eased off,' to smoke their pipes and drink their beer and be jolly; only, such hours were, so to speak, a by-product of living, not the usual and expected consummation of every day. Accepting them by no means unwillingly when they occurred, the folk still were wont normally to reduce them to a minimum, or at least to see that they did not occur too often; as if spare time, after all, was only a time of waiting until work could be conveniently resumed. So lightly was it valued that most villagers cut it short by the simple expedient of going to bed at six or seven o'clock. But then, in their peasant way, they enjoyed interesting days. The work they did, although it left their reasoning and imaginative powers un-developed, called into play enough subtle knowledge and skill to make their whole day's industry gratifying. What should they want of leisure? They wanted rest, in which to recover strength for taking up again the interesting business of living; but they approached their daily life – their pig-keeping and bread-making, their mowing and thatching and turf-cutting and gardening, and the whole round of country tasks – almost in a welcoming spirit, matching themselves against its demands and proving their man-hood by their success. But the modern labourer's employment, reduced as it is to so much greater monotony, and carried on for a master instead of for the man himself, is seldom to be approached in that spirit. The money-valuation of it is the prime consideration; it is a commercial affair; a clerk going to his office has as much reason as the labourer to welcome the morning's call to work. As in the clerk's case, so in the labourer's: the act or fruition of living is postponed during the hours in which the living is being earned; between the two processes a sharp line of division is drawn; and it is not until the clock strikes, and the leisure begins, that a man may remember that he is a man, and try to make a success of living. Hence the truth of what I say: the problem of using leisure is a new one in the village. Deprived, by the economic changes which have gone over them, of any keen enjoyment of life while at work, the labourers must make up for the deprivation when work is over, or not at all. Naturally enough, in the absence of any traditions to guide them, they fail. But self-respect forbids the old solution. To feed and go to bed would be to shirk the problem, not to solve it.

So much turns upon a proper appreciation of these truths that it will be well to illustrate them from real life, contrasting the old against the new. Fortunately the means are available. Modernized people acquainted with leisure are in every cottage, while as for the others, the valley still contains a few elderly men whose lives are reminiscent of the earlier day. . . .

The man I have in mind – I will rename him Turner – belongs to one of the old families of the village, and inherited from his father a cottage and an acre or so of ground – probably mortgaged – together with a horse and cart, a donkey, a cow or two, a few pigs, and a fair stock of the usual rustic tools and implements. Unluckily for him, he inherited no traditions – there were none in his family – to teach him how to use these possessions for making a money profit; so that, trying to go on in the old way, as if the world were not changing all round him, he muddled away his chances, and by the time that he was fifty had no property left that was worth any creditor's notice. The loss, however, came too late to have much effect on his habits. And now that he is but the weekly tenant of a tiny cottage, and owns no more than a donkey and cart and a few rabbits and fowls, he is just the same sort of man that he used to be in prosperity – thriftless from our point of view, but from the peasant point of view thrifty enough, good-tempered too, generous to a fault, indifferent to discomforts, as a rule very hard-working, yet apparently quite unacquainted with fatigue.

He gets his living now as a labourer; but, unlike his neighbours, he seems by no means careful to secure constant employment. The regularity of it would hardly suit his temper; he is too keenly desirous of being his own master. And his own master he manages to be, in a certain degree. From those who employ him he obtains some latitude of choice, not alone as to the hours of the day when he shall serve them, but even as to the days of the week.

Keeping this old-fashioned kind of life in mind as we turn again to the modern labourer's existence, we see at once where the change has come in, and why leisure, from being of small account, has become of so great importance. It is the amends due for a deprivation that has been suffered. Unlike the industry of a peasantry, commercial wage-earning cannot satisfy the cravings of a man's soul at the same time that it occupies his body, cannot exercise many of his faculties or appeal to many of his tastes; and therefore, if he would have any profit, any enjoyment, of his own human nature, he must contrive to get it in his leisure time.

In illustration of this position, I will take the case – it is fairly typical – of the coal-carter ... He is about twenty-five years old now; and his career so far, from the time when he left school, may be soon outlined. It is true, I cannot say what his first employment was; but it can be guessed; for there is no doubt that he began as an errand-boy, and that presently, growing bigger, he took a turn at driving a gravel-cart to and fro between the gravel-pits and the railway. Assuming this, I can go on to speak from my own knowledge. His growth and strength came early; I remember noticing him first as a powerful fellow, not more than seventeen or eighteen years old, but already doing a man's work as a gravel-digger. When that work slackened after two or three years, he got employment – not willingly, but because times were bad – at night-work with the 'ballast-train' on the railway. Exhausting if not brutalizing labour, that is. At ten or eleven at night the gangs of men start off, travelling in open trucks to the part of the line they are to repair, and there they work throughout the night, on wind-swept embankment or in draughty cutting, taking all the weather that the nights bring up. This man endured it for some twelve months, until a neglected chill turned to bronchitis and pleurisy, and nearly ended his life. After that he had a long spell of unemployment, and was on the point of going back to the ballast-train as a last resource when, by good fortune, he got his present job. He has been a coal-carter for three or four years – a fact which testifies to his efficiency. By half-past six o'clock in the morning he has to be in the stables; then comes the day on the road, during which he will lift on his back, into the van and out of it, and per-haps will carry for long distances, nine or ten tons of coal – say, twenty hundredweight bags every hour; by half-past five or six in the evening he has put up his horse for the night; and so his day's work is over, excepting that he has about a mile to walk home.

Of this employment, which, if the man is lucky, will continue until he is old and worn-out, we may admit that it is more useful by far – to the community – than the old village industries were wont to be. Concentrated upon one kind of effort, it perhaps doubles the productivity of a day's work. But just because it is so concentrated it cannot yield to the man himself any variety of delights such as men occupied in the old way were wont to enjoy. It demands from him but little skill; it neither requires him to possess a great fund of local information and useful lore, nor yet takes him where he could gather such a store for his own pleasure. The zest and fascination of living, with the senses alert, the tastes awake, and manifold sights and sounds appealing to his happy recognition – all these have to be forgotten until he gets home and is free for a little while. Then he may seek them if he can, using art or pastimes – what we call 'civilization' – for that end. The two hours or so of leisure are his opportunity.

But after a day like the coal-carter's, where is the man that could even begin to refresh himself with the arts, or even the games, of civilization? For all the active use he can make of them those spare hours of his do not deserve to be called leisure; they are the fagged end of the day. Slouching home to them, as it were from under ten tons of coal, he has no energy left for further effort. The community has had all his energy, all his power to enjoy civilization; and has paid him three shillings and sixpence for it. It is small wonder that he seems not to avail himself of the opportunity, prize it though he may.

Yet there is still a possibility to be considered. Albeit any active use of leisure is out of the question, is he therefore debarred from a more tranquil enjoyment? He sits gossiping with his family, but why should the gossip be listless and yawning? Why should not he, to say nothing of his relations, enjoy the refreshment of talk enlivened by the play of pleasant and varied thoughts? As every-one knows, the actual topic of conversation is not what makes the charm; be what it may, it will still be agreeable, provided that it goes to an accompaniment of ideas too plentiful and swift to be expressed. Every allusion then extends the interest of it; reawaken-ed memories add to its pleasure; if the minds engaged are fairly well furnished with ideas, either by experience or by education, the intercourse between them goes on in a sort of luminous medium which fills the whole being with contentment. Suppos-ing, then, that by education, or previous experience, the coal-carter's mind has been thus well furnished, his scanty leisure may still compensate him for the long dull hours of his wage-earning,

and the new thrift will after all have made amends for the deprivation of the old peasant enjoyments.

But to suppose this is to suppose a most unlikely thing. Previous
experience, at any rate, has done little for the man. The peasants
themselves were better off. Compare his chances, once more, with
those of a man like Turner. From earliest childhood, Turner's
days and nights have been bountiful to him in many-coloured
impressions. At the outset he saw and had part in those rural activities, changeful, accomplished, carried on by many forms of skill
and directed by a vast amount of traditional wisdom, whereby
the country people of England had for ages supported themselves
in their quiet valleys. His brain still teems with recollections of all
this industry. And then to those recollections must be added
memories of the scenes in which the industry went on – the wide
landscapes, the glowing cornfields, the meadows, woods, heaths;
and likewise the details of barn and rick-yard, and stable and cow-
stall, and numberless other corners into which his work has taken
him. To anyone who understands them, those details are themselves like an interesting book, full of 'idea' legible everywhere in
the shapes which country craftsmanship gave to them; and Turner
understands them through and through. Nor is this all. If not
actual adventure and romance, still many of the factors of adventure and romance have accompanied him through his life; so that
it is good even to think of all that he has seen. He has had experience (travelling down to Sussex) of the dead silence of country
roads at midnight under the stars; has known the August sunrise,
and the afternoon heat, and the chilly moonlight, high up on the
South Downs; and the glint of the sunshine in apple-orchards at
cider-making time; and the grey coming of the rain that urges a
man to hurry with his thatching; and the thickening of the white
winter fog across the heaths towards night-fall, when wayfarers
might miss the track and wander all night unless they knew well
what they were about. Of such stuff as this for the brain-
life to feed upon there has been great abundance in Turner's

career, but of such stuff what memories can the coal-carter have?

Already in his earliest childhood the principal chances were gone. The common had been enclosed; no little boys were sent out to mind cows there all day, and incidentally to look for birds'-nests and acquaint themselves with the ways of the rabbits and hedgehogs and butterflies and birds of the heath. Fenced-in pro-perty, guarded by the Policeman and the Law, restricted the boy's games to the shabby waste-places of the valley, and to the foot-paths and roads, where there was not much for a child to do or to see. At home, and in the homes of his companions, the new thrift was in vogue; he might not watch the homely cottage doings, and listen to traditional talk about them, and look up admiringly at able men and women engaged upon them, for the very good reason that no such things went on. Men slaving at their gardens he might see, and women weary at their washing and mending, amid scenes of little dignity and much poverty and makeshift un-tidiness; but that was all. The coherent and self-explanatory village life had given place to a half blind struggle of individuals against circumstances and economic processes which no child could pos-sibly understand; and it was with the pitiful stock of ideas to be derived from these conditions that the coal-carter passed out of childhood, to enter upon the wage-earning career which I have already outlined.

George Bourne, *Change in the Village*

A FORM OF INSANITY

11 October, 1906. It may be only my singular taste, but it seems to me that there is for all of us a great decrease of comfort in living. It is chiefly due to the great increase of noise, and the disappearance of peace. There is a grassy bank down the road, at which I looked this afternoon, wondering for a moment why it gave me no comfort. For I recognised that the sight of such a thing, far away in some country lane, would fill me with satisfaction, so that I should desire nothing better, and should often remember it in my day-dreams. But the explanation was forthcoming very soon. Hardly ever now is that spot quiet: always there is some noisy passing on the road: always restlessness. A fancy came to me – not for the first time – that an eight hours' working day would be a boon, if only to reduce the period of bustle on our provincial roads.

I happen to know this pain of unquiet; but I think others feel it, not recognising what it is. I think in general a living is not only harder to get as time goes on, but is less worth getting, from year to year. And, observing tendencies, I grow more and more pessimistic . . .

The race appears to be to the hustler: to the millionaire trust. (And I am glad therefore if it is true that people of the hustling ranks are ceasing to breed.) There seems no escape. For why do they hurry so? And why is it that men of better tastes have to wear themselves to death against their will? It is the pressure of the developing hustler. Into the quiet old sleepy town, there comes first some unscrupulous tradesman, greedy and possessing the business instinct. At once the old-fashioned have to toe the line with him, or be left out of the running. So it goes on, stage after stage; at last comes the syndicate with the big capital and the dead conscience. All but all hate it; yet must compete with it in its own vices. It is the victorious type.

Artists, and quiet souls, are powerless to resist this advance. It will set them to work in its factories; it will enslave them, or refuse them a living at all. For it is inspired by men whose insane genius, running to money-making, happens to be a form of insanity able to succeed in the struggle for existence; and is, indeed, the most powerful thing alive, just now. It commands the world's food supply, and the world's capital. Or at least it is towards that that we are inevitably tending. We, who hate it, have no weapons wherewith to combat it.

The one hope I see (tonight at any rate) lies not in artists; not in the humanities or religion; but in the wage-earning classes. Sooner or later these and the money-making classes must come into direct conflict; because the money-makers chiefly depend on the existence of millions of men to make but not share their wealth . . . The logical end of hustling, unless checked in time, is the corruption, dishonour, and downfall that await successful selfishness, in nations as in families.

George Sturt, Journals, pp. 502-4

THE NEED FOR GUIDANCE

Dr. Brown lent me an invitation to a 'Convocation' of the University of London, dealing, amongst other things, with proposals for giving scientific teaching in crafts, in place of the old apprenticeship now everywhere dying out.

This suggests the nature of the great change overtaking all industry; which is briefly, that what was a traditional *art* is now yielding before *science*. All civilization is involved in the transition; and the Western Powers will fall behind unless Science can indeed be a substitute for the traditional arts that enabled the English (for instance) to wrest their living from this island environment.

To my mind it is very unlikely that science will succeed soon enough – before the workers have learnt better than the arts they are already forgetting. Does science indeed know the intricacies of timber seasoning, or of sheep-breeding, or of making clay into bricks, etc. etc. etc.? Will this sort of knowledge soon serve as a national guidance for working men and women, as the old peasant *arts* served?

It is our best hope; but I think it unlikely.

The papers grow more and more excited, or say gaspy, with promises, day by day, of new things in 'wireless', 'broadcasting', 'television', and so on. Truly the things promised are very new: we are, for instance, to see with our (own) eyes what is happening in the Arctic circle, or to hear with our very ears the roar of lions in central Africa. Marvel is to become obsolete, ships are to steer themselves ... and so on. These are amongst the coming improvements announced by a professor (I forget his name) in to-day's 'Daily News'. But what I do not see is that a new type of animal is to be evolved, capable of doing for itself, with senses of its own, what Man can only achieve by machinery.

And it should be owned that this achievement, spite of all that is promised, seems unsatisfying. If we are to be still the same beings, what is the advantage? What is the good of seeing, in television, the far off Arctic, if we cannot see the winter mists like this morning's, so delicate in tint, changing hour after hour across the garden? We have not yet learnt to live in the environment well known to us, and with the senses we have, when here is Science offering us an environment altogether beyond experience.

For that is what it amounts to. With its machines Science is exploring an unknown universe, of waves and rays, of atoms and electrons, as far off as the Milky Way ... but all this unknown world remains ugly, exhausting, because we have no senses for living there, but only machines to bring it within reach of our few and undeveloped senses.

George Sturt, *Journals*, pp. 837 and 528

CIVILISATION ASTRAY

There came into my head yesterday ... a number of ideas for a new book.

This new book, which might be called 'The Sweetness of Life', would discuss the sources of well-being, and show how we shoot past them in our eagerness for wealth. Civilisation (I should argue) has gone astray: instead of finding out How to Live, we have gone on pillaging – pillaging the earth's stores with violence, when we should be getting into close personal intimacy of friendship with her ways. Already in this Journal, a number of notes show the direction of the argument . . .

That note of the rural labours that still went on, during the great Coal-strike two years ago, opens up another aspect of the same idea. Pillaging the stores of coal, England gets wealth and luxuries, but no happiness. We are too greedy, to live well. These spoliations bring us no intimacies with the Earth: they make us violators of her sweetness. Other examples of pillage would be found from the discovery and ransacking of America – the destruction of the Buffalo, of the Redwood Forests, the Indian tribes . . .

. . . this would lead up to a criticism of those conveniences, those labour-saving appliances, that we applaud so . . . How if, instead of making a trouble of getting our necessary things, we should make a delight of it? . . . Do we know how lovely a thing water is, unless we get it from the living stream, or draw it – a limpid crystalline mineral – from a well?

The pillage of England's Coal-fields has made all our life a 'Black Country', I should say in my book, and then I should want to talk of those who have known better how to live – who have not been pillagers greedy for wealth, but sane men – Thoreau,[33] for instance. Above all, there would have to be suggested a new reading of Christ.

. . . I would look at him (if only for a change) as a keen eager-eyed 'wild' man – lover of country, of craftsmanship, of animals and flowers and children – a man tinglingly alive; not half so much a man of sorrows and acquainted with grief as a man of intense enjoyments and acquainted with delight; scornful of the dead-and-alive pleasures of luxury.

And out of all this would come . . . a suggestion that the Object of Religion (as of Poetry) is to keep us in mind of, and bring us back to, our wonderful and lovely *Animal* nature; to persuade us to be, as Christ said, like little children: to remind us that the Life ('animal', mysterious, 'spiritual' as well as 'bodily') is more than meat; to draw us away from our crazy pillagings that bring no happiness, and from the folly of pulling down our barns to build greater, as the 'Rich Fool' did.[34]

George Sturt, *Journals*, pp. 692–4

CONCLUSION

Since the First World War a great deal of the countryside has been destroyed by neglect, urban sprawl and motorways. But if present tendencies continue even what is left will not survive. The pressure on farming is to compensate for a steadily diminishing area of land by stepping up yields, and the results will be yet larger farms, the monocrop cultivation by heavy machines of prairie fields, and large bills for fertilisers and pesticides. Except on high ground, trees, hedges, wild life and opportunities for human enjoyment will go. The loss will affect all of us dwellers in an industrial society, because the country is so much needed for our physical and psychic health. It was this wider aspect of change that so deeply concerned Sturt, as he reiterated the question 'How to live?' He had no confidence in a civilisation that looked for guidance, but found none, in science and technology. Nor could he find hope in the leisure culture proposed to us, wherein we work to acquire the means for the separate activity of living.

The industrial system grinds on, producing goods the taste and desire for which it has created. In a market economy production becomes an end in itself, without regard to the quality of life of those who do the work, or its impact on the environment they dwell in. The products may be soul-destroying to make, or anti-social, like tobacco and napalm, but they satisfy the requirement of adding to the gross national product. (An unhappy outcome of the failure of so many occupations to engage human interest or skill is a tendency to devalue *all* work.) Criticism of technology, advancing in directions for which the means are available rather than serving the needs of men, used to be dismissed as Luddite, but the accusation is heard less nowadays, perhaps because it is clear that some of the Luddites' demands (such as the prohibition of shoddy work) are relevant today. They looked forwards as well as backwards; 'they contained within them a shadowy image . . . of a democratic community, in which industrial growth should be regulated according to ethical priorities and the pursuit of profit be subordinated to human needs' (E. P. Thompson, *The Making of the English Working Class*). Except to politicians it is obvious enough that economic growth, as well as failing to satisfy the human spirit, has been accompanied by sinister side-effects – energy crises, ecological imbalance, and damage to the quality of air and water. Self-directed 'growth' seems often to be attended by inflation and poverty.

William Morris always assumed that after a day of useful and dignified toil the workers would wish to enjoy and practise art. In 'A Factory as it Might Be' (an article printed in *Justice* in 1884) he wrote: 'People living under the conditions of life and labour above mentioned, having manual skill, technical and general education, and leisure to use their advantages, are quite sure to develop a love of art.' He might have been less sure had he read Wordsworth's prophetic insight into a trend that had already set in:

A multitude of causes, unknown to former times, are now acting with a combined force to blunt the discriminating powers of the mind, and, unfitting it for all voluntary exertion, to reduce it to a state of almost savage torpor. The most effective of these causes are the great national events which are daily taking place, and the increasing accumulation of men in cities, where the uniformity of their occupations produces a craving for extraordinary incident, which the rapid communication of intelligence hourly gratifies.

                        Preface to the second edition of the *Lyrical Ballads*

Sturt and later observers such as Eric Gill and George Orwell felt the disenchantment that is voiced so clearly by Raymond O'Malley on p. 12. Leisure has proved a barren gift. The use made of it is conditioned by the nature of work and the prospects it holds out; there is no simple relationship between the pay a person receives and the quality of his life after hours:

He comes home at night, plops down in a chair, and just sits for about fifteen minutes. I don't know much about what he does in the plant, but it does something to him. Of course, I shouldn't complain. He gets good pay. We've been able to buy a refrigerator and a TV set.

Quoted by David Meakin in *Men and Work*

That sad little account, with its pathetic minimum of expectation, suggests that the low level of popular culture is determined by the poor chances of living while working. The generations of the leisure age are culturally disinherited. It is not only that they have no access to the high culture of concerts and museums and literature; they are deprived of the basic popular culture of folk tales, song, dance and ballad, to say nothing of crafts and skills.

For these disappointments the higher standard of living is supposed to compensate. Of this sacred cow E. F. Schumacher wrote, in an eloquent page:

It is only necessary to assert that something would reduce the 'standard of living', and every debate is instantly closed. That soul-destroying, meaningless, mechanical, monotonous, moronic work is an insult to human nature which must necessarily and inevitably produce either escapism or aggression, and that no amount of 'bread and circuses' can compensate for the damage done – these are facts which are neither denied nor acknowledged but are met with an unbreakable conspiracy of silence.

Small is Beautiful (1973)

The higher standard urgently needs redefining in more than economic terms, to include true human rights at work and in life generally. As it is, the criteria of efficiency preclude the reckoning of such items as the loss of welfare, the squeezing out of fresh by convenience foods, the development of expensive habits and diets to the detriment of cheaper and healthier ones. Almost everything that matters is lost sight of in our interpretation of the higher standard, based on what can go into a computer, that homogenising influence that hides from us exactly what we need to understand.

Any nation with an awareness of its identity and an idea of its destination must have some sense of the past, of what and where it has been. It must have something to measure itself by, other than its ability to meet immediate needs and problems. Wordsworth's peasants, for example, had such a reminder in the daily sight of their forebears' accomplishment in clearing and cultivating the land they worked, just as Conrad's young captain in *The Shadow Line* was strengthened and guided by his consciousness of being in a dynastic line. Without a sense of history, of gratitude to the past, humanity is hardly human; and unaware of past or future drops into the slot (among the other animals) allocated by reductivist views. Deprived of the nourishment that the past might offer, and of its witness to human achievement, people are left with too great a tolerance of a poor environment and too small an expectation of what life might offer.

Unrewarding work; de-creating leisure; and life in general (in Sturt's words) less worth living. There are palliatives, such as the rearrangement of tasks in a factory to reduce specialising, and they should not be despised. But if, as is so often the case in a society of docile consumers, the end-product remains trivial or useless, the gain is limited. Anyway the unregulated advance of technology may mean that early next century the necessary work of the country will be done by 5–10% of the labour force – assuming of course that there will be no problems, of power, materials, side-effects, ability to export, and so on. But if the silicon-chip future were presented starkly enough, human beings might revolt against their servitude and refuse to allow the technocratic imperative a free hand at the helm. One must hope that the media, 'the power of rapid communication', so deplored by Wordsworth, will be employed not for the gratification of 'a craving for extraordinary incident' but in the wake perhaps of some economic or ecological reverse to open our eyes to the way things are drifting and the possibilities for improvement. The first industrial revolution was unplanned, not universally wanted, and attended by unforeseen results; it is time that its later developments were taken under control instead of being accepted as more inevitable than the weather. The needed change in national consciousness might come about if some of those who hold power cared to speak what they well know in their hearts to be true, instead of regurgitating the old lies about 'growth'. Meanwhile we must be opportunist.

At this point the light of American and European experience should be turned on the developing countries of the East, Africa and elsewhere. A visitor to Africa or India, anyone with experience of the modernisation programmes (of Turkey and Iran for examples), even an alert tourist, feels impelled to say, 'Stop a moment; pause to ponder what has happened in the West; does it encourage you to continue with high-cost technology? Do you not see your countryside deserted, your towns swollen with unemployed without hope of work there, your nation pursuing ends that have proved disastrous elsewhere? What do you really want for your people?' To mention only one area, the best African writers of today are well aware of the dangers that attend wholesale westernisation and the ditching of their own cultures. Camara Laye for instance in *The African Child* (1955) gives a moving and beautiful description of the order he was brought up in, and comments (in an interview reported in Achebe's *Morning Yet on Creation Day* (1975)): 'In showing the beauty of this culture, my novel testifies to its greatness. People who had not been aware that Africa had its own culture were able to grasp the significance of our past and our civilisation, I believe that this understanding is the most meaningful contribution of African literature.' Others who write well with similar aims are Chinua Achebe (*Things Fall*

Apart (1958)), Bessie Head (*Where Rain Clouds Gather* (1969)), Amos Tutuola and the Acoli (Uganda) poet, Okot p'Bitek. The latter's 'Song of Lawino' is precisely an appeal for a pause, an expression of a longing for cultural coherence. Authors such as these put the relevant questions and show a readiness to point to the lessons that the West has neglected.

Obviously no simple prescription is possible. Large-scale organisations cannot be transformed overnight, but a start can be made with small units within the large organisation. 'Growth' cannot be replaced at the flick of a switch, but we can understand its implications, experiment with partial alternatives, and start putting the word in inverted commas. There is plenty of advice to be had from 'no-growth' economists and scientists, such as P. T. Bauer (*Dissent from Development*), H. V. Hodson (*The Diseconomics of Growth*), P. B. Medawar (*The Hope of Progress* (1967)), E. J. Mishan (*Growth: the Price We Pay*) and E. F. Schumacher (*Small is Beautiful*).

Instead of the blind application of automation and mass-production without regard to human needs, the case will be for the gradual resort (where feasible) to small-scale technology, of which two forms, 'Alternative' and 'Appropriate', have been adopted in developing countries. Destructive 'growth' will be replaced by the aim of a stable economy with smaller units of social and commercial life, in which the use of land will be a main consideration. There will be no need to start a back-to-the-land movement; it has never stopped since the peasants were dispossessed, and there is no doubt that many people grope after a more sustaining way of life than they find in our present towns. Eventually the result will be a more creative relationship between men and land than is possible in today's conditions. The inadequacy of industry-directed civilisation makes ancient traditional wisdom suddenly seem apposite and opportune. The idiom of the Zend-Avesta for example is now less fantastic than it was a few years ago, in this passage on the sacredness of agriculture:

He who would till the earth . . . with the left arm and with the right, with the right arm and with the left, unto him will she bring forth plenty of fruit: even as it were a lover sleeping with his bride on her bed; the bride will bring forth children, the earth will bring forth plenty of fruit.

Meanwhile a start should be made on restoring to function and beauty the thousands of square miles of the country that industry has ruined; the re-creation of the countryside is essential to its use for the recreation of town dwellers. Forestry, rural industry, water-supply and the conservation of wild life will need to be integrated with farming; and some farmers and the large land-exploiting companies must realise that they have responsibilities that transcend the pouring out on to the land of the poisons so assiduously vended by the chemical concerns. (Inevitably the latter are helping to develop pests resistant to pesticides.) We have the resources in men and women, skill and knowledge, but no politician seems to glimpse what is obvious to the rest of us. England could once more be the agricultural country that Sturt in his *Journals* thought she might of necessity become after some great dislocations, 'when Nature has gone on strike for ever'. Whether or not Nature does go on strike – it may be that disease and other shortcomings in plants and animals are indicative – it is certain that we shall soon be compelled to import less food and that a gradual return to self-sufficiency is desirable. Already the scope seems unlimited for improvement in the national diet and for halting the decline in palatability and probably nutritive value that has followed the introduction of battery storage of animals, the great doses of chemicals they are subjected to, and the limitless processing and packaging of all foods. People cannot want what they do not know; ignorance and poor diets are maintained by advertising and supermarkets; and food of quality has become a privilege of the wealthy. You cannot buy oatmeal at a chain store.

In recent years there has been something of a trend to look to 'primitive' peoples for the secret of contentment and quality of life believed to have been lost. At least they can help us to ask the questions that we have forgotten to put to our civilisation. Stanley Diamond for example believes that it is a task of anthropology 'to assist in the reformulation of pertinent life-preserving questions. The search for the primitive is the attempt to define a primary human potential' (*Tract* No 18). And R. L. Heilbroner finds hope in

> our knowledge that some human societies have existed for millennia, and that others can probably exist for future millennia, in a continuous rhythm of birth and coming of age and death, without pressing towards those dangerous ecological limits, or engendering those dangerous social tensions, that threaten present-day 'advanced' societies. In our discovery of 'primitive' cultures, living out their timeless histories, we may have found the single most important lesson for future man.

The Human Prospect, p. 141

But there is no need to join the searchers for clues in the cultures of primitive peoples. We have in our own country the example of a satisfying way of life, evolved in an economy of bare subsistence and continuing in the face of discouragement, injustice and material difficulties. The sober records are reprinted in this volume, but – once again – revival is neither possible nor desirable; we should be able to achieve something very much better than a narrow peasant culture. Ranged with the observers are the prophetic poets, Blake, Wordsworth, Shelley and perhaps William Morris, who are now seen to be realists ahead of their time. They interpreted the past, charted the currents of the day, and offered encouragement for the future. These writers and others like them can feed the impulse to break out from the technological civilisation that Lawrence saw as having enslaved us, and evolve an order in which technology serves human ends.

NOTES

1 1741–1820; an unsuccessful farmer turned journalist, publisher and traveller. Author of *Farmer's Letters*, starting in 1771.

2 *The Cherry Tree, Corduroy* and *Silver Ley* are at present in print.

3 The Rev. William Harrison's account of his travels, *The Description of England* (1587), is one of the main sources of information about the social life of the period.

4 A unique anthology of prose (1938) from Thomas More to Bertrand, that was intended to persuade hearers or readers to action. Cross-disciplinary and most ably edited, it is unfortunately out of print.

5 Cf. E. M. Wright, *Rustic Speech and Folk-Lore* (1913).

6 Cf. James Ayres, *British Folk Art* (1977).

7 A friendly society, enabling its members to save against contingencies.

8 See St Luke's Gospel, Ch. 16, vv. 19ff.

9 Cf. H. Orel (ed.), *Thomas Hardy's Personal Writings*, on the Dorset dialect.

10 Cf. Thomas Hardy, *Far From the Madding Crowd*, Ch. 8.

11 Botany Bay, a convict settlement, was established in 1787, 10 miles (16 km) south of Sydney; Van Diemen's Land was another Australian penal settlement. For the large scale on which transportation was used as a means of suppressing protest, see E. P. Thompson, *The Making of The English Working Class*.

12 Written in 1821, to supply labourers with useful information on such subjects as the brewing of beer, baking bread, and keeping bees and animals.

13 Quoted from F. G. Emmison, *Elizabethan Life (1): Disorder* (Essex Record Office, 1970).

14 Quoted from John Seymour, *The Companion Guide to East Anglia* (1970), p. 433.

15 *Where Men Decay* (1908).

16 *Tract* No 18, 38 Prince Edward's Road, Lewes.

17 *The Letters of Dorothy and William Wordsworth: the early years* (1935), p. 162.

18 *England and the Octopus* (1928).

19 Isaac Mead, *The Story of an Essex Lad* (1923).

20 The Rev. T. R. Malthus (1766–1834) proposed in *The Principle of Population* (1798) to limit the increase of population.

21 Elizabeth I's Statute of 1601 imposed the care of the poor upon local magistrates, under the supervision of the Privy Council, which showed a real regard for the interests of the poor. Cf. G. M. Trevelyan's *English Social History* (1944), pp. 170, 171.

22 Somerville lived from 1812 to 1885.

23 Joseph Arch (1826–1919), born at Barford near Warwick, was the great architect of unionism for the farm labourer. The first edition of his book was published in 1898 under the title *Joseph Arch: The Story of His Life, by himself.*

24 Tusser (1524–80) gave advice about farming in verse in his *A Hundred Good Pointes of Husbandrie* (1557). It was so successful that he had to think up a further 500 – and then more. See my *The Uses of Poetry* (1978), p. 39.

25 See the Book of Ruth in the Old Testament.

26 Samuel Johnson (1709–84) wrote this story-with-a-moral to pay his mother's debts and the cost of her funeral.

27 The tireless preacher and founder of Methodism, 1703–91.

28 A collection of stories by Giovanni Boccaccio (1318–75) of Florence.

29 In Wiltshire.

30 A 'holt' is a wood or wooded hill.

31 A supper and songs for the workmen.

32 *Six Weeks' Tour through the Southern Counties*, 3rd ed. (1772).

33 In revolt against the values of America, H. D. Thoreau (1817–62) lived for two years on very little money in a woodland cabin, and described his life there in *Walden* (1854).

34 For the 'Rich Fool' see St Luke's Gospel, Ch. 12, vv. 16–21.

SOURCES

Joseph Arch, *Joseph Arch: The Story of His Life, by himself* (1898)
M. K. Ashby, *Joseph Ashby of Tysoe* (1961)
Adrian Bell, *A Countryman's Notebook* (1975)
    A Selection from 'Scrutiny', ed. F. R. Leavis (1968)
    (ed.) *The Open Air* (1936)
George Bourne (pen-name of George Sturt), *A Farmer's Life* (1922)
    Change in the Village (1912)
    (as George Sturt), *The Journals*, I and II (1967)
    The Wheelwright's Shop (1923)
John Byng, *The Torrington Diaries* (one-volume abridgment) (1954)
William Cobbett, *Political Register* (1802 onwards)
    Rural Rides (first published in the *Political Register*) (1820–30)
M. L. Davies (ed.), *Life as We Have Known It* (1931)
Thomas Hardy, *Far From the Madding Crowd* (1874)
Thomas Hennell, *Change in the Farm* (1934)
W. H. Hudson, *A Shepherd's Life* (1910)
Richard Jefferies, *Field and Hedgerow* (1889)
    The Life of the Fields (1884)
Harriet Martineau, *A Complete Guide to the English Lakes* (1855)
H. J. Massingham, *Where Men Belong* (1946)
Thomas More, *Utopia* (1516)
Walter Rose, *Good Neighbours* (1942)
    The Village Carpenter (1937)
Cecil Sharp, *English Folk-Song: Some Conclusions*, 3rd ed. (1954)
    English Folk-Songs from the Southern Appalachians (1917)
Alexander Somerville, *The Autobiography of a Working Man* (1848)
George Sturt, *see* George Bourne
Edward Thomas, *Collected Poems* (1922)

Flora Thompson, *Lark Rise to Candleford* (1945)
Cecil Torr, *Small Talk at Wreyland*, abridged edition (1926)
William Wordsworth, *Guide to the Lakes*, 5th ed. (1835)

RELATED READING

General Introduction

Glen Cavaliero, *The Rural Tradition in the English Novel* (1977)
W. J. Keith, *The Rural Tradition* (1965)
Peter Laslett, *The World We Have Lost* (1965)
Raymond Williams, *The Country and the City* (1973)

Part 1   A home-made civilisation

H. S. Bennett, *Life on the English Manor* (1937)
Phyllis Deane, *The First Industrial Revolution* (1965)
Georges Duby, *Rural Economy and Country Life in the Medieval West* (1968)
Russell Garnier, *Annals of the British Peasantry* (1908)
W. G. Hoskins, *The Midland Peasant* (1957)
W. E. Tate, *The Parish Chest* (1951)
Joan Thirsk, *English Peasant Farming* (1957)

Part 2   Masters and men: the farming life

George Ewart Evans, *The Horse in the Furrow* (1960)
Thomas Hardy, *Personal Writings*, ed. H. Orel (1967)
William Howitt, *The Rural Life of England* (2 vols., 1838)
Ian Niall, *To Speed the Plough* (1977)
Raphael Samuel, *Village Life and Labour* (1975)
E. P. Thompson, *The Making of the English Working Class* (1963)
G. M. Trevelyan, *English Social History* (1942)

Part 3   Living at work: crafts and skills

James Ayres, *British Folk Art* (1977)
David Buchan, *The Ballad and the Folk* (1972)
D. K. Cameron, *The Ballad and the Plough* (1978)
Edwin Muir, *An Autobiography* (1954)
Willa Muir, *Living with Ballads* (1965)
J. M. Synge, *The Aran Islands* (1906)
Denys Thompson, *Distant Voices* (1978)
    The Uses of Poetry (1978)
Alfred Williams, *Folk-Songs of the Upper Thames* (1923)

Part 4   The future

P. T. Bauer, *Dissent from Development* (1971)
Rachel Carson, *Silent Spring* (1962)
Alasdair Clayre, *Work and Play* (1974)
G. Friedmann, *The Anatomy of Work* (1961)
R. L. Heilbroner, *The Human Prospect* (1975)
H. V. Hodson, *The Diseconomics of Growth* (1972)
D. Meakin, *Men and Work* (1976)
E. J. Mishan, *Growth: the Price We Pay* (1969)
C. Reaveley and John Winnington, *Democracy and Industry* (1947)

INDEX